Mark Twain's Aquarium

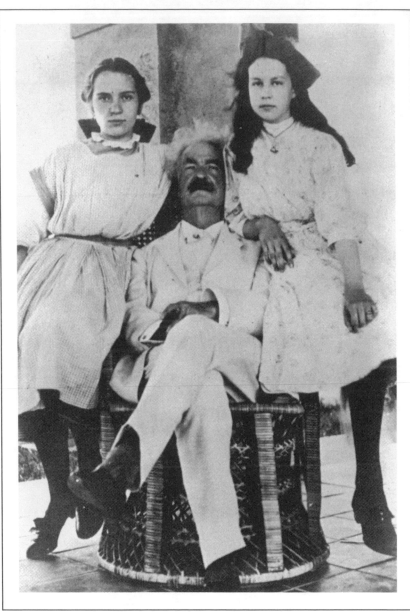

Mark Twain's
AQUARIUM

The
SAMUEL CLEMENS

Angelfish

CORRESPONDENCE

1905–1910

Edited by John Cooley

THE UNIVERSITY OF GEORGIA PRESS
Athens and London

© 1991 by the University of Georgia Press
Athens, Georgia 30602

Designed by Sandra Strother Hudson
Set in Linotron 202 10 on 14 Linotype Walbaum by Tseng Information Systems, Inc.
Printed and bound by Thomson-Shore
The paper in this book meets the guidelines for permanence and durability
of the Committee on Production Guidelines for Book Longevity of the
Council on Library Resources.

Printed in the United States of America
95 94 93 92 91   5 4 3 2 1

Library of Congress Cataloging in Publication Data
Twain, Mark, 1835–1910.
[Correspondence. Selections]
Mark Twain's Aquarium : the Samuel Clemens–Angelfish correspondence,
1905–1910 / edited by John Cooley.
p.   cm.
Includes bibliographical references.
ISBN 0-8203-1238-x (alk. paper)
1. Twain, Mark, 1835–1910—Correspondence.   2. Authors, American—20th century
—Correspondence.   3. Humorists, American—20th century—Correspondence.
4. Girls—United States—Correspondence.   I. Cooley, John R., date.   II. Title.
PS1331.A4   1991
818'.409—dc20   90-32790
[B]   CIP

British Library Cataloging in Publication Data available

Frontispiece: Louise Paine, Clemens, and Dorothy Harvey in the "Fish-Market,"
Stormfield, Summer 1908. (Courtesy, John Seelye)

for cousin Marjorie Breckenridge,
Member of the Aquarium,
and my daughters,
Carolyn and Meredith

CONTENTS

PREFACE

READERS unfamiliar with the angelfish period of Samuel Clemens's life may be surprised, perhaps even appalled, at the three hundred known letters Clemens wrote to or received from schoolgirls and the extent to which the girls occupied his thoughts during the last five years of his life. Throughout 1908, at the height of Aquarium Club activities, Clemens sent several letters a week to the angelfish and received an equal number in reply. As Clemens expressed it the Aquarium became his "chief occupation and delight" (MTAD, 17 April 1908).

Readers expecting a continuously inventive correspondence may be disappointed by the often formulaic redundancy of much of Clemens's phrasing, as he pleads for letters and visits from his young friends. Although his letters often gush sentimentality and reveal his loneliness, they also contain explosions of wit, wisdom, and humor. Patient readers will be amply rewarded with humorous and imaginative passages reminiscent of Mark Twain at his best.

This edition represents a continuous and nearly complete correspondence from December 1905 to the end of September 1908. From that date until Clemens's death in 1910, only seven letters from angelfish survive for the eighty-seven letters Clemens wrote to them during this period. Because Clemens was a diligent saver of letters, it is a reasonable guess that his daughter Clara, who strongly disapproved of the Aquarium Club, disposed of many of the angelfish letters after her return home from European travels in September 1908.

This edition's chapters reflect five significant and distinct stages in the correspondence and the development of the Aquarium Club. Chap-

ter 1 is devoted to the pre-angelfish friendship and correspondence
between Clemens and Gertrude Natkin. Chapter 2 encompasses the
period during which Clemens began "collecting" and corresponding
with schoolgirls in earnest. Soon after meeting Dorothy Butes, he became friends with Carlotta Welles and Frances Nunnally while on
shipboard en route to England. On the return voyage he met another
future angelfish, Dorothy Quick. It is not until chapter 3 (12 January
through 14 June 1908) that Clemens hits upon the idea of an aquarium
club filled with a school of bright and lively angelfish. This idea became a reality during Clemens's two winter retreats to Bermuda. While
there he met and soon began corresponding with Margaret Blackmer, Irene Gerken, Dorothy Sturgis, Hellen Martin, and Helen Allen.
Chapter 4 begins on 19 June 1908, the date Clemens moved into Innocence at Home, his new villa in Redding, Connecticut, which was
large enough to entertain the angelfish during their, by now, numerous
visits. The name of his new house referred partially to the innocence
and good fun Clemens's seven angelfish were bringing into his life.
New Aquarium arrivals during this period were Marjorie Breckenridge, Dorothy Harvey, and Louise Paine. Chapter 5, "Stormfield,"
contains the correspondence between November 1908 and Clemens's
death in April 1910. Clara Clemens had the house renamed Stormfield, which she felt was more appropriate for her father's house. There
is some evidence that Clara disliked the name Innocence at Home
because it formally associated her father's house with a gang of visiting schoolgirls. Ironically, the change of name to Stormfield marks a
period of storm in Clemens's life, caused by domestic discord, failing
health, and the death of his daughter Jean, resulting in the decline of
the Aquarium Club.

MY first knowledge of the Aquarium Club came from my second
cousin, angelfish Marjorie Breckenridge, who still had in her possession the letters Clemens had sent her. Fascinated with my cousin's
teenage friendship with Mark Twain, I set out for the Mark Twain
Papers at the University of California at Berkeley and eventually to the
other collections listed in the Acknowledgments. This edition contains

nearly every known written communication between Samuel Clemens and the young women who constituted his Aquarium Club, including letters, telegrams, personal notes, cards, and inscriptions. There is no way of knowing, of course, how many of the letters have been lost. In addition to casting light on this virtually unknown aspect of Clemens's life, this edition hopes to bring to light additional letters belonging to the Samuel Clemens–angelfish correspondence. Also included in the edition are a number of relevant pieces written by Clemens (notebook entries, autobiographical dictations, short manuscripts) and a few pertinent letters written by persons close to him. Approximately fifteen items judged insignificant to the correspondence have not been included; most of these are inscriptions or brief telegrams.

The transcriptions have been taken from the original letters Clemens and the angelfish sent, rather than from copies, whenever the original was available. The Calendar of Letters at the back of this edition, chronologically arranged, presents a complete list of the known correspondence, giving place and date of origin and the location of the manuscript or a reliable copy.

The position of each letter's date, place of origin, salutation, and closing has been standardized. The date indicated is the day on which the letter was written unless unavailable, in which case the date of the postmark on the envelope is given. Brackets enclose places or dates the editor has derived from envelopes, postmarks, or other sources. In cases where a partial date or no date is available, letters have been placed where they most likely belong in the context of the correspondence.

Unconventional spelling and punctuation have been transcribed literally; similarly, ampersands, which Clemens used often, have not been expanded to *and*. Any editorial alterations or additions appear within brackets. A bracketed question mark has been placed after any place, date, or word of sufficient uncertainty. Even though Clemens sometimes double and triple underlined words for emphasis, all such words have merely been italicized. His use of a varying number of dashes has been standardized to a single dash, and superscript letters within the letters have been lowered.

ACKNOWLEDGMENTS

WITHOUT THE GENEROUS SUPPORT of Western Michigan University this edition would not exist. The university provided a faculty leave, a research fellowship, and travel grants, and the English department gave me time to work on the letters. Though many colleagues provided assistance, I must single out Edward Galligan for his careful reading of the manuscript. Graduate assistants John Hanley and Scott Mattison were invaluable aides in transcribing and editing the letters. I appreciate the support given the edition by Robert Hirst, general editor of the Mark Twain Papers, and by his staff. My thanks also to Jim Dayton for giving me Marjorie Breckenridge's letters, and to the American Arts staff at the University of Exeter. I am indebted to Hamlin Hill, Everett Emerson, Louis J. Budd, and Elizabeth David for their suggestions and advice. Finally, I give heartfelt appreciation to my wife, Barbara, for her help, patience, and understanding.

Formal acknowledgment and thanks are extended to the following manuscript collections for permission to publish letters from their collections: Mark Twain Papers, The Bancroft Library; The Huntington Library, San Marino, California; the Rare Book and Manuscript Library, Columbia University; the Henry W. and Albert A. Berg Collection, The New York Public Library, Astor, Lenox and Tilden Foundations; and the Collection of American Literature, Beinecke Rare Book and Manuscript Library, Yale University.

ABBREVIATIONS

The following abbreviations and shortened references have been used throughout this edition:

Collections

Berg   Henry W. and Albert A. Berg Collection, New York Public Library

Columbia   Columbia University Library, New York City

Cooley   John Cooley, Western Michigan University, Kalamazoo

Huntington   Huntington Library, San Marino, California

MTP   Mark Twain Papers, University of California, Berkeley

Pr. Col.   Private collection

Yale   Mark Twain Collections, Yale University Library, New Haven, Connecticut

Previously Published Works and Unpublished Manuscripts

EMT   Dorothy Quick. *Enchantment: A Little Girl's Friendship with Mark Twain*. Norman: University of Oklahoma Press, 1961

GND   Gertrude Natkin's diary, MTP

HAM   Helen Allen manuscripts, MTP

IE   Albert E. Stone, Jr. *The Innocent Eye: Childhood in Mark Twain's Imagination*. New Haven: Yale University Press, 1961

IVLD	Isabel V. Lyon's diary, MTP
MCMT	Justin Kaplan. *Mr. Clemens and Mark Twain*. New York: Simon and Schuster, 1966
MMT	William Dean Howells. *My Mark Twain*. New York: Harper and Brothers, 1910
MSO	Mark Twain. *The Mysterious Stranger and Other Stories*. New York: Harper and Brothers, 1922
MTA	Charles Neider, ed. *The Autobiography of Mark Twain*. New York: Harper and Row, 1959
MTAD	Mark Twain's Autobiographical Dictations, MTP
MTAP	Albert Bigelow Paine, ed. *Mark Twain's Autobiography*. 2 vols. New York: Harper and Brothers, 1924
MTB	Albert Bigelow Paine. *Mark Twain: A Biography*. New York: Harper and Brothers, 1912
MTGF	Hamlin Hill. *Mark Twain: God's Fool*. New York: Harper and Row, 1973
MTHI	Elizabeth Wallace. *Mark Twain and the Happy Island*. Chicago: A. C. McClure & Co., 1913
MTHL	Henry Nash Smith and William M. Gibson, eds. *Mark Twain–Howells Letters: The Correspondence of Samuel L. Clemens and William Dean Howells, 1872–1910*. Cambridge, Mass.: Harvard University Press, 1960
MTL	Albert Bigelow Paine, ed. *Mark Twain's Letters*. New York: Harper and Brothers, 1917
MTM	Lewis Leary, ed. *Mark Twain's Letters to Mary*. New York: Columbia University Press, 1961

INTRODUCTION

"As for me, I collect . . . young girls"

I suppose we are all collectors, and I suppose each of us thinks that his fad is a more rational one than any of the others. Pierpont Morgan collects rare and precious works of art and pays millions per year for them; an old friend of mine, a Roman prince, collects and stores up in his palace in Rome every kind of strange and odd thing he can find in the several continents and archipelagos, and as a side issue—a pastime, and unimportant—has collected four hundred thousand dollars' worth of postage-stamps. Other collectors collect rare books, at war prices, which they don't read, and which they wouldn't value if a page were lacking. Still other collectors collect menus; still others collect playbills; still others collect ancient andirons. As for me, I collect pets: young girls—girls from ten to sixteen years old; girls who are pretty and sweet and naive and innocent—dear young creatures to whom life is a perfect joy and to whom it has brought no wounds, no bitterness, and few tears. My collection consists of gems of the first water. (MTAD, 12 February 1908‡)

As Samuel Clemens so vividly described his retirement pastime, he became a collector of "pets": "young girls—girls from ten to sixteen years old." In 1907, at the age of seventy-two, Clemens began collecting surrogate granddaughters. He was so successful that within a year his collection numbered a dozen young women. In the spring of 1908 he began calling them "angelfish" and inducting them into the Aquarium Club, an organization he devised to keep them in frequent contact and to formalize his hobby. Clemens's correspondence with school-age girls includes approximately 300 letters dating from December 1905 to the time of his death in 1910. Although Clemens's last years were often dominated by loneliness, illness, and depression, his angelfish letters are nearly always optimistic, loving, and playful; they reveal the depths of his loneliness and the size of his need for attention and affection.

The angelfish correspondence not only reveals the extent of his interest in schoolgirls during his last years but also helps complete the picture of this period, which has for so long remained hazy. Hamlin Hill's important biography of Clemens's last decade, *Mark Twain: God's Fool*, reveals many aspects of Clemens's last years that strongly contrast with the image of him perpetuated by his daughter Clara and his official biographer, Albert Bigelow Paine. Until Hill's biography appeared, it was possible to believe that Clemens remained, until his final illness, the "king" of American humor—a devoted family man and playful public cynic, passing gracefully into retirement and old age.

Recent biographical criticism has helped us see the extent to which, after Olivia Clemens's death in 1904, the family virtually ceased to exist. Clemens's relationship with his surviving daughters, Clara and Jean, became so strained that neither spent much time with her father during his last years. Clemens's overwhelming vanity and unpredictable rage made him, at the very least, extremely difficult to live with. Jean was institutionalized, perhaps unnecessarily, during this period for treatment of her epilepsy and possibly because living in her father's house caused great emotional strain. Clara absented herself through extensive travel, officially in pursuit of her singing career but perhaps privately in exile from her father, as well. Quite routinely, after prolonged visits with her father, Clara would place herself in a rest home to regain her emotional stability. Clemens also showed the strain of trying to adjust to the injured and diminished circumstances of his life: the loss of his wife and eldest daughter, his estrangement from Jean and Clara, and the decline of his health and literary powers.

Indeed, given the conditions of his life, it is remarkable that he had the resilience to attempt any humor at all during his last years, and equally remarkable that he found the energy and frame of mind with which to write hundreds of playful, loving letters to schoolgirls—a correspondence that continued until the very last weeks of his life. As one might guess, it became increasingly difficult for Clemens to maintain the public image of himself, the Mark Twain that he had so painstakingly constructed over the years. As Hill expresses Clemens's inner conflict during his last decade: "The impulse to be humorous choked a man whose sense of rage at the world in which he lived grew and grew to mammoth proportions" (*MTGF* xxiii–iv).

Clemens's own awareness of his destructive pessimism, of his great rage at the swindle of life, must have driven him all the harder to construct about himself a small court of happiness, innocence, and youthfulness, which he set against the ever painful reality of his life. Thus, his indulgence in stories and tales involving young female characters and his collection of young angelfish serve as a surprising antistrophe to the strophe of his rage and despair.

Equally as important as reading the letters in biographical context is reading them in the literary context of Clemens's last decade, as revealed in his autobiography, in *The Mysterious Stranger*, and in his late stories, essays, and letters. It is perhaps only when the youthfulness, playfulness, and affection of these letters is placed in contrast to his other writings of the same period, with their predominant fatalism and barely contained rage, that the angelfish period can be fully appreciated as counterpoint to the prevailing mood of Samuel Clemens's last decade.

"What I Needed was Grandchildren"

One day at Riverdale-on-Hudson Mrs. Clemens and I were mourning for our lost little ones. Not that they were dead, but lost to us all the same. Gone out of our lives forever—*as little children*. They were still with us, but they were become women, and they walked with us upon our own level. There was a wide gulf, a gulf as wide as the horizons, between *these* children and *those*. We were always having vague dream-glimpses of them as they had used to be in the long-vanished years—glimpses of them playing and romping, with short frocks on, and spindle legs, and hair-tails down their backs—and always they were far and dim, and we could not hear their shouts and their laughter. How we longed to gather them to our arms! but they were only dainty and darling spectres, and they faded away and vanished, and left us desolate.

That day I put into verse, as well as I could, the feeling that was haunting us. The verses were not for publication, and were never published, but I will insert

them here as being qualified to throw light upon my worship of school girls—
if worship be the right name, and I know it is. . . .

After my wife's death, June 5, 1904, I experienced a long period of unrest
and loneliness. Clara and Jean were busy with their studies and their labors,
and I was washing about on a forlorn sea of banquets and speechmaking in
high and holy causes—industries which furnished me intellectual cheer and
entertainment, but got at my heart for an evening only, then left it dry and
dusty. I had reached the grandpapa stage of life; and what I lacked and what
I needed, was grandchildren, but I didn't know it. By and by this knowledge
came by accident, on a fortunate day, a golden day, and my heart has never
been empty of grandchildren since. No, it is a treasure-palace of little people
whom I worship, and whose degraded and willing slave I am. In grandchildren
I am the richest man that lives today: for I *select* my grandchildren, whereas
all other grandfathers have to take them as they come, good, bad or indifferent.
(MTAD, 17 April 1908‡)

With uncharacteristic candor Samuel Clemens reveals in this passage from his autobiographical dictations the extent of his loneliness
and aimless "washing about" during the years between his wife's death
and the beginning of his angelfish period. The "golden day" he refers
to occurred in the late winter of 1907 when a fourteen-year-old English
girl and her mother came to visit. Dorothy Butes and Clemens began a
correspondence soon afterward, and he considered her his first angelfish. Dorothy and the other young girls Clemens "collected" within
the next year satisfied his expressed need for granddaughters. As this
edition reveals, he was indeed able to select grandchildren who were
affectionate, charming, and interesting; he was under no obligation to
"take them as they come, good, bad or indifferent," as is the fate of
real grandparents. The dozen young women who filled his Aquarium
Club were, in addition to being surrogate granddaughters, no doubt
reminders of the happy years when his own daughters were younger,
and of his girlfriends from that happiest of times, his own adolescence.

Although Clemens immersed himself in a whirl of adolescent girls
during the last five years of his life, he had always been fascinated with
schoolgirls. During the period of his daughters' childhood, Susy, Clara,
and Jean Clemens more than filled his need for contact with teenage
girls. He teased and played with them and frequently created stories

for their entertainment. As his daughters grew up, the longing to be surrounded by school-age girls returned. This desire was made more acute by the death of his eldest daughter, Susy, in 1896, the epilepsy of his youngest, Jean, and his lack of grandchildren.

A reading of Clemens's two manuscripts devoted to his family, "A Family Sketch" and "The Children's Record" (MTP) reveals how much pleasure his young daughters gave him. When Susy was eight he wrote, "Both of the children are sweet, gentle, humane, tractable, and lovable creatures, with sharply marked and differing characters"—a sentence he could just as easily have written about the angelfish. Clemens often played with his daughters, inventing plays and sketches to be acted out. They would challenge his storytelling ability too by pointing to a picture in a magazine and demanding a story about it. He collected sayings and writings by his daughters and took great pleasure in them, just as he would some forty years later with the angelfish.

Clemens's youthful sweethearts Laura Wright and Laura Frazer are also part of the complex background to the angelfish. Laura Wright was fourteen when she met Clemens, a point of some significance. Years later his rules of the Aquarium Club stipulated that only school-age girls were eligible for active membership. On 30 July 1906, Clemens dictated a remarkably detailed passage for his autobiography concerning his brief romance with Laura Wright. He commented that a "chance remark" called to mind this short-lived love that erupted forty-eight years earlier. "I found that I remembered her quite vividly and that she possessed a lively interest for me notwithstanding the prodigious interval of time that had spread its vacancy between her and me. She wasn't yet fifteen when I knew her." It was summertime and Laura had sailed with her parents from St. Louis to New Orleans on a freighter named the *John J. Roe*. The next four pages recall, with fine detail, the boat and the circumstances of their meeting. Clemens had a job steering on a swift passenger packet, the *Pennsylvania*, which tied up alongside the *Roe* in New Orleans.

I can state the rest, I think, in a very few words. I was not four inches from that girl's elbow during our waking hours for the next three days. . . . That comely child, that charming child, was Laura M. Wright, and I could see her with perfect distinctness in the unfaded bloom of her youth, with her plaited tails dangling from her young head and her white summer frock puffing about in the wind of that ancient Mississippi time. . . . I never saw her afterward. It is now forty-eight years, one month and twenty-seven days since that parting, and no word has ever passed between us since. (*MTA* 80)

Laura Wright's parents did not approve of her continued association with the cub pilot. Although he wrote her many letters, they were intercepted and disposed of, and the young lovers neither saw nor heard from each other for the next forty-eight years.

Two weeks after he wrote this passage Clemens received a letter from his old sweetheart, reestablishing contact and asking for money. She hoped he would ask his good friend Andrew Carnegie to contribute one thousand dollars to help her friend with college expenses. Clemens sent her a check for the amount himself and probably took immense pleasure in doing so. In his dictation of 31 August 1906, he quoted a flattering passage from her letter: "I really forget that I am writing to one of the world's most famous and sought-after men, which shows you that I am still roaming in the Forest of Arden." Twain reflected on his humble adolescence, "And so I am a hero to Laura Wright! . . . One can be a hero to other folk . . . but that a person can really be a hero to a near and familiar friend [is inconceivable]." One can speculate that Clemens was flattered to be Laura's hero beyond what words could fully say. He also called her a "near and familiar friend," an indication of the important role this fourteen-year-old had played in his imagination over the intervening forty-eight years.

Clemens's reaction to her career as a teacher and to her modest circumstances is also noteworthy: "When I knew that child her father was an honored judge . . . What had that girl done, what crime had she committed that she must be punished with poverty and drudgery in her old age? . . . It shook me to the foundations. The plaited tails fell away; the peachy young face vanished; the fluffy short frock along with it; and in the place of that care-free little girl of forty-eight years ago, I imagined the world-worn and trouble-worn widow of sixty-two" (MTAD, 31 August 1906‡). There was no record of correspondence following Laura's letter of appreciation, nor is there any indication that they ever met again. It seems likely that Clemens preferred his image of the fourteen-year-old Laura with her peach complexion and fluffy frock to what time and circumstance had made of her.

Two years later, in the early fall of 1908, Clemens heard from his other childhood sweetheart, Laura Hawkins (Frazer). As a child she was a blond, blue-eyed "charmer" who wore white summer frocks, plaited her hair into two long tails, and lived across the street from the Clemenses in Hannibal. She was also the source for Twain's Becky Thatcher in *Tom Sawyer* and several of his stories. Clemens invited Laura Frazer to visit him in Stormfield, his home in Redding, Connecticut. Clemens anticipated her visit in a letter to Margaret Blackmer: "About next Tuesday or Wednesday a Missouri sweetheart of mine, is coming here from Missouri to visit me—the very best sweetheart I ever had. It was 68 years ago. She was 5 years old and I the same. I had an apple, & fell in love with her and gave her the core. . . . She figures in 'Tom Sawyer' as 'Becky Thatcher' " (6–9 October 1908‡). Laura Frazer did visit him a few days later and received a Mark Twain photograph inscribed, "To Laura Frazer, with the love of her earliest sweetheart." Although the actual roles played by these two early sweethearts in his imagination and in his fiction can only be surmised, it is clear that they held prominent places in his memory.

An understanding of Clemens's lifelong affection for adolescent females involves a consideration not only of biographical matters but also of the many young women who were created by the pen of Mark Twain. It hardly needs saying that Clemens devoted his career to writing about children, including important childhood characters and themes in five novels, several novelettes, and a host of stories, essays, and sketches. For Clemens, childhood was the most important time —the central experience—of life. Although boyhood portraits figured prominently in what would become Mark Twain's best-known and greatest works, in his later years Clemens turned his attention to the adolescent female.

Clemens's repeated concern for the innocence of his angelfish suggests that he believed young women became spoiled or perhaps cor-

rupted once they entered the age of sexual activity. In both his fictional and his autobiographical writing, Clemens returns with some
frequency to the idea of the "platonic sweetheart," in which a somewhat older and more experienced male both longs for and wishes to
protect his school-age sweetheart from whom he has been separated
and with whom he is now reunited. This idea is staged in the short
story "My Platonic Sweetheart" (1898), which purports to be a report of
Twain's recurring dreams in which he is always seventeen and his love
is an innocent maid of fifteen. Although he kisses her and they walk
arms-about-waists, he insists that it "was not the love of sweethearts,
for there was no fire in it." Nor was it the mere affection of brother
and sister, but something "finer than either, and more exquisite, more
profoundly contenting" (*MSO* 289).

Clemens worked out his concept of young female innocence and
purity in greatest detail in his *Personal Recollections of Joan of Arc*
(1895). Clemens remarked that *Joan of Arc* was written out of love, not
for money, and that his heroine reminded him of his daughter Susy:
"I liked *Joan of Arc* best of all my books; and it is the best; I know it
perfectly well" (MTAD 1034‡). In writing *Joan of Arc* Clemens was expressing his love for his eldest daughter, as well as for childhood innocence and heroic potential, but he was also riding on a surge of public
interest in Joan of Arc during the last two decades of the nineteenth
century. The preface to his *Joan of Arc* cited eleven books on the topic
of the Maid from Orléans, nearly all of which he owned. Throughout his career Twain had difficulty with issues of sex and sexuality in
his writing and generally avoided them. No doubt part of Joan's ap-
peal to Clemens was her innocence, incorruptibility, and lack of sexual
development. She came the closest of any of his characters to repre-
senting perfection in a corrupt world. Interestingly enough, Clemens
used some of the same terms of endearment, love, and devotion when
writing about his angelfish a decade later.

Other revealing though minor portraits of young women appear during Clemens's last decade of writing: "The Death Disk" (1901), "Eve's
Diary" (1905), "A Horse's Tale" (1906), and an essay, "Marjorie Flem-

ing, Wonder Child" (1909). "A Horse's Tale" returns to the heroic heroine figure. Cathy is something of an American Saint Joan; adults and
horses intuitively recognize her innate goodness and natural leader-
ship. Like Joan, Cathy is too powerful a force for the good to survive,
but in her death purity shines forth. Again, Clemens returned to the
memory of his daughter Susy. He wrote to his editor, F. A. Duneka,
in 1906: "The heroine is my daughter, Susy, whom we lost. It was not
intentional—it was a good while before I found it out" (*MTL* 779).

Clemens's writing during the last decade that does not include young
female characters reveals his preoccupation with predestination and a
corruption seemingly inevitable in adult society. In one of the bleakest yet most important works of his last years, *The Mysterious Stranger*,
Twain has his cosmic representative, a young cousin to Satan named
Philip Traum, reveal that human and earthly reality are purely an illusion, a dream. Despairing as this seems, he concludes that the great,
unbeatable weapon of the human race is laughter: "Against the assault
of laughter nothing can stand" (*MSO* 132). For a humorist suffering
from a nihilistic world view, this is a reasonably reassuring conclusion.
Similarly, at the conclusion of *What is Man?* the "old man" declares
that nothing is able to shake humanity of its fundamental cheerfulness,
not even the bleakest facts of existence.

Those two words, *cheerfulness* and *laughter*, suggest an effort on
Clemens's part to create a counterforce, albeit fragile and threatened,
against the awesome forces of despair that overpowered his view of the
human condition. Throughout this last decade and its angelfish period,
Clemens seems fixed on a dichotomy between evil and good, darkness
and light. Against the forces of nihilism and determinism on the one
side, he gives us the weapons of cheerfulness and laughter on the other.

Thus for Clemens the memory of his daughter Susy, her fictional rep-
resentatives—Joan of Arc and Cathy Alison—and the clutch of young
angelfish who visited and wrote him until he was too ill to reply, all
played important parts in his polarized state of mind. As Albert Stone
expresses this dichotomy, Clemens sought to maintain a "desperately
delicate balance between despising mankind and loving certain indi-

viduals, between intellectual assertion of a meaningless universe and intuitive awareness of ' love's reality" (*IE* 249). Although readers of this volume will find little of Clemens's misanthropy and despair, they will find ample evidence of his love for certain individuals, and through them his rekindled awareness of love's reality.

MARK TWAIN'S AQUARIUM

CHAPTER ONE

"Marjorie"

27 December 1905 – 20 February 1907

ONE DAY in December 1905, fifteen-year-old Gertrude Natkin caught Samuel Clemens's eye while he was leaving Carnegie Hall. He introduced himself, discovered her name, and soon afterward began corresponding with her. Clemens wrote Gertrude a half dozen letters a month during the first three months of their friendship, each of which received her enthusiastic reply. He soon nicknamed her "Marjorie" after Marjorie Fleming, a young Scottish writer whom he admired.

Marjorie Fleming died before her ninth birthday, but her journals were published through the efforts of Clemens's friend Dr. John Brown of Edinburgh, whom Clemens praised for rescuing Marjorie from oblivion. As Clemens described Marjorie Fleming: "She was made up of thunderstorms and sunshine" (MTAD 212‡). In the last year of his life he wrote an article titled "Marjorie Fleming, The Wonder-Child," a further indication that this remarkable child who reminded him of his daughter Susy remained in his mind throughout the angelfish years. Although she could not have fully appreciated the gesture, it was a significant compliment he paid Gertrude Natkin by conferring on her the nickname Marjorie.

Even though Gertrude Natkin never became an angelfish, Clemens's correspondence with her points the way to the Aquarium and the dozen young ladies who were to become angelfish. The Natkin correspondence is characterized by a freshness and playfulness many of his later letters do not achieve. Clemens is disarmingly honest here. He admits to longing for his former brightness and to despairing over his present lackluster mind. Throughout the exchange of letters Marjorie appears almost giddy with infatuation. One notices that she often writes in the privacy of her room, or during boring school lessons, admitting a pleasantly secretive aspect to their friendship. Clemens appears perfectly at ease in these letters, parodying his own vanity and his difficulty writing poetry. During this exchange Clemens discovers the pleasures of corresponding with a young lady and reinforces his long-standing conviction that youth is the finest and most valuable time of life, a time not to be parted with unless one must. He also seems to have discovered here that he could recapture some of the liveliness and innocent fire of youth through association with a school-age girl. By vicariously participating in her life, he felt younger and more fully engaged in life himself.

The tone of Clemens's letters to Gertrude Natkin began to shift after 9 April 1906, the day on which she turned sixteen. Even though Gertrude pleaded with him to continue their friendship, she sensed that their relationship had irrevocably changed because of her birthday. When she proudly announced her sixteenth birthday, Gertrude had no way of knowing that she had just crossed the boundary, in Clemens's mind, between childhood innocence on the one side, and the spoilage and corruption he associated with adulthood on the other. Now that she was sixteen, he told her, she could no longer be his little girl—it would be almost improper to send her a "blot" (a kiss), but if she could, like Alice in Wonderland, eat a cake or drink a dram that would make her younger, why then there would be no impropriety in sending her a kiss. He closed his letter of 8 April with "Good night, sweet fourteen," denying her new age and pushing her back an extra year for added safety. Of course, the passage is light and charmingly put, but beneath it, as Gertrude soon discovered, lay the heart of Clemens's belief in the innocence of girls and of youth. A month later Gertrude wrote pleadingly, "I hope you will love me just the same, you know I have taken away those two years long ago" (early May 1906), and in her next letter, "Dear Grandpa, please don't love me any the less because I am sixteen" (late May 1906). But Clemens stuck to his concept of innocence. He opened his last letter to her, "Hail & Aufwiedersehen" (10 May 1906). Although he was leaving New York for a long summer in Dublin, New Hampshire, it becomes obvious that he was bidding Gertrude goodbye and Godspeed. Gertrude wrote several additional letters, but they either went unanswered or were given the briefest possible replies, discouraging further contact. If Gertrude's behavior toward Clemens was as warm and fervent as her letters, he may have felt she needed a boyfriend more than a friendship with Mark Twain. Oddly enough, Clemens seemed to have eliminated her from his memory as well as from his friendship, for he makes no mention of her in any of the autobiographical dictations regarding the angelfish.

During the period of Clemens's correspondence with Gertrude Natkin he was living in a substantial brownstone house in New York at 21 Fifth Avenue, on the corner of Ninth Street. It was a home Clemens never cared much for, frequently complaining that he was lonely there. His dissatisfaction was a reflection more on his state of mind than on the house, since he filled his life there with dinner and lunch engagements, lectures, curtain speeches for benefit programs, and the like. During this period he came to rely increasingly on the energy and efficiency of his secretary, Isabel Lyon, to manage his household as well as his financial and literary affairs.

Just before he met Gertrude Natkin, Clemens had celebrated his seventieth birthday. It was a gala celebration arranged by his publisher, George Harvey, editor of both the *North American Review* and *Harper's Weekly*. The birthday banquet was held at the posh Delmonico's restaurant where an impressive collection of social and literary notables enjoyed five hours of dining and tributes to Mark Twain. Mindful of the marvelous publicity to be gained for his most valuable author, Harvey ran a thirty-two-page supplement to the Christmas issue of *Harper's Weekly*, recording the full text of the tributes paid by William Dean Howells, Willa Cather, George Washington Cable, Emily Post, Henry

Rogers, Andrew Carnegie, and others. Present at the banquet was a writer with an especially keen interest in Mark Twain: a young man named Albert Bigelow Paine.

On 7 January 1906 Albert Paine called on Mark Twain and was ushered upstairs to the dark-red bedroom that also served as his study. Since Clemens did not dress until noon, Paine found him sitting up in his carved mahogany bed, answering correspondence and smoking a cigar. Paine expressed his admiration for the great author's works and then proposed that he be given permission to write a biography. It was apparently an irresistible idea, for after a moment or two of silence, Clemens quipped, "When would you like to begin?" (*MCMT* 447). Three days later Paine started working in an adjoining room. Thus began a literary relationship and friendship that lasted until Clemens's death.

As Paine read through the Mark Twain manuscripts and Clemens's letters he quickly realized the need to fill in many blanks and encouraged Clemens to resume work on his autobiography. Clemens had worked intermittently on an autobiography from as early as 1870, but the project had lain idle in recent years. Not long after Paine's arrival at 21 Fifth Avenue, Clemens hired Josephine Hobby, a stenographer, to take down his autobiographical dictations. The project was so successful that between January 1906 and April 1909 he dictated a half million words, as he randomly recalled and reconstructed events from his earlier years. Clemens insisted that his autobiography was going to be an absolutely "true" book, for he would be speaking "as from the grave," with the added inducement toward truth telling that came from insisting it not be published until a century after his death. On this delicate point he told Howells, "The remorseless truth *is* there, between the lines, where the author-cat is raking dust upon it which hides from the disinterested spectator neither it nor its smell" (*MTHL* 782). It was obviously important for Clemens either to believe or to pretend he was telling the searing truth, but his dictations kept to safe topics and comments. Soon after Paine began work on the biography he understood that Clemens's reminiscences bore the inevitable mark of the humorist and storyteller, and "only atmospheric relation to history" (*MTB* 1268).

The autobiography that emerged that spring and summer also adjusted to the immediate financial advantage dangled by Harvey of publishing it in serial form in the *North American Review*. For the next year Clemens kept up a steady pace of dictations, for the *Review* had agreed to pay him two thousand dollars a month for installments that would total one hundred thousand words. As the sessions with Josephine Hobby continued through the spring and summer, they became more a record of Clemens talking, his compelling voice creating a shapeless, rambling magic out of his life. Naturally, many of the dictations vividly recalled his own adolescence, his early infatuations, and the years of his daughters' childhood and adolescence. It was a project ripe with recollections of youth and of happier times.

During the spring of 1906 a new court of admirers formed around Clemens, composed of Isabel Lyon, Albert Paine, and Josephine Hobby. They encouraged his various interests—the dictations, his correspondence with Gertrude Natkin, a great whirl of social engagements—and helped drive his loneliness into a corner. Paine originated the idea of purchasing some land in Redding, Connecticut, and, with Lyon's encouragement, Clemens sent the owner one hundred dollars on 19 March as a deposit to secure the eventual purchase. As money came in from the *North American Review*, it was decided this income should go toward the eventual construction of a house in Redding to be called the Autobiography House. The handsome Italianate villa that was to rise on a hilltop of land outside Redding would become Innocence at Home, the official headquarters of his Aquarium Club, when Clemens moved there in June 1908.

In April 1906 Clemens gave a speech at the Majestic Theatre to benefit the YMCA, and Gertrude Natkin attended, apparently presenting flowers and kisses to the celebrated speaker afterward. Clemens especially enjoyed young female audiences; he gave lectures at Smith, Vassar, and Barnard colleges that spring and boasted that he got kisses from all the girls present. "Girls are charming creatures," he declared, "I shall have to be twice seventy years old before I change my mind as to that" (*MTM* 29).

On 15 May, after wishing *auf wiedersehen* to "Marjorie" Natkin,

Clemens and his immediate family set out for a second long summer in Dublin, New Hampshire. The Upton house, which he had rented, afforded splendid views but seemed isolated from human community. Clemens became irritable with everyone in his household at Dublin, with the possible exception of Isabel Lyon, and his dictations became less frequent and less cohesive, as the summer wore on. Still, a great deal was written that summer, more by free association than by any sense of plan or logic. He often dictated from bed, propped up on pillows with the inevitable cigar in hand. Alternatively, he walked up and down the long veranda of the New Hampshire house, filling the air with words; during periods of rain he shuffled back and forth in the living room, talking as he walked. Paine recalled, "When I think of that time I shall always hear the ceaseless slippered, shuffling walk, and see the white figure with its rocking, rolling movement passing up and down the long gallery" (*MTB* 1323).

Among Clemens's closest and most supportive friends during this period was H. H. Rogers, not only one of the nation's wealthiest and most successful businessmen but also an enthusiastic devotee of Mark Twain's works. Clemens visited the Rogerses occasionally, both in New York and at their country home in Fairhaven, Massachusetts, and enjoyed the company of Rogers's son, Harry. But, as is typical of Clemens's late years, he struck up a closer friendship and correspondence with Harry's young wife, Mary Benjamin Rogers. Although Clemens's first letter to her dates from October 1900, on the occasion of her engagement, a rich correspondence with Mary emerged during the summer of 1906 and continued with some frequency for the following year. Although Mary was too old to become an angelfish, she posed no threat to his reputation because she was a married woman. *Mark Twain's Letters to Mary* contains ample evidence that she brought out of her "Uncle Mark" a brighter, more youthful voice and mood. He made Mary his "honorary niece" and asked quite candidly for her flattery.

In October, Clemens and his entourage moved back to 21 Fifth Avenue, and he resumed his busy city schedule of social engagements, and, perhaps less often than before, his dictations. His daughter Clara and Isabel Lyon continued to work over plans for the building of a country home at Redding, a project that Clemens entirely approved but on which he had no desire to spend his time. His youngest daughter, Jean, had suffered from deteriorating health during the summer, including a number of epileptic seizures, and she was sent to a sanitorium in Katonah, New York, later the same month. It was the start of something akin to an exile, which continued for the next three years, as Jean was moved from one sanitorium to another. Apparently Clemens was not able to create easy or enjoyable relationships with Clara or Jean. Clara found his "overbearing" presence intolerable for sustained periods and would frequently place herself in a sanitorium to restore her delicate psychological equilibrium. By contrast, Jean, who frequently pleaded to be either visited often or returned home, was kept at a distance from her father until the last few months of her life. Because of these strained relationships with his own daughters, he craved for and found happy, playful relationships with Gertrude Natkin, Mary Rogers, and, a year later, with the first of his angelfish.

Soon after Clemens's return to New York, a seventy-first birthday present arrived from the Rogerses—a very handsome billiards table. It opened up a new world of pleasure for Clemens to have the table, and it turned out to be medicine "better than the doctors." He claimed that he walked "not less than ten miles every day with the cue in my hand" (*MTM* 83). Unfortunately, Clara laid down the law as to when he must dress in the morning, how many cigars he could smoke, and how late at night he could play billiards. He confessed to Mary that he had to "lead a life of chicane and deception" with Clara in order to enjoy himself, and asked Mary to affirm anything he asked, if Clara should seek validation. "At this very moment I am only waiting for Clara to depart for her train, then I am going to get up and do some forbidden things and have a pleasant time" (*MTM* 90). Clemens enjoyed the role of rebellious boy, which no doubt reminded him of his own youth and of his fictional adolescents Tom and Huck and gave occasion for a slightly subversive relationship with Mary and, later, the angelfish.

Sometime during the fall of 1906 Clemens decided to clothe himself entirely in white. His insatiable vanity liked the conspicuousness of the white uniform, as well as the symbolic cleanliness and purity it connoted. As Isabel Lyon expressed this new obsession, "The King is filled with the idea of defying conventionalities, and wearing his suitable white clothing all winter, so he has bidden me to order five new suits from his tailor" (IVLD, 21 December 1906). In December he traveled to Washington to testify before a joint congressional committee on copyright legislation. Howells was also present and witnessed Clemens emerging from his overcoat, a ghostly white figure, from his mane of white hair to his white shoes. "Nothing could have been more dramatic. It was a magnificent *coup*," Howells recalled (*MMT* 96). Slowly a new mood and style were falling into place for Clemens: billiards, white suits, card games, his autobiography, young women, and other pleasant diversions from the unhappiness that otherwise filled his life. As far as he was concerned, Samuel Clemens had gone on "permanent holiday."

GERTRUDE NATKIN TO CLEMENS

[New York]
December twenty-seventh, 1905

My dear Mr. Clemens:

Yesterday a very happy little girl went home, thinking only of dear Mr. Clemens. I wish to thank you very much for being so kind, I really think you must have seen in my face that I was yearning to speak to you and it was kind of you to gratify my wish. I am very glad that I can go up and speak to you now (if ever I have that pleasure again) as I think we know each other. Trusting you will favor me with "little business" (grand treasure) which you said I should leave to you (and which I shall, as an obedient child) I am the little girl who loves you.

                                        Gertrude Natkin

Clemens to Gertrude Natkin

21 Fifth Avenue
Dec. 28 [1905]

To Gertrude
It was very sweet of you, dear, to let me shake hands with you, that day; & mind, don't you forget to remember that you are to be just as sweet & dear *next* time, and shake *again*, you charming child.

This from your oldest & latest conquest—

SL Clemens (M.T.)

Gertrude Natkin to Clemens

138 West 98 St.
Sunday Dec. 31 [1905]

My dear dear Mr. Clemens
The old year which was so *happy* toward the last is nearing its end and I want to wish you a very happy new year. I hope that I will have as pleasant an incident this new year as I had the fortune to have last year. Thanking you for your sweet letter, I am the little girl who loves you.

Gertrude

Clemens to Gertrude Natkin

21 Fifth Avenue
[1 January 1906]
Don't forget, dear, to make your New Year good resolutions. Not that *I* think you need any reforming, for I don't: I love you plenty well enough, just as you are.

Happy New-Year! I forgot to say it before: this comes of being 17 times as old as you are, and accordingly crippled in my mind & forgetful.

SLC

CLEMENS TO GERTRUDE NATKIN

21 Fifth Avenue
Feb 3/06

Now then, dear, I will recall myself to your remembrance—then I will proceed. Do you remember coming out of Carnegie Hall one day & exchanging views concerning the weather with a white-headed patriarch with a limp and a glass eye? Very well, I am that patriarch.

And so, to business. A gentleman has just been here who represents the West Side Y.M.C.A.,[1] & he says that every Sunday afternoon at 3.30 p.m. he fills the Majestic Theatre, 59th & Broadway, with his young fellows and they listen to lectures furnished by prominent men. I don't lecture any more, but I promised to introduce one of his lecturers for him. I chose Gen. Horace Porter, late Ambassador to France, because I have known him 30 years. He is to talk on the 18th of this month unless he is obliged to go to Washington on Hague Tribunal business; in which case he will do his talk a week later, on the 25th.

Would you like to hear him? A few ladies are admitted—very few. They stick them around, here & there in boxes—none on the floor, which is reserved for the young fellows. My secretary (whom you saw with me) is invited, & is going. Could you come, with your father or your mother, or both?

If you come I shall want to send you a written order on those people to see to it that you are not left outside or there will be trouble. And won't you be a good child & come & speak to us?

I kiss your hand, dear.

Your oldest friend
S L Clemens

1. Charles Powlison

Gertrude Natkin to Clemens

138 West 98 St.

February third 1906

My *darl*ing Mr. Clemens,

(You will notice that I have expressed myself a little stronger than usual, but there is cause for it, after having received your dear letter.)

The old adage, "All good things come in threes," certainly proved itself true when I received your third letter this morning. When I saw it was from you, I was delighted but on reading its contents, I—well really, I could have kissed you; but perhaps that will hold good for another time

Not meaning to flatter you, dear Mr. Clemens, this acquaintance which has so oddly sprung up between us has made me very happy. Although you are my oldest friend you are certainly my dearest.

Now to come to business, as you call it,—I shall be more than de-lighted to accept your kind invitation for mother and myself.

Anticipating the pleasure of seeing you again, I am the little girl who loves you

Gertrude

Clemens to Gertrude Natkin

21 Fifth Avenue

Feb. 8/06

Aren't you the dearest child there is? I am perfectly sure of it. I was never surer of anything in my life. When a person gets to be as old as I am he can't take new friends into his heart easily—they don't seem as dear as the old ones; but you, oh you *are* an exception! I wouldn't trade you for dozens & dozens of these gray-heads I've been so fond of all these ages.

If Gen. Porter should postpone his lecture to the 25th we will write or telephone in time, so that you & your mother will be saved from making a fruitless journey to 59th street.

Meantime, don't forget me, & don't forget my name. Set it down on a piece of paper; & if you lose the paper, call me up & inquire: "3907 Gramercy"—it isn't in the telephone book.

Indeed, yes, you are a dear, sweet, honest, unspoiled, adorable little maid, & I wouldn't trade you for a housefull of those gray-heads whom I have loved so long & so well.

SLC

P.S. Do you know, dear, I am lost in admiration of my own smartness. I first wrote the enclosed order, & then asked Miss Lyon to call up Mr. Powlison & say I should want a couple of friends taken care of: he broke in, at that point & said "ask Mr. Clemens to write an order; the usher will find me & deliver it, & I will see that they are shown to the seats provided for them." She brings that report this moment. Do you notice? he came near repeating the words of my order. I used to be often bright, like that, but not lately—oh, no, that is not so—I am *always* bright.

He has telephoned his name; it is Charles—or Charley—I have never seen him & so I don't know which he prefers.

GERTRUDE NATKIN TO CLEMENS

[postcard]

New York
[13 February 1906]

TO MY SWEET VALENTINE

You are a merry merry lark,
You are the noble witty Mark;
My thoughts of you to tell, I fain,
You cut my little heart in Twain.

CLEMENS TO GERTRUDE NATKIN

21 Fifth Avenue

Feb. 14/06

It was a very sweet Valentine, & you are a dear. But I have told you that before. You got ahead of me, but it was only because I was busy. Yesterday I bought my favorite book for you, but I fell to reading it, & became fascinated, as always before, & here it lies, yet—unsent. It is the book of that quaint & charming & affectionate & tempestuous & remorseful little child, Marjorie Fleming. Doubtless you are already acquainted with it. I am incurably slow & lazy, but I will send it, sure —I certainly will.

General Porter can't lecture on the 18th, but I have promised to introduce Dr. Van Dyke on the 25th.[1] I think it will be at Carnegie Hall— but I will let you know. He is a very gifted man, but I have not known him as long as I have known Porter.

Aren't you dear & sweet? Doubters are requested to inquire of

SLC

1. Dr. Henry Van Dyke, a clergyman and friend of Clemens, was unable to appear, and thus Clemens himself gave a lecture on 4 March.

GERTRUDE NATKIN TO CLEMENS

New York

February 17, 1906

My darling Mr. Clemens

My vocabulary seems quite exhausted when I want to tell you how kind and good you are. I wanted to call you "sweet and dear" but I don't know whether you have a copy-right or not on these words. But I don't suppose you will mind if I use them; I shall change them a little, you are *very sweet* and *very dear*.

I want to thank you for your kind gift. It is a sweet little story but that is quite natural since it is your favorite. May I be be your little "Marjorie"?

I can hardly wait until I see you again as you imagine that the postponement of the lecture was quite a disappointment to me I think I
will stop writing now as I am getting a little sleepy (no offense meant)
and I want my thoughts always to be bright and fresh when I write to
you I will have something nice to dream about after writing this to you.
Good Night
    The little girl who loves you
                        Gertrude

Clemens to Gertrude Natkin

                                                    21 Fifth Avenue
                                                    Feb. 20/06

Isn't it odd, you little witch! I was already thinking of calling you that
name & now you have thought of it yourself. And I am very glad to
have those other titles with you, dear, very glad indeed, notwithstanding they are pretty flattering for me, while they fit you to the shade of
a shadow.

    Dr. Van Dyke has not been able to get free of his preaching engage-
ments for next Sunday, therefore he can't lecture that afternoon. Also,
it gives me my freedom, for I am now not obliged to do any introducing
there, & I think I won't; but if I change my mind I will write & tell you.
I am become so tired & dull, these latter days, that I would like to go
to bed & stay there the rest of the season. It is a dreadfully long winter;
I wish it would quit, & try something else. It makes me sour & out of
patience, & tonight I am sour beyond expression! But you—well, you
never can be that, Marjorie dear, it's against your nature.

    Good-night & bright dreams!

                                                    SLC

                        P.S.
                Wednesday afternoon

Mr. Powlison has been here, & he is a charming man. Of course he
persuaded me. The date is March 4, 3:30 p.m., at the Majestic Theatre. You and your mother will be shown to the box, as per the order

which I sent you, & you will find Miss Lyon & her mother there. Mr. P. has to provide a clergyman to furnish respectability, & I will take care of the rest of the show myself.

I'm getting dreadfully late, I've an engagement! Good-bye, you dear little friend.

SLC

GERTRUDE NATKIN TO CLEMENS

[New York]
Feb. 22, 1906

Now darling Mr. Clemens, you know way down in the bottom of that big heart of yours that you could'ent be "sour or out of patience" no matter what the weather man is doing with the weather. That going to bed and remaining the rest of the season is like the butterfly who as a nasty horrid little caterpillar goes to bed and then blooms into a beautiful butterfly. But this is not like your case, as you could not become nicer than you are, whereas there is a great chance for improvement in the case of the caterpillar

Do you know Mr. Clemens, according to the Latin language, your name suits you perfectly. What made me think of this was because I was just translating "Cicero" and I came across the word clemens: merciful, good, kind, just like you. I like to write my letters to you in my own room away from everybody else and after I have sent the letter I keep the folks curious as to what I wrote you but finally I tell them as I keep a duplicate of my letters to you.

Now Mr. Clemens, in case you go to bed, please wake up by March 4, Good-bye, Your little girl who loves you.

Gertrude

P.S. That was force of habit, I meant to sign Marjorie.
Excuse that blot I could'ent help it
well, we shall let it go as a kiss[1]

---

1. The letter shows no sign of an inkblot, but Gertrude may have kissed and blotted the letter. Future "blots" sent by both Gertrude and Clemens are symbolic.

CLEMENS TO GERTRUDE NATKIN

21 Fifth Avenue

[2 March 1906]

Marjorie dear, Mr. Powlison has sent tickets—which is very well; it simplifies things.

The house is made up of men, you see. Certainly this is a new kind of matinee.

He has added some compliments (for me). I have destroyed them. Compliments make me vain: & when I am vain, I am insolent & overbearing. It is a pity, too, because I love compliments. I love them even when they are not so. My child, I can live on a good compliment two weeks with nothing else to eat.

Marjorie, Marjorie, listen to me—Listen, you . . . you . . .

Do you notice?—it's a poem. I've got that far all right. I expect it to be 8 or ten lines when I get it done. It will take a long time, because poetry is very difficult for me on account of its being outside the range of my great talents. I expect to finish that second line during March, & take hold of No. 3 in April. I intend that it shall be exceedingly good when I get it done, you dear little creature.

SLC

Friday afternoon

P.S. It was a very nice blot, dear: There couldn't be a nicer blot than that.

CLEMENS TO GERTRUDE NATKIN

21 Fifth Avenue

[4–9 March 1906]

Sunday night

But you *were* a delightful surprise when you did at last arrive, this afternoon! I had really given you up, & was getting into that vicious mood which comes upon a disappointed person & makes him go on a platform & say odious things to a mass of men who only think kindly of him & have never done him any harm in the world!

I supposed I had carried stupidity to the limit when I failed to instruct Miss Lyon to telephone you to come to the stage door—but it wasn't so, I was stupid again in letting you & your sister go in that. . . [page missing] [1]

I thought I had made a step & added a word, but I was mistaken.

Marjorie, Marjorie, listen to me—Listen, you (elf?).

No, elf won't do because I must have a word that can furnish a proper rhyme at the end of the fourth line, & there isn't anything that rhymes with elf except self & pelf & shelf. Those are inelegant; there are not going to be any inelegant words in *this* work of art, my precious little maid. But I'm not worrying—I'll have that word inside of three weeks, *sure*. For I am full of talent. The noun is the only difficulty, not the adjective. I can manage the adjective; any two-syllable one that hasn't the emphasis on the wrong end & has sugar enough in it, will do, & I know several of those.

Thursday afternoon

Marjorie, I've got the words!

The words that rhyme. The rest is easy, because No. 3 doesn't have to rhyme with anything. Observe:

TO THAT BONNY CHILD, MARJORIE

Marjorie, Marjorie, listen to me—
    Listen, you winsome witch:
Whomever you bless with Your innocent love,
    That person is passing rich.

There, dear—that poem is as good as half done, *I* think. All in good time I shall finish it. Will see

Friday

I knew I could do it, dear. By going without rest or food for a day

and a night I have compressed the proper work of months into a single
cataclysmal explosion. And so, as you see, it is finished:

> Rich, though he have not a grain of gold
>   Save that which is in his mouth,
> Rich, though his silver be all on his head
> And crusts for his craw be all his bread
>   And his wine-tank rusty with drouth:

> *Saturday Evening*

> For your love has the power of the fabled purse
>   That wrought charms in the old romaunt:
> Who had it might live in a shack or worse
> And feed on dreams & dew & verse,
>   Yet never could *he* know want.

(There, Marjorie dear—I charge you a blot for that.)

---

1. Page 2 of this letter was missing when Gertrude received it. According to Isabel
Lyon's notes, Gertrude telephoned Clemens to report the missing page. The page presumably contained Clemens's apologies for the "riot" that had occurred at his lecture.
Albert Bigelow Paine described the incident: "When we arrived the streets were packed
from side to side for a considerable distance and a riot was in progress." Paine also quoted
newspaper headlines: " '10,000 Stampeded at the Mark Twain Meeting. Well-dressed
Men and Women Clubbed by Police at Majestic Theatre' " (*MTB* 1276n).

GERTRUDE NATKIN TO CLEMENS

138 West 98 St. [New York]
[10 March 1906]

Dear, dear Mr. Clemens

   After I phoned to you yesterday afternoon I waited very anxiously for
every mail to see whether your note you sent was stored away in the
mail bag. But I did not receive your letter last night so I had to go to bed
content only with the consolation that the morning mail would bring

better results Quite true to the prediction of my dream I did receive your dear little note this morning.

I am very glad I was a "pleasant surprise" to you as that is not always the case since anticipation is usually greater than realization and I am so happy that your little thoughts and ideas of me did not have to be changed. I think I had better keep a little account of the blots I owe you as I must give you all that are due you

Do you know, I really did'ent know whether I should phone you or not but it was this way, I came home from college after having played basket-ball all afternoon and I was tired and I felt like speaking to you so badly; I knew that your voice would comfort me. It seems that words cannot express the pleasure which you afforded me yesterday so I think I shall have to owe you another blot. Even you did not understand all the nice things I said to you, you shall hear them sometime. Anyway I do not think that Cupid did his work well at all yesterday, he should have taken these messages better than that.

Oh dear, I almost forgot to speak about the poem, oh no, I did'ent, I wanted to leave the best until last. I always knew you were a genius but this poem is certainly a work of art which I did not know lay within your power. Mr. Clemens I certainly will have to give you some compliments or blots (which ever you prefer) for the rest and food which you lost, writing that poem.

Mr. Clemens I shall close now with this little—no I shall not insult the word poetry by calling it a poem. It is a what ever you wish to call it that the children in ancient Rome would probably have sung if they had had the pleasure of knowing my dear dear Mr. Clemens

LAY OF ANCIENT ROME

Ole *Marcus* was a Roman,
A Roman good was he,
No dagger was seen neath his toga blue
But there a heart brave and true

But dear what have you done so unkindly to me that I should make you suffer at my poor attempts at poetry. Good Bye

Gertrude

ISABEL LYON TO GERTRUDE NATKIN

[New York]
[13 March 1906]

To whom these presents shall
come—greeting:
One unto you unknown—
& yet a Friend—instructs
me to beg you to hold free
of engagements the evening
of April fifth. This, from
Another Unknown Friend.

CLEMENS TO GERTRUDE NATKIN

[21 Fifth Avenue]
[16 March 1906]

To whom these presents shall come—greeting & salutation.
And thereto—this:
It's postponed to April 10th, you little rascal.[1]

Unknown Friend

1. In her diary Gertrude Natkin wrote the following: "Next evening Saturday, March 17, Miss Lyon rang up. She said that Mr. C. had not forgotten me but he was in bed as he had a cold. The next morning I sent Mr. C a box of flowers. Miss Lyon rang up the next day to thank me for Mr. C. That evening I rang up Miss Lyon to see how Mr. C was and also to send my love" (GND, 17 March 1906).

Gertrude Natkin to Clemens

[New York]
[17 March 1906]

To whom these presents shall come, greeting:
Kindly notify my unknown friend that your little known friend will take due notice of the postponement and try to remain in utter darkness until then.

Your Little Known Friend

Clemens to Gertrude Natkin

21 Fifth Avenue
March 18/06
Sunday, 6 p.m.

Aren't you dear! Aren't you the dearest child there is? To think to send me those lovely flowers, you sweet little Marjorie. Marjorie! don't get any older—I can't have it. Stay always just as you are—youth is the golden time.

Miss Lyon came up & arranged the flowers for me, & they certainly do look like you. Consequently they are very acceptable company. I was writing a short article on the Carnegie Spelling-Reform, to put in The Times, but I have finished it now.

Miss Lyon brought me your messages from the telephone, & I was very glad to have them, Marjorie dear. To-morrow or next day I can leave this bed, then I can talk to you myself. No, to your shadows—for that is all a telephone can furnish of you. It makes you vague & unreal; & the voice is somebody else's & unfamiliar.

Good-night (blot) & sleep well, you dear little rascal!

SLC

Miss Lyon, my secretary, is the other Unknown Friend—but perhaps you have arrived at that guess already.

GERTRUDE NATKIN TO CLEMENS

New York
[21 March 1906]

My poor, dear Mr. Clemens:

To think of you confined to your room on this first day of Spring makes me down hearted. Your wish is almost justified, as Winter is gone, but only in name, as we have not the beautiful Spring weather yet. Did you think I had forgotten you! I took a dreadfully long time to answer your note, but I thought my messages from the telephone would be just as acceptable.

This morning I was writing a note to you during the—perhaps I better not say, yes, I must confess all to you. Well, to continue, I was writing a note during the French period. I had written a few lines when Mademoiselle looked at me and of course I dropped my pencil and my eyes wandered to my book with a very knowing and intelligent air. You see I am usually very fond of French, but I was thinking of you and could I turn my thoughts to French when I love you. Oh! how I love you! (blot)—so that explains this little delay.

I must not write any more, I am too impatient. I must go right down and telephone Miss Lyon and see how you are.

"Your own little Marjorie"

CLEMENS TO GERTRUDE NATKIN

[New York]
March 24/06

Are you listening, you little rascal? You have been thinking about me? That is quite proper—when there is nothing else on hand; but not in lesson time, *that* won't do. Why, not even Marjorie Fleming was so lawless as that, altho she was a good deal of a rule-breaker. Dr. John Brown never saw Marjorie, of course, yet she was so alive to him, & so vivid & so dear & sweet, that he told me she was the same to him as a grandchild, & that he couldn't love a real grandchild any more than he loved this little comrade of his musings & his dreams. So he spoke of her as his dream grandchild. And you are mine. I shouldn't want a sweeter one, & there couldn't be a dearer one. For a year & more I have been calling this house a hospital, & now at last I am a patient myself—but I'm only a "temporary," not a "permanent," like the rest of the family—& I shall be up to-morrow, I suppose, & maybe this evening, and will hunt for you on the telephone, & thank you for those dear messages you sent me. I am cross, for our being restrained of my liberty, but not with you, dear, only with the rest of the human race. No, I couldn't be cross with you, you dear little Marjorie—on the contrary I blow you a volley of blots!

SLC

Gertrude Natkin to Clemens

[New York]

[early April 1906]

My dear Mr. Clemens

—You see, I do not wish to appear as a reckless little law breaker in your sight so I have tried to restrain myself from setting forth my love on paper during school time and I have succeeded. I am just overflowing with love for you and there is likely to be an inundation at any time, hence this violation of rules.

It was very dear of you to telephone to me that evening, but you are such a dear, I knew you would telephone if you said you would. I am so glad that Apr. 10th comes during Holiday week for then I can think of you as much as I please without breaking any rules. Oh, that I could give you a real blot right now, well I will have to make the best of it and store it up for the eventful evening.

Good Night, Sweet Dreams

Marjorie

Isabel Lyon to Gertrude Natkin

New York

April 3, 1906

Dear Gertrude:

Mr. Clemens has asked me to send you these tickets for a box for the evening of the 19th,[1] and to say that he would write you himself, but that these are very very busy days—when he is not working he is too tired to do anything but rest up for the busy day that comes tomorrow.

He sends his love to you as always & will be glad when the days come when he will not be so driven.

Sincerely yours,

I.V. Lyon

Secretary

1. The event referred to is the Robert Fulton Association gathering in Carnegie Hall, where Clemens was to deliver a lecture. The association was named after Robert Fulton, inventor of the steamboat.

Clemens to Gertrude Natkin

21 Fifth Avenue

[8 April 1906]

3 p.m. Sunday

You are the sweetest grandchild I've got, Marjorie dear, & the best. Am I a long time sending that stage-door order? Yes; & it is partly because I was born lazy, & partly because I have been very very busy gadding around & very very tired and

Interrupted

10.30 p.m.

This is an hour later than usual for me to return to bed. So you are 16 to-day you dear little rascal! Oh, come, this won't do—you mustn't move along so fast; at this rate you will soon be a young lady, & next you will be getting married. I shall be sorry, then; & moreover if you don't appoint me your head bridesmaid & be exceedingly good to me I will do everything I can to break off the match.

I was going to give you this pen, & now it will do for a birth-day token. It is the best one I have ever had; I have used no other for 4 years. I asked Miss Lyon to send to Toledo for another one for me, & it will arrive before the 19th I guess.

Marjorie dear, the stage-door is on the *side* of the Carnegie building, back toward the rear. If I remember rightly, you go up a short flight of stairs & enter a reception room which is back of the stage. There will be lots of gentlemen there but I'll see that they don't bite you. Miss Lyon says it is easy to get from there to the boxes. But whether it's easy or not, we'll *make* it easy. When I say "lots" of gentlemen, I mean a dozen. They are going to sit on the platform & keep game.

Sixteen! Ah, what has become of my little girl? I am almost afraid to send a blot, but I venture it. Bless your heart it comes within an ace of being improper! Now back you go to 14!—then there's no impropriety. Good night, sweet fourteen.

SLC

GERTRUDE NATKIN TO CLEMENS

[New York]
Monday evening April 16

Dear Mr. Clemens

Perhaps it is rather inconsiderate of me to write to you at such a busy time but I cant restrain myself from sending you some love and blots. Of course I shall keep a good many of these imaginary blots and bring them forth into real ones for Thursday evening. I am quite sure you will accept them then.

I was going to send you a cartoon that was in the paper Friday evening but Miss Lyon has told me that you have already seen it.

I almost forgot, I am taking up too much of your time because when

you are not busy I want you to rest. Now I hope you will be already to
receive a volley of "real" blots.
Good night

Your own Marjorie

Gertrude Natkin to Clemens

New York
[18 April 1906]

NOTICE !

A little girl is very anxious waiting for the eve of the 19th. *Reward!* of
ten blots to the one identifying this little girl.

Clemens to Gertrude Natkin

[stage pass]

21 Fifth Avenue
[19 April 1906]

Please admit these friends of mine by the stage door, & greatly oblige.[1]
   Yours very truly
   Mark Twain

---

1. Gertrude wrote in her diary that she visited Clemens backstage before and after his
Fulton Association lecture. "Mr. Clemens was dear; he threw me kisses from the stage.
After the lecture we went behind again and Mr. Clemens gave me the pen" (see his letter
of 8 April) (GND, 19 April 1906). Clemens told his adoring audience during the standing
ovation, "In saying good-bye to you, I am saying good-bye to the Nation" (*MTM* 33).

CLEMENS TO GERTRUDE NATKIN

21 Fifth Avenue

27 April 1906

Friday evening

Those lovely flowers & that precious volley!—certainly you are a dear sweet little girl, Marjorie; there's none dearer nor sweeter. I am hereby answering that volley with another, you dear child; also I am sending an Auf wiedersehen along with it, & thereto the injunction that when the wiedersehen occurs next fall it shall find you a little girl *still*. Cling to your blessed youth—the valuable time of life—don't part with it till you must.

With love & good-byes, & lots of blots—

SLC

GERTRUDE NATKIN TO CLEMENS

[New York]

[early May 1906]

My dear Mr. Clemens.

It seems such a long time since I have written to you that I thought I would write you a few lines this evening. What a disappointment to you to be confined to your room when I suppose you are contemplating the enjoyment of the green meadows, of driving, riding, and other pleasures. But I suppose you will enjoy it all the more after your unexpected delay.

I have just seen three very good pictures of you in the "Literary Digest" and I am going to mount them for my room. Oh Mr. Clemens I should just love to have an autographed photograph of you for my room. I have always wanted it but I thought you might think of it yourself.

Mr. Clemens, if you only could realize how I love you. I can not express it but I suppose sending a few blots will help a little. I hope you will love me just the same, you know I have taken away those two years long ago. Now I must take your time where you might be resting or sleeping so Good Night dear. (blot).

Your little girl Marjorie

Clemens to Gertrude Natkin

21 Fifth Avenue
May 10/06

Hail & Aufwiedersehen,

Marjorie Dear! & thank you for the blots—which I duplicate. Indeed it has been a troublesome capitivity, but the end is near by, now, for if the weather permits, I am to leave my room day after tomorrow (or at furthest Monday) & break for the woods & freedom—that is to say, Dublin, N.H.

An autographed photograph? Why I *did* think of it long ago, you little witch, but of course it wouldn't have been proper etiquette for me to offer it, you know. If there is one in the house you shall have it right away; & if there isn't, Miss Lyon will send out & get one.[1]

Good-night & good-bye. I love you dearly, you dear little Marjorie (blot) & I'm glad you have shed those two unnecessary years (blot.)

SLC

1. In her diary Gertrude comments, "I received the photo the next week." (GND, early May 1906).

Gertrude Natkin to Clemens

[New York]
[late May 1906]

Dear Mr. Clemens

That letter you sent in the morning was very dear. You see I had the added pleasure of reading it in bed and taking my time about it, whereas other mornings I have to read it through quickly while eating breakfast.

Dear Grandpa, please dont love me any the less because I am sixteen. No matter how old I am in years, I shall always be your young little Marjorie as long as you wish it. That was very sweet of you to think of a little gift for me and such a gift!! Something you have used yourself. It shall receive shower upon shower of blots. When I use your pen I certainly [*page missing*]

Gertrude Natkin to Clemens

[New York]
[after 30 June 1906]

Dear Mr. Clemens.

How good of you to think of me and especially in such a sweet way as I prize very highly any of your works.[1]

I hope you will excuse my neglegence in acknowledging your gift as I have been down to the seashore for a few days and I just returned this morning.

I have already [read] your book which I laughed over heartily

After my sister's wedding which is Sunday we are going to the Adirondacks. Of course I am glad to get away but still am looking forward to the autumn when I can see my dear Mr. Clemens again. Now continue to have a good rest which I know you need after your strenuous winter. Mother wishes to be remembered and I also wish to send my regard to Miss Lyon.

Au revoir, dear

Your little Marjorie

1. In her diary Gertrude Natkin wrote the following about this letter: "On June 30, Mr. Clemens sent me Eve's Diary with his autograph. I sent this letter—" (GND, early July 1906).

GERTRUDE NATKIN TO CLEMENS

[telegram]

[New York]

[30 November 1906]

Congratulations & best wishes with love and blots
Marjorie [1]

1. In her diary Gertrude notes, "I sent this telegram early in the morning. In the evening I sent Mr. Clemens my birthday gift which was a leather case. Soon after this Mr. Clemens went to Washington on business, that is to try to have a copyright bill passed to have the rights of the published preserved fifty years after he is dead" (GND, December 1906).

CLEMENS TO GERTRUDE NATKIN

[telegram]

[30 November 1906]

The same to you and good health and happiness

SLC

Gertrude Natkin to Clemens

[New York]
[25 December 1906]

Dear Mr. Clemens

Knowing how busy you are and also how tired you are I do not wish to make you more so by taking up time but I do want to wish you a very merry Christmas.   I hope that Santa has many good things in store for you, the Coming Year, including your copywright law.

From Marjorie.[1]

1. "On Christmas I sent Mr. Clemens this letter" (GND, December 1906).

Clemens to Gertrude Natkin

[telegram]

[New York]
[December 1906]

Wish you same and good health and happiness.

SLC

Gertrude Natkin to Clemens

[New York]
[20 February 1907]

My dear Mr. Clemens—

Although this is very late, to thank you for your sweet New Year greeting and also wish you a Happy New Year, I know that you will forgive me after I tell the reason of this delay.

A very sad misfortune has occurred in our family which naturally has upset us all   My sister (who you met and) who was with us at the Majestic Theatre on that memorable afternoon died. I wanted to write sooner but I had not the heart to write on such a sad occasion and thought I would wait until I became more reconciled to this loss.

My mother has not been well since this misfortune happened and is now in Lakewood but I hope she will come back in better health.

Now I know that you will accept my greetings for this New Year even though it is late

Your little Marjorie

CHAPTER TWO

First Angelfish

April 1907 – 30 December 1907

IN HIS AUTOBIOGRAPHICAL DICTATION of 17 April 1908 Clemens recalled a certain fortuitous spring day in 1907. It was "a fortunate
day, a golden day, and my heart has never been empty of grandchildren since." The specific reference is to his meeting Dorothy Butes,
a fourteen-year-old English girl, whose mother asked if they might
briefly visit Mark Twain during their travels in America. Clemens described Dorothy as "simple, sincere, frank and straightforward, as became her time in life" (MTAD, 17 April 1908‡). Although his correspondence with Dorothy was limited, he considered her, not Gertrude
Natkin, his first angelfish.

Except on special occasions, such as the visit of Dorothy Butes,
Clemens disliked his life in the house he rented at 21 Fifth Avenue.
In her diary Isabel Lyon described Clemens's mental outlook this way:
"This is too dreadful, this loneliness, for the King. . . . I telephone
in every direction to get people to come in for billiards, but no one
is to be reached. Mr. Dooley is South, Col. Harvey is busy, or skit-
tish, Dr. Rice is busy, the Coes are in Florida, the Benjamins in Lake
Placid, the Broughtons en route to some Southern place, and the rest
of the world can't play: and I am afraid for him" (IVLD, 26 Febru-

ary 1907). Although he received more correspondence in 1907 than any other year, it hardly dented the armor of unhappiness in which he had steeled himself. He sent out a continuous stream of regrets to invitations to give lectures and to attend dinners, teas, and other social occasions. Seldom did he show any enthusiasm for the activities his correspondents offered, unless, of course, the offer came from an old friend or a young lady. To ensure as agreeable a summer as possible, he rented the William Boss house in Tuxedo Park, New York, and also signed a contract for the construction of his "Autobiography House" in Redding, Connecticut.

Of course, Clemens continued his correspondence with certain old friends, such as William Dean Howells and H. H. Rogers. As in the past, Howell's sober personality brought out lightheartedness, even tomfoolery, on Clemens's part, as evidenced in the following letter of 1907:

To the Editor
Sir to you, I would like to know what kind of a goddam govment this is that discriminates between two common carriers & makes a goddam railroad charge everybody equal and lets a goddam man charge any goddam price he wants to for his goddam opera box
W D Howels
Tuxedo Park Oct 4
(goddam it)

Howells it is an outrage the way the govment is acting so I sent this complaint to the N.Y. Times with your name signed because it would have more weight.
Mark   (*MTHL* 827)

In early May 1907 Clemens received a cablegram from Oxford University inviting him to receive an honorary degree on 26 June. He readily accepted the invitation, for it redressed a grievance he had harbored for years that only Yale and Missouri had conferred honorary degrees on him. In his autobiography Clemens spoke heatedly on the inequity in degree giving, in which "persons of small and temporary consequence—persons of local and evanescent notoriety, persons who drift into obscurity and are forgotten inside ten years" receive most of the honorary degrees. He felt that the Oxford degree was certainly worth "twenty-five of any other" and would thus allow him to purge himself of "thirty-five years' accumulation of bile and injured pride" (*MTA* 349). He sailed for London on board the *Minneapolis* on 8 June, carrying with him explicit instructions from Clara regarding his behavior. She was especially concerned that he dress properly at all times, and that he wear something other than his white uniform.

On the *Minneapolis* he attempted to establish another friendship with a young lady, but this time he met with less success. Carlotta Welles apparently reminded him of his daughter Susy, and consequently he showed greater interest in "Charlie," as he nicknamed her, than she did in him. Despite his charming advances and hyperbolic notes, Carlotta Welles was unmoved. Many years later she recalled her experience with the famous author: "I used to get restless and chafed at times at being expected to sit quietly with him when my inclination was to race around" (Carlotta Welles Briggs to Dixon Wecter, MTP, 4 November 1947). Far more receptive to Clemens's endearments was Frances Nunnally, a schoolgirl from Atlanta, whom he met at Brown's Hotel in London and was soon calling "Francesca." She accompanied him on various social calls in London, and became a faithful correspondent and loyal angelfish.

In his biography, Paine observed that Clemens was no more able to resist all the London attention and invitations "than a débutante in her first season." His festive mood continued throughout the visit, and various of his eccentric habits were reported in the papers. One morning he paraded through the lobby of Brown's Hotel attired in his bathrobe, and marched down Dover Street for a swim at the public baths. The *London Times* reported that "after his bath Mark Twain returned to his hotel in his three-piece costume of one bathrobe and two slippers, and had the pleasure of making a lot more people open their eyes very wide" (IVLD, 3 June 1907). His unconventional street attire was even reported in the American papers, and Clara cabled to admonish her father for his unacceptable behavior.

Clemens apparently dressed suitably for the king's garden party at Windsor Castle and for luncheon with George Bernard Shaw, as well as at the Oxford degree ceremony on 26 June. He was honored along with

Rodin, Saint-Saëns, Kipling, General William Booth (of the Salvation Army), and British Prime Minister Campbell-Bannerman. Not only had the trip and its crowning event provided respite from his boredom at home, it had given him the highest recognition he could receive, save the Nobel prize. It did seem, as Paine expressed it, that "the great career . . . in a sense now had been completed since he had touched its highest point" (*MTB* 1405). Clemens may have felt this way about the event, but he also commented that he took careful mental notes on the pomp and pageantry for the planning of his own funeral procession.

He was greatly impressed with his scarlet Oxford robe and academic hood and on the ship home strolled the decks displaying his new regalia, still glowing with the euphoria of London and Oxford. Thus embellished, Clemens met an eleven-year-old American girl named Dorothy Quick, who had been watching him for some time, fascinated by his robe and crop of snowy hair. "It was soft as the down of a thistle and whiter than the gleaming feathers of a swan," she recalled (*EMT* 4). The famous snowy head with the drooping mustache and the brilliant blue eyes came up to her and said, "Aren't you going to speak to me, little girl?" (*EMT* 5). Dorothy recognized the robe and white head from newspaper photographs, and she had just been in England where her grandfather had been reading aloud from *Life on the Mississippi*. Clemens and Dorothy talked about his writing and her desire to become a serious fiction writer when she grew up. When she told him *Tom Sawyer* was her favorite book, he "revealed" to her that "all the bright things Tom did I took from my own youth; the other things I just made up. Of course, I was never bad" (*EMT* 10). According to Dorothy's published reminiscence, *Enchantment: A Little Girl's Friendship with Mark Twain*, they both suffered from bronchitis, liked to wear white, and they both adored Mark Twain. To honor their new friendship, Dorothy and Clemens vowed to wear white all the rest of the voyage. For her skillful play at shuffleboard, which Clemens called "horse billiards," he gave her an inscribed copy of his recent book, *Eve's Diary*.

One day a ship's officer came to Dorothy and asked if he was addressing Mark Twain's business manager. Dorothy nodded and was informed that Mr. Twain had announced he would not perform in the ship's program, a benefit for the sailors' fund, unless she gave her permission. The printed program for the event even announced him as "Mark Twain (by courtesy of Miss Dorothy Quick)." Their growing friendship moved so many of the ship's passengers that a photo session was arranged. Dorothy stood between Clemens and Captain Layland, while dozens of passengers snapped their Kodaks. When the prints were developed by the ship's photographer, there were many requests for the inseparable duo's autographs. Once they arrived in New York, the process was repeated for newspaper photographers. Dorothy recalled, "There was not a paper in New York the next day that didn't carry a photograph of 'Mark Twain and Dorothy Quick.'" One headline reported, "Mark Twain Home—Captive of Little Girl" (*EMT* 33). Before they separated at the New York docks, Clemens introduced Dorothy to his publishers, Frederick Duneka of Harpers and David Munro of the *North American Review*, who had come to meet him, and exacted a promise that she would visit him at Tuxedo Park, New York.

Dorothy's first visit (5–9 August 1907) made Clemens an enormously happy man, as his subsequent letters and dictations amply demonstrate. She remained in motion from 9 A.M. to 9 P.M., and Clemens tried his best to keep up with her. Not all the activities were exhausting, however; Dorothy spent her mornings writing or reading while Clemens worked on his autobiography, and in the afternoons there were often carriage rides in Clemens's open victoria. The evenings were occupied until well past Dorothy's usual bedtime with games of "cutthroat hearts." Isabel Lyon and Ralph Ashcroft, his young business manager, completed the table and subtly engineered Clemens's victories, knowing how important they were to him.

One night they heard a moth thumping against a lamp-lit window. Their game of hearts quickly gave way to a new activity, and within minutes Clemens had Isabel Lyon running about in the garden, net and chloroform in hand, capturing moths for Dorothy to collect. Dorothy recalled that in her enthusiasm she called one of them a "beaut"; it was probably the only time she displeased Clemens, who, his secretary whispered to Dorothy, absolutely detested slang (*EMT* 70).

On a few occasions Dorothy tiptoed into Clemens's room to witness a dictation session. "His dictation was like a mountain stream, swiftly flowing," she recalled. "The sentences came one after the other, with scarcely a pause between" (*EMT* 62). When he had finished dictating and correcting his day's work on the autobiography, he would often work with Dorothy on her writing. On one occasion he read Dorothy one of his unfinished stories and asked her to write a solution for his hero's dilemma, which she gladly did. Soon afterward they formed an "author's league for two," which was to cement their common interest and provide good writing experience for Dorothy (who did in fact become a professional writer and author of at least sixteen books). Clemens took great pleasure in recording Dorothy's dictations, after which he would read aloud from *A Connecticut Yankee in King Arthur's Court* or tell her about the writing of his novels and the experiences they were based upon.

Dorothy returned a month later for an even longer visit (3–12 September), and the exhausting good times continued. In her memoirs Dorothy recalled that there were ashtrays all about the house to receive the ashes from Clemens's perpetual cigars, and that after dinner they listened to the orchestrelle (a player organ), or had a session at the Parcheesi board. One afternoon, as Dorothy was pumping the orchestrelle and pretending she was giving a concert, a lady who stopped in for a visit was heard to remark, "It doesn't seem possible a child could play the organ like that." Clemens kept a serious face, while steering the woman to a porch so as not to shatter her illusion, and commented, "Dorothy does everything beautifully" (*EMT* 116).

During the second visit activities of the author's league continued, and Dorothy wrote a story about an Indian princess. In order to illustrate the finished story properly, Clemens had Dorothy dress up as an Indian rani, with a long embroidered skirt, a headband across her forehead, and a turquoise chiffon veil draped all about. The result was so dramatic that Clemens had photographs taken, probably chuckling under his breath the entire time. The finished photographs were tinted to capture Dorothy's exotic brilliance and eventually hung in the billiard room. Here was the first step toward the billiard room–Aquarium

Club headquarters at Stormfield, its walls to be eventually covered with framed photographs of a dozen angelfish.

Clemens greatly enjoyed receiving letters and read them aloud to Dorothy during her visit. Since many of the correspondents were seeking Mark Twain's autograph, Dorothy decided it would be easy to start an autograph collection. Clemens told her that from vast experience in such matters he would suggest she keep her requests brief and direct. They agreed on the wording of the following sample request:

Dear ———

Will you please send your autograph to a little girl who is anxious to add it to her collection?

Dorothy Quick

To get the collection started, Clemens purchased a small leather-bound book of blank pages and wrote the first entry himself (see 8 September 1907).

Although little else in 1907 could rival the pleasure Clemens derived from Dorothy's visits, other activities were planned to keep him from further boredom and loneliness. On 23 September he joined Harry and Mary Rogers on the Rogers family yacht, the *Kanawha*, and sailed to Jamestown, Virginia, to participate in a Robert Fulton Day celebration. The Rogerses' yacht joined a three-mile-long parade of vessels participating in the centennial celebration of the invention of the steamboat. Throughout the fall and winter, Clemens maintained a humorous correspondence with Mary Rogers. Playing on his own insatiable appetite for compliments, Clemens tellingly called his own game in this letter to Mary:

BUTTER WANTED

Any kind:
New; Old;
Salted; Unsalted;
Odorless; Fragrant;
Real preferred, but
Oleomargarine not turned away.

Apply at the old stand,
21 Fifth Ave.,
at the
Sign of the Butterfly . . . .
(*MTM* 106–7)

Clemens's candid confession need not be confined to his relationship
with Mary Rogers and Dorothy Quick. In fact, "Butter Wanted" cap-
tures his prevailing mood during the latter half of 1907 and all of 1908.

CLEMENS TO DOROTHY BUTES

[inscription]

[New York]
April 22/07

To Dorothy—
with the affectionate regards of
The Author

On the whole, it is better to deserve honors & not have them than have
them & not deserve them.

Truly Yours
Mark Twain

CLEMENS TO CARLOTTA WELLES

[aboard the SS *Minneapolis*]
[June 1907]

Charlie Dear,

    You don't know what you are missing. There's more than two thou-
sand porpoises in sight, and eleven whales, and sixty icebergs, and both
Dippers, and seven rainbows, and all the battleships of all the navies,
and me.

SLC

CLEMENS TO CARLOTTA WELLES

[note]

[aboard the SS *Minneapolis*]
[17 June 1907]

Please tell the story of the Twins, one got drunk and affected the other.[1]

1. This note was written across the top of a concert program. The event in aid of the Seamen's Orphanage included the sale of Mark Twain postcards and a reading by Clemens from his autobiography.

CLEMENS TO CARLOTTA WELLES

[inscription]

[aboard the SS *Minneapolis*]
[17 June 1907]

There's many a maid that's dear & sweet,
In Paris, Versailles, Marly
But not one maid in any of those several before-mentioned towns
That can compare with Charley.

M. T.

Front seat—don't forget.

RALPH ASHCROFT TO CARLOTTA WELLES

London
July 5/07

Dear Miss Welles:
    You didn't know he was a handwriting expert, did you? [1]
        Yours, truly,
            R. W. Ashcroft

1. Clemens had received an unsigned note that read, "Please send audograph Imme-diadely." He guessed it to have come from Carlotta and instructed Ralph Ashcroft: "The

puzzle *X* is beyond me. The *X X X* two *d*s in the above words, also the two *d*s & the *L* on the envelope, were written by Charlie. I wonder why she suppresses her name and address. Send this to her: for it is of course just barely possible that my divination is in error. In which case I am ashamed, & I beg her pardon." Clemens probably had Ashcroft send her an autographed photograph.

CLEMENS TO FRANCES NUNNALLY

London
[7 July 1907]

Itinerary.
(Subject to Frances's approval.)
2.30. Visit the Neac Slister family—a visit of some length.
3. E. H. Abbey, artist.
3.30. or 3.45. Visit Lord & Lady Slargatlock—15 or 20 minutes.
About 4. The Earl & Countess of Portsmouth. Formal.
Then Mrs. General McCook.
5, or a trifle later: tea with Lord & Lady Avebury.

SLC

CLEMENS TO CARLOTTA WELLES

London
July 8/07

Didn't I *say* you were a little rascal![1] Didn't I say it a dozen times? You wouldn't believe it then, but you believe it now. The idea of your playing jokes on an innocent old dilapidation that had such unlimited confidence in you! Well, it only shows that there are all sorts of criminals in this world; but never never never would I have taken you for one, Charlie dear.

However, it *did* please me—your instinct was right. And you were right again in supposing I was troubled: I *was;* for I was not absolutely sure that you were the joker, therefore in making the charge I might be in error & you might not like it—then I should be sorry & ashamed; and not just a little ashamed, but a good deal. For there is nothing that smarts & blisters a smarty's vanity like being caught in the act of being *over*-smart—oh, yes, as I know by experience!

I am leaving London for home next Saturday the 13th. Be a good child, & send me a good-bye per post, you convicted little rascal!

SL Clemens

1. Clemens has apparently received a reply from Carlotta Welles, proving he correctly guessed she was author of the mysterious note of about 5 July.

FRANCES NUNNALLY TO CLEMENS

[London]
July 12, 1907

Dear Mr. Clemens,—

You have done so much for me since I have been in London, and given me so much pleasure, that I just wanted to write a little note to thank you for your many kindnesses. I should certainly never have seen so many delightful English people and their beautiful homes, if it had not been for your kindness in taking me calling with you.

You must be sure not to forget to come to Catonsville to see those sixty girls[1] next November.

Wishing you the pleasantest of voyages over, I am
Your little friend,
Francesca.

1. A reference to her school, St. Timothy's, in Catonsville, Maryland.

CLEMENS TO CARLOTTA WELLES

London
July 12, [1907] late p.m.

Dear Charlie—

Indeed you *are* good—& although I do like to call you a little rascal, it is only because you are charming. I was afraid you wouldn't send me

Frances Nunnally and Clemens, London, July 1907. (Reproduced by permission of The Huntington Library, San Marino, California)

a good-bye, but you have sent me a lovely one, & by that gentle deed I know you are good.

You thought I couldn't trace my joker out, but I did. When I had been a day or so in this house I found that Mrs. Nunnally & Miss Frances were guests. Miss Frances had your address in her notebook, in your own handwriting. The d's & the Ls betrayed you. So I knew what little rascal it was that was playing jokes upon her guileless old shipmate.

You are right, Charlie, I didn't steal the cup; & if I even tried to steal it, it wasn't for myself, I only wanted to give it to you. I wouldn't take a thing like that for a selfish reason.

We sail in the morning. Good-bye, dear, & continue to be happy in that beautiful foreign home of yours.

Doctor S L C

CLEMENS TO DOROTHY QUICK

Tuxedo Park, New York
[late July 1907]

Dorothy dear, will you come & make me a visit? do you think your mother could spare you a week? Miss Lyon is 43 years old & quite able to take care of you. She would take the best of care of you, for she has been a governess, & knows all about it. I would send her to Plainville (or Plain*field*) to fetch you; also she would take you back at the end of your visit. Will you come? If you can't come for a whole week will you come for half a week? But I hope you can make it a whole one.

It is beautiful here—lakes, woods, hills, & everything! Yes, quite beautiful & satisfactory, but I miss you, all the same.

I hope you will remember me most kindly to your mother, & to your grandfather & grandmother; & that you will allow me to keep my place as

your ancient &
affectionate friend
S L Clemens

Clemens to Dorothy Butes

Tuxedo Park, New York
[late July 1907] [1]

Your letter has arrived tonight. Tried to telephone you but you are out. To-day mailed letter to you to New Hampshire. I have engagement here tomorrow or would go and see you. Please telephone me here first thing in the morning. Call 113 Tuxedo. I am unspeakably sorry you are going without seeing you. If I had known you were in town I would have called last night.

S.L. Clemens

1. This letter, one of three from Clemens to Dorothy Butes that have survived, appears to have been written just as she was returning to England, probably in late July or August 1907, rather than May 1907 as indicated on the letter.

Dorothy Quick to Clemens

Truell Inn, Plainfield, N.J.
[31 July 1907]

My dear Mr. Clemens,

On my return from Long Island I found your telegram and letter waiting for me. I was so glad to get them and to know you missed me too for I have missed you so much, and will be so glad to see you again so soon   I have never been away from Mother at all but I have promised her to be very brave and not to get home sick if she would let me go to you so she has promised and will write you by this mail thanking you so much for wanting me with you. I am with lots of love and kisses,

Your little friend
Dorothy

CLEMENS TO DOROTHY QUICK

Tuxedo Park, New York
[early August 1907]
Wednesday

Dorothy dear, I am writing you a *real* letter, and it will go to you in a day or two. But *this* is only just a line, to send you my love & say how glad we are that you are coming, and that we can have you one day *earlier*—which is delightful.

SLC

CLEMENS TO FRANCES NUNNALLY

Tuxedo Park, New York
August 3/07

Dear Francesca, if you sail Sept. 14 in the Minnewhatyoumay call um you are to reach New York on the 23d, which is the day after I sail for the Jamestown Fair. I may have to be absent 4 or 5 days—I can't tell yet.

When you arrive will you telephone or telegraph your address to
R. W. Ashcroft
    The Koy-lo Co, 11 Broadway
and to
S. L. Clemens, Tuxedo Park—so that Ashcroft or Miss Lyon can let me know at Old Point Comfort, Va.

This because we have shut up 21 Fifth ave till November, put it on the General Burglar Alarm, over the telephone wires, & brought the servants here. So there will be no one there to answer a message, not even a care-taker.

I don't know how to reach you, but I will try by way of Atlanta & take the chances.

I hope you & your mother are well.
Affectionately
    S L Clemens

FRANCES NUNNALLY TO CLEMENS

Brown's Hotel, London

August 3, 1907

Dear Mr. Clemens,—

By now I suppose you have become entirely rested from all the festivities you had over here, and I do not doubt but that you were very glad to get home, where you could find rest from luncheons, dinners, and such things. I hope you had a pleasant and smooth voyage over, and if the weather on sea was anything like it was over here the week you sailed, I am sure you did. I hear that the "Minnetonka" had a colision with a sailing vessel, but I was very glad to know that nothing serious came of it. I think if nobody was hurt, I should rather like the excitement of having such an accident.

We came back to London two or three days ago after a very nice little trip. As you know, we first went to Oxford for a few days, and while we were there, Mr. and Mrs. Porter were just as nice to us as they could be. They invited us to their home, and we enjoyed meeting the family very much. I think they are all over on the continent now.

From Oxford we went to Seamington and then down into Devonshire. This certainly is a beautiful part of the country, and though the rainy weather was rather against us, we had some lovely trips down there. We went everywhere we could by coach, for this is such a splendid way to see the pretty parts of the country.

Hoping that you have not forgotten your engagement at St. Timothy's next fall, I am

With love,

Francesca

CLEMENS TO DOROTHY QUICK

Tuxedo Park
[9 August 1907]
Friday eve

Dorothy, dear, one of these days I am going to write you a letter the first time I write my other children, but not now, now I haven't time, because I haven't anything to do, & I can't write letters except when I am rushed.

I went to bed as soon as you departed, there being nothing to live for after that, & the sunshine all gone. How do you suppose I am going to get along without you? For five hours this has been a dreary place, a sober & solemn place, a hushed & brooding & lifeless place, for the blessed Spirit of Youth has gone out of it, & left nothing that's worth while. Aren't you sorry for me, you fresh breeze blown from fragrant fields of flowers? I thought this was a home. It was a superstition. What is a home without a child? particularly a home that's had such a child as you in it. It isn't a home at all, it's merely a wreck. *Now* I hope you see what you've done by going away, you little witch.

It's odd: this morning I dated that "recommend" August 5 instead of 9. I think it is because you seemed to have been here only one day— just one short beautiful day, without a break in it. I am very grateful to your mother for lending you to me, you dear sweet child. I am aware that you can't come again in August, but I hope you can come after Sept. 2 & stay a *whole* week, not a broken one. I mean to expect it & count upon it; & I do hope I shall not have to make any engagements that would interfere.

The Lioness is back, & has given me a nice long account of your journey down, & about the turtle; & and has told me that she delivered you safe & sound & happy into your mother's hands—which is very good news for me.

Are you an idol? I suspect it; for I know you have left a lot of idola-ters behind you in this house. Of whom the very principalest one is the undersigned.

Please give my kind regards to all your household.

S.L.C.

Dorothy Quick and Clemens, Tuxedo Park, August 1907.
(Courtesy, The Mark Twain Project, The Bancroft Library)

Clemens to Dorothy Quick

Tuxedo Park

Sunday, Aug. 11 [1907]

This isn't a letter, Dorothy dear, yet I know I ought to write you a letter, because I said I would write you every time I wrote the other children, & I've just finished a letter to Clara. But I never *could* keep promises very well. However, I shall certainly write you a letter before very long. I wrote to Clara:

"When Dorothy went away she took the sun & the moon & the constellations with her, & left silence & solitude & night & desolation behind her."

And *that's* a true word, if ever *I've* spoken a true word!

Thursday, 15th. I have been away several days, but am home again —and no Dorothy! And so I go mourning around, like an old cat that's lost her kittens. But you are coming soon again, & that is a large comfort to me. You are the best reader, of your age, I have yet encountered; & when I finish teaching you & drilling you you will read still better than you do now. It's a great accomplishment, a very great & very rare accomplishment, & *I'm* the expert that knows how to teach it! There'll be grand times in my class of one pupil, Dorothy dear!

Thank you for your letter, which was very sweet & welcome. I am glad you arrived safe—you & the other butterflies. And the turtle with the warlike name.

A wonderful thing has happened here. You remember the central bed of nasturtiums—the round one. Well, Miss Lyon planted some seeds there, & raised a family of rabbits. She asked me to tell you that. The nest is under the nasturtiums, in the middle of the bed. There are 3 little rabbits, & they are about the size of mice. Their eyes are not open yet. I hope they will still be there when you come. I have named them Dorothy. One name is plenty for all of them, they are so little.

Hugs & kisses—well, I'm[?] sending them—along with the love of your most devoted admirer & friend

SLC

DOROTHY QUICK TO CLEMENS

Truell Inn, Plainfield, N.J.
16 August, 1907

My dear Mr. Clemens

It's just a week since I last saw you and I miss you very much indeed I did not go to Long Island on Tuesday but I am going this Tuesday you see my Granpa wanted me this week but mother and I will surely go next week it is lovely down there but I like it much better here, the pictures I took did not turn out well but I am enclosing those that did there is one very good one of you and me which Miss Lyon took and I will send you one when I get it, I wish I could read to you a little while this morning: would you like it too? I am going to study very very hard this winter for I want to write stories when I grow up if I do what do you think would be a good name to use? I forgot to tell you I have Mr. Roosevelt and Grover Cleveland signatures and I have written for lots of others with lots of love a big hug and a great many kisses I am your

Little Dorothy

Lots of love and kisses for Miss Lyon.

CLEMENS TO DOROTHY QUICK

Tuxedo Park
[17–22 August 1907]
Saturday

Do you know what that is? It is a butterfly. Drawn by the artist. The gifted artist. I am the gifted artist. Self-taught.

No, I find it is a grasshopper. It is for your collection. Miss Lyon has nailed it to a box, with pins. It took more chloroform than was good for it. And so it is sleeping with its fathers.

Sunday

We talk about you all the time. You are not a large subject, but a very entertaining one.

"Would I like to have you read to me?" Indeed I should. I shouldn't like anything better.

Don't you be troubled about your hand, Dorothy. It is a good hand, & has the chiefest of all merits: that it is as easy to read as print.

Miss Lyon didn't count right: there are 4 little rabbits. She can count horses very well, but not rabbits, on account of being near-sighted.

Monday, A.M.

"Just a *week*" since I saw you! Why, you little humbug, it is over 3 months; even Miss Lyon, who never gets anything straight but cork-screws & potato peelings & things like that, concedes that it's upwards of *two* months. What is the matter with your veracity-mill?

Night.

It is a good idea, to choose a name in advance, & then fit the litera-ture onto it when the literature comes. I will keep on the lookout for a fortunate name, dear. Write another little story now, & send it to me. It will take you several years to learn to do a story even *tolerably* well, & it will cost lots of good hard work, & patient thought, & sharp attention & close observation, & ever so much tearing-up & re-writing—but no matter, it's worth the trouble; & no trade is ever well learned on any other terms.

Good-night it's sleep-time.

Wednesday, Aug. 21.

THE BUSY BEE

About tomorrow or next day there'll be a note from the same, I hope, containing that picture of the same & me which the same Kodak'd when the same was here.

I suppose you will return to Plainfield for your birthday?

If a parcel arrives there from Harper & Brothers in a day or two, it is for your birthday.

That thing the bee is chasing is a dog, or a rat, or something of that kind, I think but there is room for conjecture. This does not settle it. What do you think it is, if you've got time?

You are coming Tuesday the 3d. Now then, *that's* settled, lassie. Shall you be welcome? There isn't any doubt about it, dear.

Afternoon.

The Harpers have sent the books here. It's just as well: I will write my name in them, then forward them.

Thursday, 22

I'm collecting red cigar-belts for you against you coming—but I love you—notwithstanding.

SLC

CLEMENS TO FRANCES NUNNALLY

Tuxedo Park
Aug. 18/07

I am very glad to hear from you, Francesca dear.

Mr. Porter wrote me of your visit, with your mother, & it was clear that he & his family enjoyed the visit very much. Very nice folks they are.

No indeed, I have not forgotten the proposed visit to St. Vincent's in the fall. I shall be there.

It occurred to me that you might reach New York & telephone my house & get no answer & not understand why; so I started the enclosed explanatory note after your August 3rd. It may miss you, but the present one won't for I shall enclose it to Captain Gates before he sails for England the last day of this month & you will get it when you board his ship Sept. 14th.

You will be pretty sure to have a pleasant voyage: a little frosty, perhaps, but sunny & smooth.

With love to you & kindest regards to your mother.

SLC

DOROTHY QUICK TO CLEMENS

East Rockaway
Long Island
26 August 1907

My Dear Mr Clemens

I have just gotten your letter I have been watching for it every mail the butterflys are grand I think I like your kind best because they dont have to die still I am very proud of my collection and I hope I can get some more when I come back Oh please Mr Clemens try and keep the little baby rabbits I love them so much it will be such fun to see them play around the flower beds We will take thier pictures yesterday I went on my first real picnic we went on a lovely sail boat the gentlemen got off and dug clams then we sailed up the beach and they got off again and cooked the clams while we got the lunch ready it was such fun of course I didint like the clams I never like anything other people think is fine it seems to me but I enjoyed the picnic and had a very find day we left at ten and returned at eight oclock I shall spend my birthday here

Grandpa and Grandma are coming down on Saturday and stay over Sunday which is my birthday but any mail or parcel sent to Plainfield will be alright and thank you so much for sending me a present I know it is a book and I shall be very happy when it comes Mother says I must confess to you that I read the Dogs Tail it was sad and I cried but I am glad I read it now for I should not have been quite happy untill I had you don't mind do you? Mother wants me too ask you if I come Wed. instead of Tues. Will it be just as convenient for you I shall be so happy to be with you again and am not a bit afraid of being homesick this time with lots of love and kisses for yourself and Miss Lyon
　　your little
　　　　Dorothy

P.S. Mother wants to know what train Miss Lyon will take down and would like her too have luncheon with us at the Hardware Club. We would meet Miss Lyon at the down town ferry if we know the time on Wednesday if this is as convenient as Tuesday with love.

Clemens to Dorothy Quick

> Tuxedo Park
> Aug. 26/07
> Monday

At last, you dear little tardy rascal! This morning I was going to stick up a notice on the back porch:

LOST CHILD!
=

Answers to the name of Dorothy.
=

Strayed, Stolen or Mislaid.

DISAPPEARED
On or about the 9th of August.
=

Any one restoring this inestimably
precious asset to the
SORROWING
Will be richly
REWARDED!

—and right away this evening came your letter, & takes every bit of the uneasiness out of me! I had gone to bed, but Miss Lyon brought it anyway, because she knew I would break her furniture & throw all her things out of the window if she delayed it till morning.

Very well. You have been having good times; so I am satisfied, & will go to sleep now.

But wait! Where is that picture of you & me? You have forgotten it, dear, but I must have it.

Tuesday.

Yes, Wednesday will be perfectly convenient—and we'll have you a whole week, which is grand! Provided you don't get homesick—& we *do* hope you won't. We'll do our very best to keep you happy & content.

Miss Lyon will arrange about the trains with your mother by telephone, if she can: otherwise by letter.

I've got a birthday [?] for you, but I will keep it till you come, because it isn't the [?] & I shall need to [?] Guess what it is. [1]

You've written me a good letter: simple, lucid, straightforward, well expressed.

FLIGHT
Of the Rabbit Family

Alas, they have deserted us, & I am so sorry. We were hoping to keep them for you, & we never dreamed that they would go away & leave us. I am just as sorry as I can be.

That big one that has three ears & looks like an angel, isn't an angel at all, it is the mother rabbit.

She isn't swimming, she is praying—praying for succor, I reckon: that is, I *think* that that is her idea . . . No, that isn't it: she is jumping —jumping over a rope-walk, or a stone wall, or something of that kind, & has bumped her stomach against it, poor thing. It is very difficult to tell what a rabbit is really trying to do, in a picture, because rabbits are so irrelevant. It is their nature, when excited.

Do I mind? (that you read the dog's tale.) Indeed, no. I don't mind anything you do, because you never mean any harm; & you are a dear good child all the time.

You have written the *very letter* I was going to propose that you write: a letter telling me all about your activities & industries & enjoyments, all the things your busy hands & head find to interest themselves in. It is good practice for you, in observing & remembering, & good entertainment for me, because I am fond of you, & so whatever you do, & think, & feel, interests me.

AFTERNOON

The Lioness[2] has just received good news by telephone: you are coming *Tuesday*. It's fine! You will reach this house at 5.30 p.m. You will most certainly be welcome.

EVENING

DEER

There were several of them. They came down hill from the woods above the house, & stopped a while behind the kitchen to look at the cook. You can see by their eager expression & enthusiastic delight, that they had never seen a cook before. Sometimes they go down through the woods below the house to get a drink at the lake. If ever they come into the house you must be ready, for we will have them to luncheon & then photograph them in the act.

With love & good night,

SLC

1. The three bracketed question marks here are in Clemens's hand. He is teasing Dorothy so that she will pay him a visit to receive her birthday gift.
2. Clemens's secretary Isabel Lyon.

ISABEL LYON TO DOROTHY QUICK

[Tuxedo Park N.Y.]
Aug. 31. 1907

Dear Dorothy:

I wanted to write you two days ago, but one of *my* headaches came along, & so I couldn't tell you how glad I am you are coming back again to Tuxedo. You will need some warmer clothes perhaps, for even now in August it is like September—real September. The laundress told me yesterday that she saw the mother rabbit up under a hedge, nursing her four children. She doesn't often come to the nasturtium bed now, for Charles the workman didn't know she & her family were there & so he turned the hose upon it, & of course they fled.

Please thank your mother for her nice note & tell her how glad I shall be to see you both on Tuesday.

With much love to you dear, & warm regards to Mrs. Quick, Ever yours

Isabel Lyon

Dear, will you bring with you, the one or two letters Mr. Clemens has written you since you ran away from us? There is something I want very much to see in one of them.[1] It has been dreadful of me, but since you left I haven't been very well, & I have been very busy, & so my films haven't been developed even yet. We'll try to be more successful this time.

1. Isabel Lyon was perhaps interested in seeing Clemens's drawings in his letters of 17 and 26 August. Clemens may have wished to chuckle some more over his drawings and other enticements to win a visit from Dorothy.

CLEMENS TO DOROTHY QUICK

[telegram]

Tuxedo Park
[1 September 1907]

To Miss Dorothy Quick

I tried to get some elephants for your birthday but they charge ten thousand dollars apiece, 3 for twenty-five thousand, I can get one elephant & sixteen hundred monkeys for the same money if you prefer. Telephone answer.

S.L.C.

Isabel Lyon to Dorothy Quick

Tuxedo Park
[2 September 1907]
Monday

Dear Dorothy:

Mr. Clemens has just left for town, & he asks me to write your mother & you to come up here on Thursday the second leaving N.Y. Central on the 4:15 train for Redding. Mr. Clemens and Mr. Paine will be on the same train. Please do not disappoint Mr. Clemens. He sends you much love, & to your mother too.

Yours ever
I. V. Lyon

Clemens to Dorothy Quick

[inscription]

Tuxedo Park
Sept. 8, 1907

Consider well the proportions of things: It is better to be a young june-bug than an old bird of paradise.[1]

Truly Yours
Mark Twain

To Dorothy—
With the love of S.L.C.

1. At Clemens's suggestion, Dorothy had become interested in collecting autographs. He gave her a small leather-bound book of blank pages and wrote this inscription on the first page.

Clemens to Dorothy Quick

Tuxedo Park, New York
September 12, 1907
Thursday

Dorothy Dear, you are gone, & I am dissatisfied.

Friday

You are still gone, & I am still dissatisfied.

Subsequently

You are still gone, & I am still more dissatisfieder than ever. This is a long day.

Homeward the bandit plods her weary way and leaves the world to darkness and to me:[1]

I will to bed.

Saturday

Which I did. But a cricket was hiding somewhere in the room, & continuously & monotonously shrieking. I endured it an hour (until 10), then removed to another room. I returned at 11, at 1, & at 4, but was driven out each time.

Last night he drove me out at 9:30, & I returned no more. To-night Miss Lyon will occupy my room & capture him if possible.

———

Meantime your letter has come, you very dear child, & I think it is the best typewritten handwriting I have ever seen.[2] I would not have believed a type-machine could spell so well. I'm a-missing you, Dorothy.

(Anyway I *think* it's an axe, but some think it's a bonnet.) But it's for the cricket when I get him—I am quite certain as to that.

I'm going to Fairhaven, Mass.,[3] day after tomorrow—Monday—& return Thursday night.

I sail for Jamestown three days later, to be gone several days.

I've had a misfortune, Dear: a page of the Indian story is missing. I shall find it, but meantime I want you to rewrite it—it's good practice —& send it here.

With lots of love, you dear little rascal.

SLC

1. Here Clemens parodies the following line from Thomas Gray's "Elegy Written in a Country Churchyard": "The plowman homeward plods his weary way, / And leaves the world to darkness and to me."

2. "Typewritten handwriting" refers to Dorothy's clear and very regular script as opposed to her "lawless" spelling.

3. Fairhaven was the home of Clemens's good friend H. H. Rogers.

DOROTHY QUICK TO CLEMENS

[Plainfield, N.J.]
Sept. 13. 07

My Dear Mr Clemens

I have arrived safely of course I always do. I find it very hot here. to hot for me I miss you very very much but I can write to you and have letters which will be very very nice I hope Miss Lyon got home safely. I am afraid I can not write any more but send lots and lots of love to you and Miss Lyon

your very loving
Dorothy

ISABEL LYON TO DOROTHY QUICK

Tuxedo Park
Sept. 19, 1907

Dearest Dorothy:

This is just the beginning of the photographs that I am to send you. The others have not yet arrived from N.Y. Mr. Wark[1] developed the Indian Princess & cut down the photo a little, but I think that improves it and isn't it lovely? Mr. Clemens is away & will not be home until some time on Friday. It is very very desolate without him. But to relieve the situation a beautiful young grey & white cat followed Claude & Katie home one night not long since, in fact since Mr. Clemens went away. & the beautiful creature has spent a lot of time with me.

Thank you very much too for the little photos you sent; they are nice, but do not forget that you are going to send me the whole batch of negatives. I quite forgot to give you the sixty-cents, or the roll of films for the one I am having developed, so here is the check for 60 cents dear.

Mr. Robert P. Porter of Oxford who spent last Sunday here, gave me these English cigar bands; have you any like them?

With much love to you dear, & warm regards to your mother, & to your grandfather I am yours always

Isabel Lyon

1. Charles E. "Will" Wark, Clara Clemens's accompanist and a family friend, appeared at Tuxedo Park with some frequency.

Dorothy Quick to Clemens

[Plainfield, N.J.]
[20 September 1907]

My Dear Mr Clemens

I spent Saturday and Sunday with my uncle and just recieved your letter and was very glad to get it I am very glad you had such a nice time at Jamestown   My uncle invited Mother and I to go down last week but Mother thought it would be too much for me so we did not go I am going to see Robert Mantell in King Lear to-night I know he will be fine in it we have a very nice theather out here and all the best actors come out here I enclose some pictures for you I also sent Miss Lyon a lot I am having a lovely time at school and like it very much I must close now as it is dinner time.

with lots and lots of love hugs and kisses I am your loving little
Dorothy

Clemens to Frances Nunnally

The Waldorf Astoria
New York
September 25, 1907, 11.30 AM

Dear Francesca:

I have just come ashore from the Yacht, & am passing by to take the 12.55 Erie RR train for Tuxedo Park.[1] You & your mother are out—naturally, at this time of day. I would have telephoned in advance, but there wasn't time.

Won't you & your mother come out to Tuxedo Park on Saturday & stay over Sunday? I hope you can & will. There's a good train, with parlor car, leaving the New York side at 12.40 p.m. (only on Saturdays.)

Mr. Ashcroft (11 Broadway) can give you all needful information if you will call him up. And I shall want to know when to meet you at Tuxedo station & pass you by the guard.

With love

SLC

I shall wait here until 12.05.

1. Clemens had most likely been yachting with H. H. Rogers and was returning to Tuxedo Park. He wrote this letter at the Waldorf, leaving it for Frances and her mother. They were returning from their summer in England.

Clemens to Dorothy Quick

Tuxedo Park

Sept. 26/07

Dorothy dear, I hear that you are at school, & that you greatly like it & are very busy—all of which is good to hear, & naturally is a great pleasure & comfort to your mother.

I am back from Jamestown & am glad. Still, we had reasonable weather & a swift voyage & altogether a good time. Miss Lyon & her mother went down on another boat & enjoyed the trip. Meantime the cricket has joined the union & cleaned out. This room is quiet now.

Delia's gone. She meant well, but she wasn't of much account & was a troublebreeder with the other servants, so Miss Lyon discharged her. Maggie is back, & now it's a model household. I think you knew Maggie. In about a week Catherine will be back from Ireland—*she's* a bird!

It is milking time, now. I mean I am taking my noonday glass of milk. Several drops have gone down the wrong way. Try it—it is ever so much fun.

I miss you, dear—I miss you a *lot*. If I had you here we would start the Author's League again.

And now Miss Lyon has come up to say some ladies are calling & I must go down & see them.

You remember Miss Lyon?

You remember how she looks?

The way she looks.
Good-bye, I love you very much.

SLC

FRANCES NUNNALLY TO CLEMENS

The Waldorf-Astoria, New York
[September 1907]

Dear Mr. Clemens,—

I received your note yesterday and was so sorry that we missed you, for I should like so much to have seen you.

It is lovely of you to give Mama and I that kind invitation and we appreciate it ever so much. We shall be delighted to accept it, and as you suggested we shall come to Tuxedo on Saturday by the train which leaves the New York side at 12:40 p.m. I hope you enjoyed your trip to Jamestown and I am glad you did not stay down there too long, so that we can have the pleasure of seeing you before we leave for Baltimore.

Thanking you again for the invitation, I am

With love,
Francesca

Clemens to Dorothy Quick

[Tuxedo Park]
2 October 1907

It is a very good photograph, Dorothy dear, & I am very glad to have it. I wish I could have you here, too—I miss you all the time. Goodness! What makes you think I have forgotten you? Indeed I haven't, but I have been so busy lately that I haven't written my daughters and they are scolding me. I hope to do better, now, and be good, for a while. It will attract attention. I like that.

I wish I *could* go & see you, dear, but I know you couldn't save me from the reporters—they would find me out in spite of all you could do to prevent it. You dear child. But I'll be back in New York, just at the end of this month & then I hope you can come to us on Saturdays and stay over. We can have very good times together.

Mr. Ashcroft is here to-day.

=====

Oct. 3

Last night we played "hearts"—a very good game, I think, because it is simple, and doesn't require any mental labor. I wish we had thought of it when you were here. But next time we'll play it. It is more interesting than those other games.

You should see our cat. It is half grown, & is gay & wise & courteous, & very handsome. It has a tail at one end, & two sets of legs, one set at the bow & the other at the stern, & is just as astonishing in other ways.

This cat is trying to look like Miss Lyon, but I think it does not succeed very well—& won't, until it has had more practice. It sits up like this. Always on the same end. Everybody admires it and thinks it is full of talent.

We drove over the bigger-pond road and all around the lake, yesterday afternoon—remember that road? It is very beautiful now. We'll make a longer drive today. I wish you were here to go with us.

Evening

Your letter & the pictures have come, dear. The one where you are standing by my chair is the very *very* best one of you I have ever seen, & you are next best in the one where I am a nice old white headed nigger.

That little cat caught a bird to-day & brought it in, & it got away & flew out of the window.

There is a heavenly dog here, but he is not ours; he came down the hill on a visit, & will have to be sent back. He is the long kind.

With love & lots of kisses
SLC

FRANCES NUNNALLY TO CLEMENS

St. Timothy's
Catonsville, Md.
October 2, 1907

Dear Mr. Clemens,—

I just wanted to write you a note and tell you again how much we enjoyed our visit at your home. It was a very great pleasure to both mama and myself, and we certainly had lots of fun playing hearts as we did.

It is half grown, & is gay &
wise & courteous, & very handsome. It has a tail at one
end, & two sets of legs, one set
at the bow & the other at the
stern, & is just as astonishing
in other ways.

This cat is trying to look
like Miss Lyon, but I think
it does not succeed very well
— & won't until it has had
more practice.

up like this. Always on the
same end. Everybody admires
it & thinks it is full of talent.
We drove over the nigger-pond
road & all around the lake, yesterday afternoon — remember
that road? It is very beautiful now.
We'll make a longer drive today.
I wish you were here to go with
us.

Clemens to Dorothy Quick, 2 October 1907.
(Courtesy, The Mark Twain Project, The Bancroft Library)

4

Evening.
=

Your letter & the pictures have come, dear. The one where you are standing by my chair is the very very best one of you I have ever seen, & you are next best in the one where I am a nice old white-headed nigger.

That little cat caught a bird to-day & brought it in, & it got away & flew out of the window.

There is a heavenly dog here, but he is not ours; he come down the hill on a visit, & will have to be sent back. He is the long kind.

With love & lots of kisses — SLC

Clemens to Dorothy Quick, 2 October 1907.
(Courtesy, The Mark Twain Project, The Bancroft Library)

When we got back to New York after this delightful little visit, we went back to our shopping and were kept busy until the very moment we left yesterday morning.

We reached Baltimore yesterday afternoon and this morning I shall enter school. All the girls will come some time to-day and then to-morrow I suppose our work and study will begin. It will seem very strange at first, but I am sure I shall soon get used to it and shall like it very much.

Hoping to see you down here next month, I am

With love,

Francesca

Clemens to Frances Nunnally

Tuxedo Park

Oct. 4/07

Thank you very much, for letting me know you arrived safely, Dear Francesca. It was hard for us to let you & your mother go; however it wouldn't have been any easier if the visit had been many times longer than it was.

I hope Governor Warfield really has a daughter that's coming out. I don't know. But he *said* he had. I hope so; & that it will happen in November, & not in the holidays, so that I can see you. If you please, Dear, give my kindest regard to your mother, & thank her again for the visit.

With love,

SLC

Ashcroft came & we played the game. When it was through he was about bankrupt, & Miss Lyon owed 94 buttons.

AUTOBIOGRAPHICAL DICTATION, 5 OCTOBER 1907

Francesca and her mother arrived from England ten days ago, and spent a couple of days with us. Ten days earlier Dorothy, my latest little shipmate, arrived here and we had her delightful society during seven days and nights. She is just eleven years old, and seems to be made of watch-springs and happiness. The child was never still a moment, when she wasn't asleep, and she lit up this place like the sun. It was a tremendous week, and an uninterruptedly joyful one for us all. After she was gone, and silence and solitude had resumed their sway, we felt as if we had been through a storm in heaven.

Dorothy is possessed with the idea of becoming a writer of literature, and particularly of romance, and it was a precious privilege to me to egg her on, and beguile her into working her imagination. I never betrayed myself with a laugh, but the strain which I had to put upon every muscle and nerve and tendon in me, to keep from breaking out, almost made a physical wreck of me sometimes. She is swift with the pen, she is hampered by no hesitations when she is dictating, and she is even a more desperate speller than ever Susy was. We began our mornings early—as early as half-past eight and from that time until nine in the evening there were no breaks in our industries. I say *our* industries because I always assisted her in them until I broke down at noon; then Miss Lyon stood a watch till about three; then I resumed my watch. In order to save myself from perishing, I usually persuaded Dorothy to devote this half-afternoon watch to literature. By grace of this subterfuge, I was enabled to lie down and perform; I lay on one lounge on the back porch and she on another one at my side; then she dictated her stories glibly, and I set them down. When a story was finished I dictated it to her from my manuscript, and she wrote it down. I got around telling her why I observed this practice; I didn't want her to know my reason, which was that I wanted the tale in her own brisk and tumultuous handwriting, adorned with her own punctuation —I mean the absence of it—and steeped in the charm of her incomparable spelling. Her tales were of a highly romantic order, and she chose highly romantic scenes and episodes for them; but at that point romance usually took a rest; it didn't extend itself to the names of her characters; *any* sort of name would appear for her heroes—and five times in six they bore names of so plebeian and flat & pulpy a sort as to almost disqualify those persons from doing heroic things. But to me those forlorn names were golden, and I wouldn't have traded them for the most high-sounding ones in the world's romantic literature. One day she dictated an Indian romance, and I set it down. The little rascal was all innocence and candor, and was seldom suspicious, but it cost me many lies to keep her so, because every now and then as the sentences fell felicitously from her lips they hit me hard, and my suppressed laughter made my body shake; and when she detected that, I could notice a vague suspicion in her voice when she would ask what was the matter with me. The answer which came nearest to satisfying her was that I was feeling a little chilly; but that had also another effect, which was not a happy one for me, for it aroused her affectionate solicitude and she would not rest until I had taken some whisky to keep me from catching cold. Before we got through with the brief Indian tale—which I am going to insert here just as she wrote it, just as she spelled it, just as she punctuated it—the loving little creature had inflicted so many whiskies on me that my efficiency as an amanuensis was a little damaged and rickety; and if the tale had gone on a little longer I should have been incapable.

    in the very depts of the forest the day was a sultry day and Henry Potter was tiered of hunting when suddenly a wild war hoop sounded very near him great heavens it's the Idains what can I do the hoop was coming nearer and nearer I must run for my life now he thought but then yes I must oh what can I do—the hoop was almost upon him now and from the other direction was comming another hoop good heavens it must be a band there is no chance I must hide in that hollow tree the indains by this time were there they at once began to camp then one of the Idains said we must have some wood for our fire there is a good tree there he pointed to the one where Henry was Hiding the men of the tribe began to approach the tree with tomahaks one of the Idains saw the hollow in the tree and said oh there must be an annimal in that tree I will get that for my supper Henry was thinking a nice supper you'll have out of me and even in all the danger that was around him he could not help smailing the Idain split the hole in the tree wider and when Henry saw his eye he knew no

more— — — — — — — — — — — — — — — — — — —m— —
— — —— —— —— —— — — —— — —— —— —— —— —— — — —

——when he awoke he was in a large tent the tent of the chife who was glaring
down upon him I wish I could make you see that tent with all the grim old
warriors in thier coustans[1] ranged about thier chief eager to see what was to
be done with this new captive—he will be burned cried some others he will be
stoned with a lot of other opinions—at last the chief said put him under gaurd
for tonight tomorrow we will decide what to do with him. Henry saw an Indain
girl in the ranks of women start and look toward him—then he was led away it
was about 11 oclock that night when a gentle footstep came lightly into the tent
then said a voice he thought he knew come with me at once who are you asked
Henry I am Margearet oh Margearet cried Henry Margearet was a girl who
had dissepered from the seltement 2 years ago she was dressed as an Indain
girl and was taned[2] she and Henry loved each other and were to be married
she said we have no time for talking now come Henry followed her and she led
him safely to the edge of the forest where they lived happily ever afterwards.

    1. costumes [Clemens's note]
    2. tanned [Clemens's note]

After this she reeled off this masterful tale just as she had punctuated
it—without a pause anywhere, and just as if Henry's adventures were
passing before her eyes at the moment and she was simply setting them
down according to facts. I was glad when "Margearet" got her young
man safely out to the edge of the forest where they lived happily ever
afterwards—without the formality of a marriage—for I thought for a
moment that she was going to furnish the pair a family without any
superfluous preliminaries and I would get another whisky-drench by
consequence.

Isabel Lyon to Dorothy Quick

Tuxedo Park
Oct. 7. 1907

Dear Dorothy:
    Two days ago these prints arrived & twice I tried to get them ready to
send to you, but things and people interrupted me. One was a woman

who came all the way from Philadelphia to ask Mr. Clemens to lecture there; but of course he couldn't do it, & I had a hard time trying to induce her to let me send for a jigger. You are busy in these days & so am I.

Tonight Mr. Clemens & I are going to dine with Mr. & Mrs. Lord. Do you remember Mr. Lord who called while we were on the porch one afternoon and Mr. Clemens was reading aloud from the dear "Yankee at King Arthur's Court?"

I think some of these photographs are charming, but some of the others came out very badly & are not worth having & I am disappointed.

Two weeks from yesterday we go to New York. I have been in several times opening the house & now Miss Clara Clemens is there.

Please give my very kind regards to your Mamma & to Mr. & Mrs. Aaron.

Very affectionately yours,
Isabel Lyon

CLEMENS TO DOROTHY QUICK

Tuxedo Park
[19 October 1907]

Dorothy dear, it is perfectly lovely here, now—with brilliant skies, brilliant water, sleek as a mirror, & all the brilliant colors of the hills painted on it like a picture. And there's rabbits—oh no end! They've got a nest in that tree that leans over the nasturtium bed, & they scamper up & down it all day long & jabber. And as for squirrels, & deer, & Italians, & other game, They're everywhere. And nobody shoots them, for it isn't allowed, I don't know why. And there are owls, & cows, & bears; & nights you can hear them hooting. Sometimes they make the kind of a noise a preacher makes. It is awful, but I am not afraid. The others are afraid, but I am calm, & go down cellar.

I believe that that is about all the news there is, except that we leave

Dorothy Quick and Clemens, Tuxedo Park, August 1907.
(Courtesy, The Mark Twain Project, The Bancroft Library)

Tuxedo the 31st, to live in town—21-Fifth ave—where you must come & stay over Sundays every time you can be spared.

Dear heart, you must'nt send stories to St. Nicholas, yet, it is too soon.[1] You must learn the trade first, & nobody can do that without a long & diligent apprenticeship—not anything short of 10 years. Write the stories—write lots & lots of them for practice—& when the Literary League gets together again, we'll examine into your progress & take note of such improvement as we find.

We have a very nice thoughtful little cat, & it catches snakes & brings them into the house for Miss Lyon to play with.

3.30 p.m. Time to get up.

With love & many kisses

SLC—who misses you, dear.

1. *St. Nicholas* magazine had run a contest for stories by children under age twelve. Dorothy was disappointed at his mild admonishment after she had won "honorable mention" in the contest. Years later she was able to comment, "His words did me more good than any amount of praise" (*EMT* 105).

DOROTHY QUICK TO CLEMENS

[Plainfield, N.J.]
[after 19 October 1907]

My Dear Mr Clemens

I have been watching the mail for a long while expecting a letter every day I feel very lonesome for you when you dont write for so long Mother says you are a very busy man and I should have patience but I cant. Please write me soon if only a tiny little letter I had a reply from the St. Nickolas yesterday they said my story was very good but too long so I think I will take your advice and wait until I am older before I try again I copied a lead in the Ladies Home journal and it was so good I won the prize please write to me very soon. I am well and happy but I miss you very very much with love to Miss Lyon and lots and lots of love and kisses for you I am

Your fond little
Dorothy

Frances Nunnally to Clemens

St. Timothy's
Catonsville, Md.
Oct. 27, 1907

Dear Mr. Clemens,—

I was so glad to get your letter and have been trying to find time to write to you ever since, but something is planned for us to do every minute of the day, and I do not have any time to myself. We have to study awfully hard, but then we have to take a certain amount of recreation every day, so that we keep in good health. We are outdoors almost all the afternoon, playing basket ball, or tennis, or some game like that. I have never been better in my life and my appetite is perfectly enormous, so that I am really getting fat.

It is almost November now and I hope you know positively that you are coming down to Annapolis, and you must be sure to stop by Baltimore. I should so love to have you come out here to our school, and all the other girls are crazy to have you come too. So if you find that you really can come down, please let me know, and come out to see us. The girls here are just as nice as they can be and I am sure you will like all of them.

Hoping to see you down here before very long, I am

With love,
Francesca

Clemens to Frances Nunnally

New York
Oct. 28/07

Now, dear Francesca. This is to admonish you—& please remember: your studies, & your outdoor & indoor amusement activities are very important, in fact are *essentials* & any time filched from them for a courtesy's sake means a loss not warrantable & not justifiable. You are a dear sweet Francesca but you must not write letters to people on those costly terms. Neither must you filch time to read letters *from* people, except when they are very brief. Read part of this one: that will be sufficient.

I perceive, with pleasure that you are having a very prosperous time down there, both mentally or physically. Let it continue!

I came home last Thursday, Miss Lyon followed late on Saturday, with the Tuxedo servants. My daughter had already been domiciled in the house several days.

Dear me, I must stop making November engagements, right away! For there is Annapolis to be thought of. Of the five or six already made I can excuse myself from all but one—Nov. 19th. I will make only confidential ones henceforth.

Yes, indeed, as soon as we hear from Gov. Warfield I shan't fail to let you know. Also I shall allow myself time to kiss you & the rest of the 70. You, anyway, shipmate!

With Love

SLC

DOROTHY QUICK TO CLEMENS

[Plainfield, N.J.]

[1 November 1907]

My Dear Mr Clemens

I just simply love the pictures Miss Lyon sent me they are all so good of you I wished I was back again at Tuxedo when I saw them Grandpa and Grandma and everyone in fact say they are the very best Kodak pictures they ever saw I read in the paper that you were down town I think you were very brave I should have been frightened to death you dont know how I miss you or how I long to see you we play cards every night and have lots of fun please tell Miss Lyon I will write to her very soon

with lots and lots of love kisses and hugs your very loving

Dorothy

Please give my love to Miss Lyon.

CLEMENS TO MARGARET BLACKMER

[New York]

[14 November 1907]

This is only a copy so it won't matter if it should get injured in the mails; but you must come & get the original which is more valuable than anybody can imagine. Tell me when you are coming.

SLC

Be good, be good, be always good,
And now and then be clever,
But don't you ever be *too* good,
Nor ever be too clever;

For each as be too awful good
The awful lonely are,
And such as often clever be
Get cut and stung and trodden on by
persons of lesser mental capacity, for
this kind do by a law of their construction
regard exhibitions of superior intellectuality
as an offensive impertinence levelled at
their lack of this high gift, and are
prompt to resent such-like exhibitions
in the manner above indicated—and are
they justifiable? alas, alas they

(It is best not to go on; I think the line is already longer than it ought to be for real true poetry.)

Mark Twain

Clemens to Frances Nunnally

21 Fifth Avenue
Nov. 18/07

Francesca dear, I am so disappointed! We are due in Annapolis 7 days hence—25th—& I have to be in Boston that very day, & remain 2 days & probably 3. And so we are writing to Governor Warfield to explain. But although I've *got* to be in Boston I am not sure that I can go. because I have had a cold ten days & cannot manage to get rid of it; if it continues I can't risk traveling in draughty trains, lest I bring on the bronchitis again. I wanted to see you, you dear child, & it's a great disappointment. It would be a charming change to look at you— a change from watching the stocks go down!

This isn't a bright day—it is the other way: my daughter is leaving to-night, to be gone a good while, & she will be missed—nobody left but Miss Lyon & me.

Goodbye—& good health—& all sorts of happiness to you dear!

With love

SLC

Clemens to Dorothy Quick

21 Fifth Avenue
Nov. 18/07

Why you sweet little rascal! Don't you suppose *I* am doing any long-ing? Indeed I am. I'm longing to see you. Of course you've got a lot of other lovers, & of course they pine to see you—Bache & the rest—but when they pine it's only a individual pine, whereas when I pine for you it's a whole forest! Now then, try & remember that, dear.

I think it is very nice—the faithful industry you are devoting to your studies & the gymnasium. And the drawing lessons—that's a great thing. Drawing will educate your eye, & give you a correct perception of forms & proportions which you couldn't get in any other way. I've never had a drawing lesson myself, but I know the great value of that art in training the eye to observe—also to see things as they *are*. Go on with your pleasant labors, dear heart, you dear little Dorothy.

This with the love of

SLC

Just think—71 years[1] from now you'll be 72. It seems impossible. Why, I am only that old *myself*.

1. Since Dorothy was eleven, Clemens must have meant "61 years."

FRANCES NUNNALLY TO CLEMENS

St. Timothy's
Catonsville, Md.
Nov. 23, 1907

Dear Mr. Clemens,—

You don't know how sorry I am that you can not come down here to school, for I had looked forward to your visit with a great deal of pleasure. I wish your engagement in Boston had been just a little later, so [you] could have made the Annapolis trip too. I sincerely hope that your cold is entirely over now, so that you will not be deprived of both these trips, and that you will not have bronchitis again.

I still am just as well as I can be, and am studying hard all the time. I can hardly realize that it is almost Thanksgiving and that in about four weeks I am going home for the holidays. On Thanksgiving Day we have a match game of basket-ball, and we are getting excited over it already, as we always do over things like that. On that day there are absolutely no rules on, and I know we will have all sorts of fun. We have a great many rules here, so I know it will seem exceedingly queer not to have any.

Hoping that your cold is very much better, I am

With love,
Francesca

CLEMENS TO FRANCES NUNNALLY

[telegram]

St Timothys School
Catonsville Md
Nov 27-1907

Miss Francesca Nunnally

I hope your team will win Francesca dear I could not go to Boston
S L Clemens

DOROTHY QUICK TO CLEMENS

[Plainfield, N.J.]
[27 November 1907]

My Dear Mr Clemens
   I was so glad to get your letter and to know you are well I often see your name in the paper so I suppose you are very busy   My Grandpa and Grandma expect to sail for Europe next Saturday on the new boat I shall be lonely without them especially Grandpa for as you know we are great chums I wish I was a big girl and all through school so I could go with him I have been very well so far and have only lost a few days at school which is doing very well for me our Sunday school class has gotten up a League and we have to make clothes for poor children it is lots of fun please write me very soon with lots of love to Miss Lyons and lots of hugs and kisses for you

lots of love
Dorothy

Frances Nunnally to Clemens

St. Timothy's
Catonsville, Md.
Nov. 29, 1907

Dear Mr. Clemens,—

This is just a note to say that I hope you will have many very happy returns of the thirtieth.[1]

I received your telegram, and I can't tell you how much I appreciate your thinking of our game, and so do all the girls of our team. I think it must have brought our good luck to us, for we won with a score of seven to three. We are so happy over our victory that we don't know what to do, and we have sung and cheered ourselves hoarse over it. I wish you could have been here to see it, for it really was a very pretty game, and both teams played splendidly We had an awfully nice Thanksgiving Day, and I hope you did too.

I was sorry to hear that you were not well enough to go to Boston, and I certainly hope you are all right now.

Wishing you a very happy birthday.

I am
    With love,
            Francesca

1. Clemens's seventy-second birthday.

Gertrude Natkin to Clemens

[telegram]

New York
Nov. 30, 1907

My sincerest wishes for many bright and happy years.

Marjorie

DOROTHY QUICK TO CLEMENS

[Plainfield, N.J.]
[19 December 1907]
Wednesday

My Dear Mr Clemens

I am waiting for Saturday when I shall see you most impatiently but it will soon be here   please write to me when you have time   my Teddy Bear is sitting on the top of the dressing table and he has just fallen down and is hanging on with one leg and is in danger of falling on the floor any minute   it is snowing here now   I have written to Bache and am waiting for an answer   I have not been to school for one week and am not going this week as I have a cold and mama is afraid to let me go to school for fear I shall take more cold   hopeing to see you on Saturday   with lots of love
I am

your loving
Dorothy

P.S. Please give my very best love to Miss Lyon but keep some for yourself

CLEMENS TO FRANCES NUNNALLY

21 Fifth Avenue
Dec. 20/07

I suppose you are about to leave for home, dear Francesca, so I am hasting to wish you a happy holiday-time before you get away down there out of my reach. Indeed you are much too far out of my reach even when you are in Catonsville. I wish you were going home by way of New York, so that I could have a glimpse of you, you dear little rascal.

It is hard times, now;[1] still I am going on with the house & our building in the country, & there'll be plenty of room for you, & you must come & see us next summer, & stay as long as you can. That Tuxedo visit was *much* too short.

Please remember me to your mother when you get home. You are going to be a glad child soon!

With love & merry Xmas,

SLC

1. Clemens was concerned about his finances, including the cost of the new home in Redding, because of the closing of the Knickerbocker Trust Company, in which he had $51,000 on deposit. The Knickerbocker Trust did soon reopen and resume payments.

CLEMENS TO FRANCES NUNNALLY

21 Fifth Avenue

Dec. 29/07

Ah, you dear Francesca, you & your mother gave me a pleasant surprise in that beautiful & valuable addition to my winter comforts, & I thank you cordially; & I wish also to thank you, dear, for the fine album of Rembrandts. I am the better, bodily & spiritually, for these welcome remembrances.

Yesterday I went with 70 other slaves of Harper & Brothers to Lakewood to lunch Mr. Howells out of the country & give him God-speed.[1] The distance was greater than I was expecting it would be: multiplied by 2 or 3 it would have reached Baltimore, & so if you had been in Catonsville I would have gone on. But you had already escaped South: you had probably already started before I wrote you the other day.

If you see Uncle Remus Harris you must give him a good hearty Xmas hand-squeeze for me, for I am very fond of him.

Half-hour later. I wish you were here, so that I could have you at dinner This evening & show you off, as I did to those admiring families in London. It's a small dinner, for stage friends: John Drew & his wife,

Will Gillette, & Billie Burke—excellent folk, & Billie is as good as she is pretty.[2] And Gillette is *such* a bright talker. He has just gone from the room, it is 1:30 p.m, & now I will get up & play billiards with Mr. Paine.

I may have to go to Washington by & by, & then I will fall off the train at Baltimore & have a glimpse of you.

With my kindest regards to your mother, & my love to you dear.

SLC

1. The occasion for the Harpers luncheon was Howells's departure for Italy. There was also a farewell luncheon given by the Damned Human Race Club, with Howells, Clemens, and Colonel Harvey present.

2. Actress Billie Burke was becoming a good friend of Clemens and visited him at Stormfield in 1909. Clemens had probably seen her as Julia in *My Wife*, which was her New York debut performance in August 1907.

CLEMENS TO DOROTHY QUICK

21 Fifth Avenue
Dec. 29/07

Happy New Year, Dorothy dear!

I miss you so, you dear child—I miss you all the time, you little rascal. Your mother said you could come again, before the end of January —you will be very welcome, honey.

With love

SLC

DOROTHY QUICK TO CLEMENS

[Plainfield, N.J.]
[30 December 1907]

My Dear Mr Clemens

Here I am safe in Plainfield. Grandpa and Grandma came yesterday and I was so glad to see them   I had over 40 Christmas [presents]

when I counted them all up   It is raining here and is dark and dreary
I have not heard from Bache but expect a letter every day   will let you
know when I get it with lots of love
   your loving

                              Dorothy

P.S. Please give lots of love to Miss Lyon from me.

Clemens to Carlotta Welles

                                   21 Fifth Avenue
                                   Dec. 30/07
Dear Charley:
   Your letter has just arrived, & is a very pleasant & very welcome surprise; I thought you had forgotten me long ago. The xmas holidays have
this high value: that they remind Forgetters of the Forgotten, & repair
damaged relationships.
   Yesterday afternoon when I was breaking the Sabbath over the billiard table, word was brought up that "3 Doangivadams" were downstairs, waiting. We had a very pleasant time together, & some day I'm
going down to Bryn Mawr & return the visit.[1]
   You remember Frances Nunnally? I had xmas letters from her & her
mother day before yesterday, from their home in Georgia. They visited
me in Tuxedo in September. Frances (whom I call Francesca for short),
was very good to me in London, & drove with me two hours every afternoon, returning calls. Her school is near Baltimore; I am going down
there by & by.
   Dispeptic? Dear me, I do pity you Charley, for I was walking that vale
of tears & exasperations for many many months, & I know all about
it. I cured it two months ago, & I will tell you the process. So that you
can duplicate it? Indeed *no!*—so that you can avoid it. For what cures
one person always kills another. I stopped drinking milk—that was the
main thing. I stopped dieting. That was the next mainest thing. I dine
chiefly on radishes & celery now (I am not joking), following these with

all kinds of deadly food, & always finishing with two pears. My health is at last perfect. But don't you venture that road, you little rascal!

    With love & Happy New Years

SLC

1. Carlotta was attending the Baldwin School in Bryn Mawr, Pennsylvania; the three visitors were probably school friends.

CHAPTER THREE

Final Harvest

12 January 1908 – 14 June 1908

"IT WAS HIS FINAL HARVEST and he had the courage to claim it," commented Albert Bigelow Paine, in reference to Clemens's remarkably busy public life during the winter and spring of 1908 (*MTB* 1034). Not too surprisingly, however, Clemens was losing his appetite for a harvest of public recognition, just as he was sowing the seeds for another harvest, a harvest far closer to his heart. Dorothy Quick and Frances Nunnally had shown Clemens how much pleasure he could gain from friendships with school-age girls, and he continued making new female acquaintances as circumstances allowed. His two holiday trips to Bermuda during the winter months of 1908 provided the perfect opportunity for new acquisitions. By April 1908 Clemens had collected eight new schoolgirls, increasing the number of angelfish to ten, and he had devised a club to contain them. By mid-summer Clemens had moved into his new house in Redding and surrounded himself with a dozen angelfish. When they were not there in person, he could enjoy their framed photographs gazing at him from the walls of the billiard room, which also served as angelfish headquarters. Indeed, schoolgirls, not public notoriety, became Samuel Clemens's final harvest.

A man of Clemens's disposition could hardly have turned his back

on public fame, however, and he was occasionally seen walking up or
down Fifth Avenue, attired completely in white, from patent leather
shoes to silk top hat. He enjoyed being stared at and recognized as he
walked up Fifth Avenue, sometimes strolling the entire distance from
Washington Square to Andrew Carnegie's mansion at Ninety-Second
Street, then returning downtown on the open deck of the Fifth Avenue
bus. It was also his pleasure to walk down the Avenue from the Plaza
Hotel on Sunday mornings. As he described the ritual in his 24 May
letter to Dorothy Quick, he discovered that by the "careful and delicate art" of implication he could convince hundreds of churchgoers he
had "partaken of *their* clerical feast." Although Howells conferred on
him the title "White Sepulchre," in reference to his immaculate dress,
Clemens would not consider entering one of those churches, so long
as he could enjoy the secular pleasures of the Avenue. He described
his sartorial inclination this way: "I wear white clothes both winter and
summer . . . because I prefer to be clean in the matter of raiment—
clean in a dirty world; absolutely the only cleanly-clothed human being
in all Christendom north of the Tropics" (*MTA* 370).

Dorothy Quick continued to be Clemens's most faithful young correspondent and also paid him several visits: in the fall, just before
Christmas, in April, and in May. During her visits they toured muse-
ums, went to the theater, and played billiards for hours at a time.
Dorothy recalled that since Clemens always took a box at the theater,
she could watch with excitement as the word spread that Mark Twain
was in the house, and heads craned about to catch a glimpse of the
famous author. Clemens's proclivity for young female company was no
secret, of course, and Dorothy even received an invitation to attend a
dinner in tribute of Twain. Clemens had at the last moment decided
not to attend and sent his regrets, but when he saw the disappointment painted across Dorothy's face, he changed his mind. Dorothy and
Clemens dressed quickly, in white of course, and rushed to the dinner,
where Dorothy was given an ovation for bringing Mark Twain to the
dinner in his honor.

Clemens had stopped celebrating, even noticing, Christmas, from
the year of Olivia's death. Twenty-one Fifth Avenue pretended there

was no such day, in fact, for even to mention Christmas was to invite a Scrooge-like outburst. With her winning ways, Dorothy managed to melt Clemens's resolve and rescind his cancellation of Christmas. She quite innocently presented him with a Christmas present during her visit just before Christmas 1907. His staff held their breath, but Clemens calmly opened the gift to find a very useful smoker's jackknife. He reciprocated by presenting Dorothy with an illustrated edition of *Joan of Arc,* thus allowing Christmas into his life once again.

Dorothy had to cancel a January visit and dinner invitation because of illness. The occasion was another honorary affair, this one given by the Lotus Club. The menu read:

> Innocent Oysters Abroad
> Roughing it Soup
> Huckleberry FinnFish
> Joan of Arc filet of beef
> Jumping Frog Terrapin
> Punch Brothers Punch
> Gilded Duck
> Hadleyburg Salad
> Life on the Mississippi Ice Cream
> Prince and Pauper Cake
> Pudd'n Head Cheese
> White Elephant Coffee

When Dorothy asked, in amazement, if he had eaten all that, Clemens confessed "No. I didn't. I stayed through Joan of Arc filet, because I'm fond of Joan and wanted to do her honor" (*EMT* 151–52). Clemens stretched out in the club lounge for a good cigar and a rest, returning for the White Elephant Coffee.

Clemens took two trips to Bermuda during the winter of 1908: one from 25 January to 6 February, and the other from 1 March to 11 April. Clemens described his Bermuda vacations in such detail in his autobiographical dictations of 13 February and 17 April (both included in this chapter) that these happy periods need no more than brief mention here. During his first sojourn in the "Happy Isles" Clemens met

Margaret Blackmer and Irene Gerken in his hotel. Clemens and his impatient young friends shared many conversations at the dining table, while they endured the "leisurely" meals in the hotel dining room. Clemens sometimes entertained them with amusing history lessons, complete with sketches of the English kings and queens. These conversations were often followed with billiards lessons. Irene played billiards with Clemens and his friends so often that long after her return home they referred to a certain position of the balls as an Irene.

Clemens pretended that Margaret Blackmer was growing up so fast he would not recognize her again unless they had a secret sign by which to identify themselves. He gave her one half of a complete shell, keeping the other half himself. Later, he had gold-enameled replicas made and sent Margaret her half. When she visited Clemens back in New York, Margaret pretended not to recognize him and asked, "Do you know if there is a nice old gentleman, by the name of Mr. Clemens living here?" Clemens quickly produced his half of the shell, provoking Margaret to exclaim, "Why you are Mr. Clemens!" (*MTHI* 7–8).

Clemens and Margaret Blackmer took daily excursions by donkey cart to a picturesque spot on the coast called Spanish Point. After Margaret returned home from "Bermooda," as Clemens gleefully called the islands, Irene took over in the donkey cart. One can surmise that Clemens's other female acquisitions, Hellen Martin, Jean Spurr, and Helen Allen, also joined him on his daily donkey excursions, entertained by the stubborn, long-eared Maude, and her unflappable groom, Reginald.

During the second Bermuda trip Clemens and H. H. Rogers visited a large aquarium on the island, and Clemens fell in love with the beautiful angelfish he saw there. He quickly made the connection between these colorful, angelic fish and the bright young ladies who were beginning to swim about him. They were to be his angelfish, and he would need an aquarium, much like the one he had seen with Rogers, to keep them close to him. By the time Clemens returned home in April he could count ten angelfish in his aquarium. He quickly had little enameled angelfish pins made up by Tiffany's and sent one to each of his fish, inviting her to become a member of his Aquarium Club.

Dorothy Quick returned to 21 Fifth Avenue for visits in April and

May. She was pleased to see how handsome his cat Tammany had become, recalling the scrawny stray that had wandered onto Clemens's porch at Tuxedo when she was there the previous summer. Clemens told Dorothy he named the cat Tammany (in obvious reference to Tammany Hall) once he realized what a scrapper she was and how impossible it was to keep her in at night. Tammany insisted on keeping her five kittens in the coal bin, so Clemens and Dorothy had to crawl over the coal pile to watch them. Their white outfits somewhat the worse off from one such sooty romp, the two arrived upstairs to find Dorothy's mother and a friend, whom they had invited to tea. Quick work with hankies only set the smudges further, and Dorothy's mother let out a gasp as the sooty duo entered the sitting room. Despite Clemens's unhappiness with 21 Fifth Avenue, episodes like this surely relieved his loneliness and temporarily lightened his spirits.

During the spring and summer Clemens's letters to angelfish numbered far more than half his total correspondence: an angelfish letter went out or was received every day. Clemens moved into his previously unseen mansion in Redding, Connecticut, on 18 June and was delighted with what he found there. Anticipating many angelfish visits to his pastoral retreat, he had already rechristened it Innocence at Home.

DOROTHY QUICK TO CLEMENS

[12 January 1908]
Sunday

My Dear Mr Clemens

Thank you so much for your letter I shall be so glad to come in next Saturday and stay until Monday   dont bother about taking me to the theathre unless there is something you especially want to see and I shall be perfectly satisfied to stay home with you and play pool   I hope you are well with lots of love to Miss Lyon and a hundred hugs and kisses for yourself

I am

your loving little
Dorothy

CLEMENS TO DOROTHY QUICK

21 Fifth Avenue
[13 January 1908]
Monday

You are just a dear little Dorothy, & I am ever so glad you are coming
Saturday morning. We'll have a fine holiday together. I wish a person
could rent or buy you, just as he would other choice real estate, then I
wouldn't let you go back any more.

Love & good-night, dear.

SLC

CARLOTTA WELLES TO CLEMENS

92 Ave Henri Martin
Paris
January 14th 1908

My dear Mr. Clemens:—

I was very happy to hear from you. I should certainly have written you
long ago if I had thought that you cared to hear from me, but you must
have so many friends, so many people to remember you affectionately,
that I did'nt think you very much wanted me to tell you that I hav'nt
forgotten you. I'm afraid you're joking when you say that, anyway!

Of course I remember Frances Nunnally. We exchanged Xmas cards.
If I go to College next fall we shall be in the same class—and I hope you
will come to Bryn Mawr then, and see the whole bunch of us, the three
"doangiva-dams" and Frances and me, and, incidentally, the College.

I am getting on all right now. The lake in the "bois de Boulogne"
right near us, has actually frozen up so that you could skate on it and
I have been improving my opportunities, so you see I'm not very sick.
Yesterday they had a sort of band there and you had to pay to get in,
so it was quite stylish. I paid and went in and staggered around (not to
mention the tumbles) and had a good time watching the fancy skating.

I have been reading a book called "Fraulein Schmidt and Mr. Pustender" by the author of "Elizabeth & her German Garden" which I like ever so much. I hope your radishes still agree with you, and keep you in perfect health.

Very affectionately
Charley

CLEMENS TO FRANCES NUNNALLY

21 Fifth Avenue
Jan. 15/08

Where are you, dear? At school? I suppose so, but you haven't told me.

What I am anxious to know is, can't you steal a day or two & run up & see us? Miss Lyon & I will go down & board your train at Philadelphia & escort you up. Or, we will go all the way to Baltimore, if you prefer. And gladly.

Can you come, dear? And will you? If it isn't possible to come now, will you name a date & come later? Don't say no, dear, say yes.

With love
SLC

P.S. [*written on envelope*] I forgot to add, you dear little Francesca, that we'll see you home again—all the way, if necessary. We'll take the very very very best care of you, you precious child.

CLEMENS TO DOROTHY QUICK

[New York]
[17 January 1908]
Friday, 4 p.m.

Oh you dear child, I am so sorry for you, and also so sorry for myself! It is *such* a disappointment. I have been sick abed with a cold all day, but I was resolved to be up & dressed & ready for you tomorrow morning. We've got a box for a matinee tomorrow, and—well, we've got to bear those disappointments, so I may as well get *at* it; it's the best way & the only way.

Dear heart you must come *next* Saturday, if you are perfectly well & strong by that time; but if you aren't we'll put it off still another week.

Ashcroft was here last night, & we played hearts till two or three hours after midnight—with the beautiful cards you gave me. I captured all their chips & more besides.

With lots & lots of love,

                                        SLC

CLEMENS TO DOROTHY QUICK

[telegram]

                                        New York
                                        1/18/1908

To Miss Dorothy Quick
You are ill in bed so am I. With Bronchitis. But I am sending you a very nice picture.

                    S L Clemens

FRANCES NUNNALLY TO CLEMENS

                                        St. Timothy's
                                        Catonsville, Md.
                                        Jan. 18, 1908

Dear Mr. Clemens,—

That certainly is a lovely invitation you have given me, and I only wish I could say "yes". Miss Carter never allows us girls to go away from the school, so I can't possibly come to see you, though I surely wish I could. As I cannot persuade Miss Carter to let me come, I wish you would come down to Baltimore so I could see you. I know you don't like travelling on the train, but if you should come to Washington or any where in this direction, do stop by here.

I came back to school on the ninth after a perfectly fine holiday at home. I had had such a lovely time and I did not want to come back to work a bit. I might as well get used to it, though, as I will have to study hard now until Easter, when we have about a week or ten days holiday.

I would give anything if I could come up to see you some time soon, but as I can't, I hope I will see you down here.

I am

With Love,

Francesca

CLEMENS TO FRANCES NUNNALLY

[New York]

Jan 21/08

Francesca dear

I wish you were here and had 2 weeks to spare. Then I would pack you & Miss Lyon aboard ship & sail for Bermuda Saturday. Now you see what you are robbing her of—she needs that trip very much. I shall take nobody but Ashcroft—yet he hasn't any use for a voyage.

You are going to spend those ten Easter days here aren't you dear? We'll come to Catonsville & fetch you.

Two hours ago I didn't know I was going to Bermuda—& I can't swear to it now. But Ashcroft has secured the staterooms, & I fully expect to be out of bed by Saturday.

Good-bye, dear, With love

SLC

CLEMENS TO DOROTHY QUICK

[New York]

[21 January 1908]

Tuesday evening

Dorothy dear, tell your mother that the wisest way for her to spend money on your health will be to take you to Bermuda for a week or a fortnight: & you must tell her that the best *time* is next Saturday. (That is because I am going, then, & so is Ashcroft.) It's the big ship (The "Bermudian"). She makes the passage across in 45 hours.

In Bermuda a sick person gets well in 3 days, & strong in a week. I rather expect to be gone from New York till Feb. 11, but I may be back earlier. I tried the trip twice last year, & I know—the change made me well in 3 days.

The doctors say I shall be well enough by Saturday to sail—so Mr. Ashcroft has secured the staterooms.

I hope you are well by this time, dear. You only need the Bermuda air to make you weller than ever you were in your life before.

With lots of love

SLC

DOROTHY QUICK TO CLEMENS

[Plainfield, N.J.]
[21 January 1908]
Tuesday

My Dear Mr Clemens

Thank you so much for our picture   it is lovely and I am glad to have it   I hope your cold is better now   I am better but have not been to school yet the doctor is giving me   a tonic and in another week I ex- pect to be all right   Mother says she dont think I will be able to come this Saturday but I hope surely the Saturday after I can come if you want me with much love to Miss Lyon and lots and lots and lots for you I am your loving little

Dot

FRANCES NUNNALLY TO CLEMENS

St. Timothy's
Catonsville, Md.
Jan. 22, 1908

Dear Mr. Clemens,—

I surely do wish I could go to Bermuda for I cannot imagine anything nicer, and I should love to have a holiday like that with you. It certainly is lovely of you to ask me to spend my Easter vacation with you, and there is nothing I should like better, but I cannot promise anything now, as I don't know what Mother has planned for me.

I only have a very few minutes before I shall have to go to bed, but I just wanted to write you a line to wish you the very best of trips. So hoping you will enjoy your two-weeks voyage very much, I am

With love,
Francesca

CLEMENS TO FRANCES NUNNALLY

[New York]
Feb. 8/08

Francesca dear, I (*and* Ashcroft) got back from Bermuda night before last, after a pleasant absence of 13 days.[1] I've brought you a Bermuda jewel & Miss Lyon will presently dispatch it to you when Ashcroft sends it to the house. It is decorated with an image of Bermuda's pride, the angel-fish. It is utilitarian—this gimcrack. I think it's a hair pin, but other authorities think it's a safety.

But never mind, that isn't what I sat down to talk about. No, but to thank you & your mother again for the shawl, which has been a most handy & competent friend in time of need—that is to say, illness. For three weeks it protected me night & day against fresh colds; & was also the only bed-covering I used on Shipboard & in Bermuda.

Good-bye, dear.

With love,
SLC

1. The importance of this and a second trip to Bermuda in the winter of 1908 should be emphasized; Clemens made friends with at least four and probably six girls while there: Margaret Blackmer, Irene Gerken, Helen Allen, Dorothy Sturgis, and probably Hellen Martin and Jean Spurr. As his dictations during the next three months indicate, he formed the idea of an Aquarium club filled with angelfish either while in Bermuda or soon after his return.

AUTOBIOGRAPHICAL DICTATION, 13 FEBRUARY 1908

My first day in Bermuda paid a dividend—in fact a double dividend: it broke the back of my cold and it added a jewel to my collection. As I entered the breakfast-room the first object I saw in that spacious and far-reaching place was a little girl seated solitary at a table for two. I bent down over her and patted her cheek and said, affectionately and with compassion,

"Why you dear little rascal—do you have to eat your breakfast all by yourself in this desolate way?"

She turned up her face with a sweet friendliness in it and said, not in a tone of censure, but of approval,

"Mama *is* a little slow, but she came down here to get rested."

"She has found the right place, dear. I don't seem to remember your name; what is it?"

By the sparkle in her brown eyes, it amused her. She said,

"Why you've never known it Mr. Clemens, because you've never seen me before."

"Why that is true, now that I come to think; it certainly is true, and it must be one of the reasons why I have forgotten your name. But I remember it now perfectly—it's Mary."

She was amused again; amused beyond smiling; amused to a chuckle, a musical gurgle, and she said,

"Oh no it isn't, it's Margaret."

I feigned to be ashamed of my mistake, and said,

"Ah well, I couldn't have made that mistake a few years ago, but I am old now, and one of age's earliest infirmities is a damaged memory;

but I am clearer now—clearer-headed—it all comes back to me; I remember your whole name now, just as if it were yesterday. It's Margaret Holcomb."

She was surprised into a laugh this time; the rippling laugh that a happy brook makes when it breaks out of the shade into the sunshine, and she said,

"Oh you are wrong again; you don't get anything right. It isn't Holcomb, it's Blackmer."

I was ashamed again, and confessed it; then—

"How old are you, dear?"

"Twelve, New Year's. Twelve and a month."

"Ah, you've got it down fine, honey; it belongs to your blessed time of life; when we get to be seventy-two we don't reckon by months any more."

She said, with a fine complimentary surprise in her innocent eyes,

"Why you don't look old, Mr. Clemens."

I said I wasn't, except by the almanac—otherwise I was only fourteen. I patted her dainty brown hand and added,

"Good-bye dear, I am going to my table now; but after breakfast— Where are you going to wait for me?"

"In the big general room."

"I'll be there."

We were close comrades—inseparables in fact—for eight days. Every day we made pedestrian excursions—called them that any way, and honestly they were intended for that, and that is what they would have been but for the persistent intrusion of a gray and grave and rough-coated little donkey by the name of Maude. Maude was four feet long: she was mounted on four slender little stilts, and had ears that doubled her altitude when she stood them up straight. Which she seldom did. Her ears were a most interesting study. She was always expressing her private thoughts and opinions with them, and doing it with such nice shadings, and so intelligibly, that she had no need of speech whereby to reveal her mind. This was all new to me. The donkey had always been a sealed book to me before, but now I saw that I could read this one as easily as I could read coarse print. Sometimes she would throw

those ears straight forward, like the prongs of a fork; under the impulse of a fresh emotion she would lower the starboard one to a level;
next she would stretch it backward till it pointed nor'-nor'east; next
she would retire it to due east, and presently clear down to southeast-
by-south—all these changes revealing her thoughts to me without her
suspecting it. She always worked the port ear for a quite different set
of emotions, and sometimes she would fetch both ears rearward till
they were level and became a fork the one prong pointing southeast the
other southwest. She was a most interesting little creature, and always
self-possessed, always dignified, always resisting authority; never in
agreement with anybody, and if she ever smiled once during the eight
days I did not catch her at it. Her tender was a little bit of a cart with
seat room for two in it, and you could fall out of it without knowing
it, it was so close to the ground. This battery was in command of a
nice grave, dignified, gentle-faced little black boy whose age was about
twelve, and whose name, for some reason or other, was Reginald. Reginald and Maud—I shall not easily forget those gorgeous names, nor
the combination they stood for. Once I reproached Reginald. I said,

"Reginald, what kind of morals do you sport? You contracted to be
here with the battery yesterday afternoon—on the Sabbath Day, mind
you—at two o'clock, to assist in the usual pedestrian excursion to Spanish Point and Paradise Vale, and you violated that contract. What is
the explanation of this conduct—this conduct which in my opinion is
criminal?"

He was not flurried, not affected in any way; not humiliated, not disturbed in his mind. He didn't turn a feather, but justified his course as
calmly and as comprehensively with his tranquil voice as Maud could
have done it with her ears:

"Why I had to go to Sunday-school."

I said with severity,

"So it is Bermudian morals, is it, to break contracts in order to keep
the Sabbath? What do you think of yourself, Reginald?"

The rebuke was lost; it didn't hit him anywhere. He said, easily and
softly and contentedly,

"Why I couldn't keep 'em both; I had to break one of 'em."

I dropped the matter there. There's no use in arguing against a settled conviction.

The excursioning party always consisted of the same persons: Miss W.,[1] Margaret, Reginald, Maud and me. The trip out & return was five or six miles, and it generally took us three hours to make it. This was because Maud set the pace. She had the finest eye in the company for an ascending grade; she could detect an ascending grade where neither water nor a spirit-level could do it, and whenever she detected an ascending grade she respected it; she stopped and said with her ears,

"This is getting unsatisfactory. We will camp here."

Then all the vassals would get behind the cart and shove it up the ascending grade, and shove Maud along with it. The whole idea of these excursions was that Margaret and I should employ them for the gathering of strength, by walking—yet we were oftener in the cart than out of it. She drove and I superintended. In the course of the first excursion I found a beautiful little shell on the beach at Spanish Point; its hinge was old and dry, and the two halves came apart in my hand. I gave one of them to Margaret and said,

"Now dear, sometime or other in the future I shall run across you somewhere, and it may turn out that it is not you at all, but some girl that only resembles you. I shall be saying to myself 'I know that this is a Margaret, by the look of her, but I don't know for sure whether this is my Margaret or somebody else's;' but no matter, I can soon find out, for I shall take my half-shell out of my pocket and say 'I think you are my Margaret, but I am not certain; if you are my Margaret you will be able to produce the other half of this shell.' "

Next morning when I entered the breakfast-room and saw the child sitting solitary at her two-seated breakfast-table I approached and scanned her searchingly all over, then said sadly,

"No, I am mistaken; she looks like my Margaret, but she isn't, and I am sorry. I will go away and cry, now."

Her eyes danced triumphantly, and she cried out,

"No, you don't have to. There!" and she fetched out the identifying shell.

I was beside myself with gratitude and joyful surprise, and revealed it from every pore. The child could not have enjoyed this thrilling little drama more if we had been playing it on the stage. Many times afterward she played the chief part herself, pretending to be in doubt as to my identity and challenging me to produce my half of the shell. She was always hoping to catch me without it, but I always defeated that game—wherefore she came at last to recognize that I was not only old but very smart.

1. Elizabeth Wallace, whom Clemens met during this trip to Bermuda, continued to be a good friend and later became a member of his Juggernaut Club, which was composed of women with whom Clemens corresponded. A few years later she wrote *Mark Twain and the Happy Island* about his visits to Bermuda. Clemens's own footnote concerning Elizabeth Wallace reads: "A bright and charming lady with a touch of gray in her hair, head of a college in the University of Chicago, Margaret's most devoted friend, if I except myself."

FROM AUTOBIOGRAPHICAL DICTATION, 14 FEBRUARY 1908

I was quite willing to sit [for the magazine photographer], but I said Margaret [Blackmer] must be put into the picture with me. The picture was notably successful. I was in white, and so was Margaret. Her frock was a very white white, and her white jacket had broad lapels of an intense red; also she wore a red leather belt. My white clothes were of three slightly differing shades of white, and in the picture those shades were exactly reproduced—the coat one shade of white, the shirt-front a slightly whiter white, the necktie a slightly whiter white than the shirt-front. The Lumiere had a sharper eye than myself; I had not detected those differences until it revealed them to me. . . .

One day Miss W. betrayed to me one of Margaret's sweet little confidences. Margaret said to her, "Is Mr. Clemens married?"

"No."

Margaret, after a little pause, said, with a dear and darling earnestness, and much as if she were soliloquizing aloud, "If I were his wife

I would never leave his side for a moment; I would stay by him and watch him, and take care of him all the time."

It was the mother instinct speaking from the child of twelve; it took no note of the disparity of age; it took no note of my seventy-two years; it noticed only that I was careless, and it was affectionately prepared to protect me from my defect.

I have already spoken at some length of a couple of other gems of my collection: Francesca and Dorothy—my New Jersey Dorothy, Dorothy Quick. I have two other Dorothies beside—an American one and an English one.

DOROTHY QUICK TO CLEMENS

[Plainfield, N.J.]
[18 February 1908]

My Dear Mr Clemens

Thank you so much for your dandy valentine I had thirty one when yours came so now I have thirty-two and they were all lovely every one has admired my belt that you brought me from Bermuda very much it is really beautiful I read in the paper all about Miss Clara's musical it must have been lovely I love Miss Clara she is so beautiful Will you write me soon I always rush for the mails they are delivered here three times a day always hoping I will get a letter from you but I know you are busy and cant write so often I suppose you went out for a walk today it was so lovely out here today I went to a party yesterday had a lovely played lots of silly games but it was great fun I didn't get one prize What do you think of that lots of love and kisses

your loving
Dorothy

P.S. Please give my love to Miss Lyon

CLEMENS TO DOROTHY QUICK

[New York]
[20 February 1908]
Wednesday an hour after Midnight.

I got your dear Valentine, which I prize, & today I got your letter, & I thank you for it.

And you didn't take a single prize! Oh, you dear little rat, it was a shame, & I am sorry.

Clara was very busy, or she would have sent you a Valentine. She is grieving, now, because she forgot it.

I've been to a banquet to-night, & got away at 11, which is blessedly early, for a banquet. I played billiards for an hour, & now I have gone to bed.

I sail for Bermuda in the "Bermudian" Saturday morning, with H. H. Rogers, his son-in-law Benjamin, a man-servant, & Miss Lyon. It is for Mr. Rogers' health. We shall stop at the Princess Hotel in Hamilton, & stay a month or two. You dear child, I wish you were going.

Most lovingly
SLC

FRANCES NUNNALLY TO CLEMENS

St. Timothy's
Catonsville, Md.
Feb. 20, 1908

Dear Mr. Clemens,—

I was so surprised to get your letter the other day for I thought you were still in Bermuda. You must not have had a very short stay there, but I know you enjoyed the ocean trip. How I wish I could have been there!

We have been awfully busy lately having our mid-year examinations. We had to study hard to prepare for them and then the examinations themselves lasted for eight days. I am glad to say that I had my last one to-day and I feel like quite a weight is off my mind. Now we will go back to our regular work and classes.

The weather here has been so bad lately that we have not been able to play much hockey, and we miss it very much, as that is about the only out door game we have to play all during the winter. It is better now I think and I hope we can soon begin to play again regularly.

Though I have not seen it yet, I know that pin you told me about is lovely and I certainly appreciate your thinking of me while you were in Bermuda.

> I am
> With Love,
> Francesca

FRANCES NUNNALLY TO CLEMENS

> St. Timothy's
> Catonsville, MD
> Feb. 21, 1908

Dear Mr. Clemens,—

About two hours after I mailed that note to you the postman brought me that lovely pin. [It] certainly is pretty and you don't know how much I appreciate it. The angel-fish surely must be a beautiful fish if it has all those lovely colors. I have never seen one, but I suppose they are only found in certain waters, aren't they?

What has become of that trip to Washington you thought you might take? I certainly wish you would take it and stop by Baltimore. Miss Carter asked me to-day if you were not coming down and when you were coming, but I told her I didn't know though I wished very much you would come. All the girls wish the same thing and they ask me about it all the time.

I have just come back from dancing class and the bed bell is going to ring in just about a minute, so I will have to stop.

> With love,
> Francesca

DOROTHY QUICK TO CLEMENS

[Plainfield, N.J.]
[21 February 1908]

My Dear Mr Clemens

I am glad you are going back to Bermuda because I know you love it there but I shall not see you for so long I wish I could go to   Will you write me when ever you have time and tell me about the beautiful lillies when they come out

With lots of love and kisses your loving

Dorothy

CLARA CLEMENS TO DOROTHY QUICK

[New York]
February 23, 1908

I received a very pretty Valentine and sachet a few days ago and as the envelope is postmarked Plainfield N.J. I suspect that you are the thoughtful little person. Thank you very much for your kind thought of me and with all good wishes

Believe me
Sincerely yours
Clara Clemens

MARGARET BLACKMER TO CLEMENS

Briarcliff Manor, N.Y.
Feb. 24th, 1908

Dear Mr. Clemen;

I received your nice letter, and I was very glad to hear from you.

We had a play a few nights ago. Mother came up and stayed all night.

I wonder how Maud is. Do you miss the rides we used to have?

I am very happy and I hope you are also.

Miss Tewksbury is going to take us into New York today to go to the aquarium and to the Metropolitan Art Museum. We are coming back some time today.

I hope you will see mother soon.

With lots of love,

Yours lovingly.

Margaret B.

CLEMENS TO FRANCES NUNNALLY

[postcard]

Bermuda

Feb. 24/08

Francesca dear, I got your letter just as I was leaving New York—thank you, dear.

I am writing now because I suppose that the linchpin got lost in the mails; & if that is so, I want you to drop me a line here, so that I can replace it with another.[1]

I suppose I shall be here sometime—possibly until toward the middle of April.

It is very pleasant. I hope we are to have you with us in New York at Easter.

Goodbye, dear.

With love SLC[2]

1. A reference to the angelfish pins Clemens had purchased in Bermuda and was sending to his growing collection of schoolgirls.

2. Message written on two picture postcards with Bermuda scenes on the front.

Irene Gerken and Clemens, Bermuda, Winter 1908.
(Courtesy, The Mark Twain Project, The Bancroft Library)

MARGARET BLACKMER TO CLEMENS

Briarcliff Manor, N.Y.
[28 February 1908]

My dear Mr. Clemens;

I hear that you are going to Bermuda. I hope you will have a very nice time.

Mother wrote me and wanted me to tell you that when you came back my picture would be ready for you. And will you please aske Mr. Askcroft to send her some picture of you and me in the donkey cart.

We are having a fine time coasting. I think we will go out on the big hill after supper for a while.

I hope when I come down for Easter, I will be able to see you.

If you see Maud, give her my love, and tell her I hope I will see her again.

With lots of love
Yours lovingly
Margaret

P.S. Please give my kind regard to Mr. Askecroft.

CLEMENS TO MARGARET BLACKMER

Princess Hotel, Bermuda
March 2, [1908]

Dear Margaret:

I saw the ship coming in at 8 this morning, & very soon afterward the purser sent your letter to me, & I was glad to get it.

I will see that Mr. Ashcroft does not forget to send your mother the picture of you & me & the donkey. He gave one to Miss Lyon, & it was so good that I took it away from her. I shall be so glad to have the picture of you which your mother is saving for me.

I met Maude at the rock this morning, & gave her your message. She was all alone; Reginald had gone off somewhere. We made a trip to

Margaret Blackmer and Clemens in the cart; Maude, the donkey,
with her groom Reginald, Bermuda, March 1908.
(Courtesy, The Mark Twain Project, The Bancroft Library)

Spanish Point with Maude & Reginald the other day; Miss Lyon, Miss Wallace & Mr. Benjamin walked, and Irene & I rode in the cart. Irene is 12 years old, & lives in West 75th street.

There isn't any coasting here, but no matter, it is nicely hot & sunny & comfortable.

Don't forget that I am to see you at Easter dear. I shall be here 2 or 3 weeks yet I suppose.

With lots of love.

SLC

DOROTHY BUTES TO CLEMENS

[London]
March 4th—1908

Dear Dr. Clemens.

Your crimes follow you! In geography, the other day, the Professor said that at a little inn in Germany, where he stayed, *in the guest register he had to put down, his name & profession,* & just above *his* name was that of "S. L. Clemens, Profession, Mark Twain."!![1]

We are in a pretty flat (apartment) of our own, now—It is nice not to be in hotels—one gets so tired of living in trunks—I never saw anything which *quite* equals the slowness of *British Workmen*—They put all their pots & pans in the hall, roll up their sleeves, slap each other on the back, & solicitously enquire, "Wot's wrong, old Sport?" of one another —Then they do a little work—At eleven they go off—"for lunch"— (they arrived at *ten,* you know,) and don't turn up again till 2 o'clock— Mother has been so tormented by them that the doctor has ordered her to bed for a few weeks, so the "British Workman" will be "on his own"!

I went to a Dance at Queen's College last night. Very, very few of the girls could "lead," & very few could even "follow" decently—We had a "Waltz Gallop" amongst other things. It was too funny to see our staid and stately English Grammar teacher gallop off like a Bucking Bronco from the Wild West! I & my partner started off in her wake, and bumped into a few couples—

It has been foggy and wretched. I loathe this climate!

You have been down in the Bermudas again, havn't you? We had a lovely stay in Paris—& brought back lots of mechanical toys. I must go and do my German exercises now. I don't see why one couldn't be just as happy without German verbs!

With much love, Your little friend,

Dorothy Butes

P.S. *Arn't* you coming over for the London Pageant? London would love to have you (I speak for *London!*)

1. The guest register notation Dorothy refers to would have to have occurred in 1899 or even a few years earlier, during the period Clemens was living in Europe.

FRANCES NUNNALLY TO CLEMENS

St. Timothy's
Catonsville, Md.
March 4, 1908

Dear Mr. Clemens,—

I hope you got the letter I sent to you in New York just too late for you to get it before you sailed. In it I told you the lovely pin arrived just after I sent you the letter you received in New York. It hadn't been lost in the mails at all, and I surely am glad for I wouldn't have it lost for anything.

Bermuda must be a beautiful place and I am so glad you went down there, so you will miss the disagreeable cold weather of New York.

Last night we had great excitement here, though it all came out well. While one of the clubs was giving a party in the gymnasium, the school house caught on fire from some of the paper decorations on the walls, and all the favors just went up in one great flame. All the girls got out of the building in about two minutes and no one was hurt at all. The part that wasn't burnt was damaged by water, so we will not be able to use that building for several days. Our dwelling house was not touched, though there was a general confusion, as everything was moved out for fear the fire would spread. Everything was fixed up again to-day and I think we are going to have school to-morrow in a little parish house near here. Though we only lost one day of school, I suppose everything will be more or less confused for the next three or four days, until we can get into our school house again.

Must stop now.

With love,
Francesca

DOROTHY QUICK TO CLEMENS

[Plainfield, N.J.]
[6 March 1908]

Dear Mr Clemens

I hope you are enjoying the balmy sunshine and the lillies of Bermuda better than I am enjoying the sunshine of Plainfield for I am sick in bed and can do nothing but look at it from inside while I dose with "no 77"[1] every hour   I hope you and Miss Lyon are well and enjoying the comforts of life and the Bermuda air   I wish I were with you but as I am not I wish you would write to me occasionally but then I know you are busy enjoying yourself   Miss Clara sent me some beads which my friend's and I have enjoyed very much also a very nice note   When are you coming to New York again   But now I must close   With love to Miss Lyon and lots & lots & lots for yourself

I am your very loving

Dorothy

P.S. I have several new autographs Geraldine Farrar Govenor Fort Booker Washington and curso—I have written for Mary Garden and other people—[2]

Love
    Dorothy

1. Humphrey's #77 was a well-known cold medicine of the day.
2. Dorothy appears to have collected autographs from the famous tenor Enrico Caruso

and the black leader Booker T. Washington. Geraldine Farrar sang with the Metropolitan opera, G. F. Fort was governor of New Jersey, and Mary Garden was an American soprano associated with the Chicago Grand Opera Company.

Clemens to Dorothy Quick

Hamilton, Bermuda
March 10/08

Dorothy dear, I am so sorry, sorry, *sorry* you are sick. I *know* you ought to come here. This heavenly climate & fine air would soon make you strong & well. It is doing wonders for Miss Lyon & Mr. Rogers. Can't you come? I don't expect to go home before the 1st or 10th of April. I hope your mother can bring you. You are a frail little creature, & you need to get away from doctors & let generous & wise Nature build you up & make you strong. Come to me, you dear Dorothy! You will be so welcome.

Miss Lyon is getting strong & robust, & Mr. Rogers is improving so decidedly that he has stopped talking about going back home—so I am hoping & expecting to keep him here until April 11th.

We are having very lively times every day—sailing, driving, walking, lunching, dancing; & at night we play billiards & cards & never go out, to dinners or anywhere else. I am now so strong that I suppose I could pull up one of these islands by the roots & throw it half way to New York. In fact I know I could.

Write you? Certainly I shall. I don't intend to ever be too busy to write to my dear Dorothy.

Good-bye, with lots & lots of love—

SLC

CLEMENS TO FRANCES NUNNALLY

Hamilton, Bermuda
March 10/08

Yes, you dear Francesca, I got the letter & was very glad to have it. But if the pin had been lost it wouldn't have mattered, because I find I am likely to be here a month yet, & therefore could get another.

I am very glad no harm came of your fire, but I hope you won't have any more accidents of that kind. It makes me very uncomfortable to hear about it & think of the risks.

I wish you were here, dear. You wouldn't ever be idle. We are busy every day—sailing, driving, walking, lunching, dancing, tea-ing & so on; & at night we stay at home. We decline night-invitations, & go to bed by 10:30 or 11. Miss Lyon is getting strong & healthy, & Mr. Rogers is improving so decidedly that he is glad he came, & I expect to persuade him to stay until April 11.

The weather is perfect now. It is New York June weather, & I think there is no such thing possible as improving upon that.

Goodnight, Francesca dear.

With love
SLC

CLEMENS TO DOROTHY QUICK

Hamilton, Bermuda
March 12/08

My poor little Dorothy, I hope you are well again, & will write a line & tell me so. I wish you were here—you would be on your feet right away.

We are to be here about 20 days yet. We sail for New York April 1.

It is very pleasant. There is always something going on. Yesterday it was a large garden party at the governor's, & there was music by the best band in the British army save one—the Horseguards. I have not heard such lovely music except at the King's garden-party last summer, when the Horse Guards band played.

Day before yesterday I spent the day on a British cruiser, & had a screaming good time (the screaming was laughter over yarns in the officers' mess). And yesterday Miss Lyon & 5 other ladies were the cruiser's guests & *they* had a screaming good time too.

To-day five of us men drove to St. George's, over beautiful roads with charming scenery & the wonderful blue water always in sight—distance 12 miles—& we dined at the hotel. However, on the way there we visited a wonderful cave that was discovered in December by a couple of black boys—the most beautiful cave in the world I suppose. We descended 150 steps & stood in a splendid place 250 feet long & 30 or 40 wide, with a brilliant lake of clear water under our feet & all the roof overhead splendid with shining stolactites, thousands & thousands of them as white as sugar, & other thousands & thousands brown & pink & other tints. All lighted with acetalyne jets.

Every Friday night there's a ball in the hotel, & I look on. I go out to teas & lunches, but not to dinners. I stay at home, nights.

There's a lot of lovely sailboats, & we often go sailing in them. They are wonderfully hand led by colored sailors. You dear child, if you were only here! There's a little bit of a donkey-cart, & a little bit of a donkey named Maude, & we would make trips to Spanish Point. It is 3 miles, & Maude can go there in an hour & a half. There is a pretty beach there, & the water is crystal-clear. But you can't bathe there, for the lack of bath houses.

Friday, 9 p.m. This has been a lovely summer day, very brilliant & not uncomfortably warm. If you would only come, you could *stop* those deadly medicines & soon get well.

The ball has begun, & I think I will go down & look on.

Dear child I am taking the liberty of appointing you to membership in my "Aquarium"—if you will let me. It consists of 5 angel-fishes & one shad.[1] I am the shad. The device of the club is a very small angel-fish pin, to be worn on the breast. I will fetch it when I come. I have to wear a flying-fish pin, until I can get a shad made.

March 16. The Bermudian has arrived with 60 bags of mail & 250 passengers. She sails to-morrow.

We don't sail April 1. We have postponed to April 11. I am sorry, but Mr. Rogers is improving ever so fast, & we want him to stay as long as he will. Bermuda is better than four or five or six million doctors. Don't you forget *that*, dear.

With lots of love

SLC

1. Clemens used various titles, including "slave," "shad," "servant," and "admiral," to describe his position in the club.

IRENE GERKEN TO CLEMENS

52 West 75th Street

New York City

March 13, 1908

Dear Mr. Cleamens:

We arrived safely and found lovely spring weather. The trip was fine only I was a little sick. I met a lote of friends on board and so was not very lonesome. How is Mr. Roggers? I hope he is much better, and when he leaves I hope he will have recovered all to geather. My bird was not the least sick and now he is talking all the time. Please give my love to Miss Lion and Miss Wallace. Mother and Father wish to be remembered to you. With lots of love from all

Your little Angle Fish

Irene Gerken

Clemens to Frances Nunnally

Hamilton, Bermuda
March 14/08

I was very glad to get your letter, Francesca dear, & also glad that you all escaped uninjured from the fire. But I hope you won't be subjected to any more risks of that kind.

It is lovely summer weather here, now, splendidly sunny & yet not too hot. I believe this is the best climate in the world. The sailing, among the islands is delightful, & the water is divinely blue. The drives are very fine, too. I wish you were here.

We sail for New York April 1, arriving Thursday April 3—& then it will soon be Easter & you will let us fetch you to New York for a visit, won't you? I am depending on it, and I hope I shan't be disappointed.

Are you growing out of my knowledge? Would I know you if I met you on the street in a strange town? I hope so.

Lovingly
SLC

P.S. March 16 (Monday.)
We don't sail homeward April 1. We have postponed it to April 11.

Francesca dear, I am taking the liberty of appointing you to membership in my "*Aquarium*" (Club). It contains 5 angel-fishes & one shad. I am the shad. The badge of the club is a very small angel-fish pin, to be worn on the breast. I will bring it when I come.

I have to wear a flying fish until I can get a shad pin made.

Clemens to Frances Nunnally

Hamilton, Bermuda
March 24/08

Francesca dear, this note will leave here 4 days hence by a slow steamer, & reach you 8 days from now—April 1. We sail April 11 & reach New York April 13th—Tuesday. Miss Lyon & my daughter will then go to Redding, Conn., where we are building a house, & return at the week-end—Saturday, April 18.

Then on Monday Miss Lyon will go to Baltimore & stay over night & fetch you home to New York Tuesday, & rest you up, & take you back to your school by the time it opens.

You consent, don't you dear? There is a comfortable room for you, & I would give you two if I could—or a dozen, if I had them.

You will give us this pleasure, won't you? The ship that fetches us home will leave New York the 9th of April, & if you write me by the 7th (to above address) I shall get your letter before we go hence. I am hoping you will say yes, dear heart.

> With love,
> SLC

FRANCES NUNNALLY TO CLEMENS

> St. Timothy's
> Catonsville, MD.
> March 25, 1908

Dear Mr. Clemens,—

I am sure I have not changed so much that you would not know me in a strange place, and I really do not think I have changed at all, unless I have gained some flesh.

I am deeply honored to be a member of the "Aquarium," which from the number of members I see is a very select club.

We have not had anymore excitement of any kind since the fire, and we have once more gotten back into our school house. Everything is in running order now just like it always was. We only have three weeks now before our Easter holidays begin, and I can hardly wait until that time. I think Mother is coming up to take me to New York, but I shall certainly see you while I am there. If we go to Europe this summer as we hope to do, we will have to make our preparations and do all our shopping at Easter, as we shall probably sail as soon as school is out in June. I am making all these plans in my mind, but I am not sure that we are going abroad at all. Any how I shall be in New York in about three weeks and I surely hope to see you there.

Hoping you are still having a fine time in Bermuda, I am

With love,

Francesca

Clemens to Dorothy Quick

[postcard]

Hamilton, Bermuda
March 28/08

The weather is perfect, & if you want some of it for your own use or for sale, please let me know, & I will see that you get all you want—but our government will swindle you on the duty, as it does on all imports.

S.L.C.

Dorothy Quick to Clemens

[Plainfield, N.J.]
March 29, [1908]

Dear Mr Clemens.

I wrote you a long letter last week but by some mistake it was not mailed in time for Saturday steamer so I am writing again   I will mail this one at once so there can be no mistake   I know from your letter it must be beautiful in Bermuda and I should love to be there with you and make the acquaintance of Maud   I am sure we would all be very good friends and have lots of fun together   I have one more autograph of F. S. Church (artist) it is very nice, he drew a picture and autographed it wasn't that nice of him?[1] I am doing very well in school now. I have a lot of stamps and am getting along very well with my collections   I suppose the lillies are out now they must be beautiful I shall be very glad when you are back but I do not blame you for wanting to

stay as *long* as you [can] as the weather here is very changable. Hot one day cold the next. With lots & lots of love to you and Miss Lyon I am
your very loving Dorothy

P.S. I am so glad I am a member of the Aquariumn lots of love

1. Probably Frederic E. Church, the landscape painter who lived near Hudson, New York, and had a brief friendship with Clemens in 1888.

CLEMENS TO DOROTHY QUICK

Bermuda
March 31/08
You dear little Dorothy, this is only a line to say I hope you are not still looking out upon the snow-storms from a sick bed & taking "77", but are up & around & well again. Next time you are sick you must come to Bermuda, then you won't need any medicines.

We sail for home April 11, & then I shall see you.

Lovingly
SLC

CLEMENS TO FRANCES NUNNALLY

Hamilton, Bermuda
March 31/08
Your letter has come, Francesca dear, you dear indefinite little body! But anyway, you are coming to New York, & *that* is something. I do hope your mother will let me have you part of the time.

Won't she go to the Grosvenor? It is the nicest, quietest, genteelest little hotel in all New York. We have used it [?] for a good many years. It is on the corner of 10th & 5th avenue, just a block from our house. Tell her I know she will like the Grosvenor.

Dorothy Sturgis (?) with Clemens, Bermuda, Winter 1908.
(Courtesy, The Mark Twain Project, The Bancroft Library)

We sail April 11, arriving the 18th, a day or so before you arrive. Do you know my telephone address (it isn't in the book): "*3907 Gramercy.*"

With love
SLC

AUTOBIOGRAPHICAL DICTATION, APRIL 1908

Dorothy Quick is eleven and a half years old now, and as tirelessly active vivacious, energetic, bright, interesting, good, obedient, and sweet and companionable and charming as ever. When we were shipmates last summer, coming home from England, I discovered her the second day out, and took possession, leaving her mother, her grandfather and her grandmother to get along the best they could without her during the most of each day, for we were nearly inseparable. When the time for that ancient function, the "concert," approached—a paid show in aid of the sailor hospitals of England and America—the elected manager came to me and asked if I would take part in the performance and make a speech. I said with asperity,

"It is strange that you should come to *me* with such an errand. I am a slave; I have no authority in the matter. Go to the source of power—go to the master. I will perform if the master permits."

"If I may ask, who is the master?"

"Dorothy."

The manager hunted Dorothy up and gravely laid the proposition before her, and was as gravely answered. The result appeared in the printed program, an hour later—thus:

"Mark Twain, speech. (By permission of Dorothy Quick)"

One day last September when Dorothy spent a week with us in Tuxedo, she sat at Luncheon looking radiantly sweet and lovely in her bright summer costume, and I said,

"Dorothy, I am holding in—I am holding in all I can—but I don't think I can hold in much longer—I want to eat you!"

She responded promptly,

"Don't do it, Mr. Clemens, I should miss you so."

We fell to telling anecdotes, and Dorothy furnished one or two. One of hers was to this effect:

It was April Fools' Day, and little Johnny burst into the parlor, where a dozen ladies were taking a cup of five o'clock tea, and exclaimed excitedly,

"Mamma, there's a stranger up stairs kissing the governess!"

Mamma started indignantly toward the stairs, with battle in her eye, then Johnny cried out in triumphant delight,

"April fool! It ain't a stranger at all—it's only papa!"

Next day Col. Harvey came down to spend the day. That charming man, that gifted man, has a certain peculiarity: sometimes a humorous thing carries him off his feet; at another time the same thing would merely set him to thinking, and there would be no indication that he had even heard it. We were used to this peculiarity, but it was new to Dorothy. The Colonel was in a happy mood, and he told several anecdotes. One of them was to this effect, an incident which had fallen under his personal observation:

Scene, the grand stand; occasion, a great horserace; present, in their rich attire, ladies of high society; a little apart, a pretty creature, unattended, overdressed; under-bred, also by the look of her. She was painstakingly looking the lady of culture and high degree, and she quite successfully kept up the calm dignity proper to the part until the flying horses began to draw near; then she forgot herself and stood up—which made those other ladies transfer their attention from the race to her, though she was unaware of it. She craned her neck; her eager eyes began to flame with excitement; next she began, unconsciously, to soliloquize aloud. She uttered her thought in gasps:

"I'm going to win!——I'm going to win sure! . . . Go on—whip up—whip up! . . . he's half a nose ahead! . . . He's three-quarters of a nose ahead! . . . Oh he's dropping back! back, and back, and back! . . . Damn his soul he's lost the race!"

Then she turned on a Vesuvian irruption of profanities and indelicacies that turned the air blue, and made those staring ladies gasp! There was a pause, then the soliloquizer came to herself, took one pathetic glance—one self-reproachful glance—at those horrified people, and ejaculated,

"Naughty Mabel!"

We thought it was about time to show off our Dorothy, so I asked her to tell us the April Fool story. She told it in her dearest and sweetest and most winningly simple and matter-of-fact fashion—and there was no result; that is, from the Colonel. His reflecting-mill was at work; he probably had not heard Dorothy's effort. The child looked mortified, but didn't say anything. The cut was deep—as appeared after a long, long interval; an interval of twenty-four whole hours, during which Dorothy had not mentioned the episode—but that it had been rankling all that time was evidenced in the fact that now at last when she came to comment upon it there was no subject at all before the house, yet she dropped her comment right into the midst of that vacancy without any word of introduction, and didn't even couple the Colonel's name with it, but said "he"—

"He laughs at his own jokes, but he doesn't care for other peoples."

Dorothy came last Saturday and staid over Sunday, and she was her same old dear self all the time. We occupied the billiard-room all day; again Dorothy read Shakespeare aloud, always selecting from each play her favorite passages and skipping the rest of it—which is her fashion. Now and then, between billiard games, she browsed among the books, making selection after selection, and always good selections; she would read aloud about twenty minutes, then require me to read aloud for about twenty; then she would inaugurate a game of "500" and discard it in twenty minutes; next she would play euchre twenty minutes; next it would be a game of verbarium, and so on all the day long—twenty minutes of billiards sandwiched between every two of them. And all the day long, from nine in the morning till her bedtime—nine at night —she was an immeasurable delight.

If you don't know what verbarium is I will explain. You write a great long word at the top of a sheet of paper; then you begin with the first letter of that word and build words out of the letters of the long word with that letter as a beginner; and the contestant who builds the most

words in a given length of time is the winner. Then you take the second letter, and continue the process. Dorothy would laboriously harvest
six or seven words; then she would discover that the text-word needed
another vowel or another consonant to make it really effective, and she
would suggest that we add the letter which she needed. I never ob-
jected; I always said it would be a fortunate addition—and as I never
smiled, I never fell under suspicion. But there was opportunity to smile,
for usually by the time Dorothy was tired of the game the text-word
which originally contained only seventeen letters, had, in the course of
the game, accumulated the rest of the alphabet. She's a darling little
billiard player; and when she plays the game you can recognize that
it is Dorothy, and not another, because under her sway all rules fail
and new ones are introduced, on her sole and sufficient authority and
without any vote, which improve that game beyond imagination. When
the balls do not lie favorably she makes no remark, but groups them
in a better position and goes on with her performance without any
comments.

A letter has come from Dorothy, and I will insert it here to show how
much she hasn't improved in punctuation and in slowing her swift pen
down, and in curbing and taming her dear headlong eagerness.

My dear Mr. Clemens
   Thank you so much for your lovely valentine I had thirty-one when yours
came so now I have thirty-two and they were all lovely every one has admired
my belt that you brought me from Bermuda very much it is really beautiful
I read in the paper all about Miss Clara's musical it must have been lovely I
love Miss Clara she is so beautiful Will you write me soon I always rush for the
mails they are delivered here three times a day always hoping I will get a letter
from you but I know you are busy and cant write so often I suppose you went
out for a walk today it was so lovely out here today I went to a party yesterday
and had a lovely played lots of silly games but it was great fun I didn't get one
prize what do you think of that lots and lots of love and kisses
                                                              Your loving
                                                                Dorothy

Her letter exposes another small defect or two, but they are like
all her defects—for they go to make up Dorothy, and anything that

goes to the making up of Dorothy is precious, and cannot be discarded without loss. What would a letter from Dorothy be if its express-train pace were obstructed and retarded at every mile-stone by commas, and semicolons, and periods; and if it didn't revel in tautologies; and if the rushing floods from the child's golden heart were tamed by cold literary calculation and made to flow in an orderly stream between the banks and never overflow them? I couldn't have it, it wouldn't be Dorothy. Dorothy is perfect, just as she is; Dorothy the child cannot be improved; let Dorothy the woman wait till the proper time comes.

Last summer I thoughtlessly gave Dorothy an instructive hint, and afterwards mourned about it; but the mourning was premature—the hint went wide of the mark and produced no result, achieved no damage. That hint was to this effect: I told her there was a wide difference between repetition and tautology; that she must never be afraid to repeat a word where the repetition could help to uncloud her meaning and make it clear, bright, distinct, and unmistakable, but that she must be cautious about repeating a word when it would not have that effect, for then the repetition would be tautological, and by consequence, commonplace and slovenly in the result. This letter is evidence to me, with its prodigal repetitions of "love" and "lovely," that even to this happy day the difference between helpful repetition and tautology has no existence for Dorothy.

MARGARET BLACKMER TO CLEMENS

Briarcliff Manor
April 1st, 1908

Dear Mr. Clemens:—

I received your nice letter and card.

I would like very much to join your club. I think it would be a very nice one.

I like the shell more and more every day, don't you?

Mother is out west and will be out for a long time. Maybe I can get miss Tewksbury to bring me down to see you in the Easter vacation.

Today lots of pie beds[1] were made and we played a lot of jokes on each other.

With lots of love.

Yours lovingly.
Margaret B.

1. A prank involving the shortsheeting of a bed.

FRANCES NUNNALLY TO CLEMENS

St. Timothy's
Catonsville, Md.
April 4, 1908

Dear Mr. Clemens,—

Your letter reached me this morning, and I am awfully sorry to have to tell you that I will not be able to come to New York at all during the holidays. I did not know this until two days ago, when Mother wrote and said she thought I had better come home. I certainly am disappointed that I will not be able to pay you a visit, for I had been looking forward to it with a great deal of pleasure. We have about decided to go abroad right after school closes in June, and as I will not have time to go home then, Mother thinks it best that I come at Easter. So I will have to give up my trip to New York.

Must stop so this letter will get mailed right away.

Hoping you will have a very pleasant ocean trip up, I am

With love,
Francesca

CLEMENS TO DOROTHY STURGIS

21 Fifth Avenue
13 April 1908
midnight

Good-night, Dear, *und schlafen Sie wohl!*[1] It was a great disappointment, for I was confident that you would fail to catch the train. I never gave you up until dinner time. Then Miss Lyon telephoned Plainfield, New Jersey, & asked the Youngest (no, next-youngest)[2] angel-fish in the Aquarium to come up & spend a few days, but her mother cannot bring her until Monday—so that was another disappointment, & the Aquarium is going to be empty all that interval.

Mr. Littleton was called to Washington this afternoon, & could not keep his appointment to play billiards to-night—still another disappointment. But my biographer (Albert Bigelow Paine), was in the house, & agreed to stay all night. We left Miss Lyon on guard against the reporters & went up stairs at 5 p.m. & played until 5 minutes ago (barring the dinner hour). My cat came up from the basement to superintend. She leaped upon the table & spread herself out, after her sociable habit, & we had to play around her for half an hour, then she went about her other affairs.

The house is looking very homelike & inviting, & I am not sorry to be in my own bed again.

Mr. Ashcroft came up with the trunks, but he had an engagement & could not stay; but Mrs. Littleton came over & sat with Miss Lyon in the billiard room until 11. It has been a pleasant evening, but if you had been here it would have been pleasanter.

I hope you reached home safely—but I am very very sorry you caught the train. I beg to be remembered kindly to your father & mother & your brother; & with love to you, I am

SLC

Chief Slave[3] of the Aquarium

8:10 a.m. The Major is pining. *Hoffentlich hast du gut geschlafen.*[4] Go on with it—there is no hurry about getting up.

Miss L. and Benares[5] are at breakfast—I've had mine.

1. The German translates: "and sleep well."
2. Dorothy Quick.
3. Clemens crossed out *servant* and added *slave.*
4. The German translates: "Hopefully you have slept well."
5. Benares was the household nickname for Ralph Ashcroft.

MARGARET BLACKMER TO CLEMENS

Briarcliff Manor, N.Y.

April 14th, 1908

Dear Mr. Clemens:—

My Easter vacation begins Thursday. I am going away with papa for a little while. But if you will write and tell me when you will be home I will come and see you.[1] I will be away with papa for about a week but after I come back I will come.

I love my shell so much.

With lots of love

Your loving friend

Margaret

1. Clemens wrote the following note on the letter: "Have asked her to go with us to the Children's Theatre April 23."

CLEMENS TO MARGARET BLACKMER

Telephone	21 Fifth Avenue
(not in the book)	Apl. 14/08
"3907 Gramercy"	Tuesday

Dear Margaret, we arrived from Bermuda yesterday afternoon, & in the accumulation of letters I find yours of a fortnight ago. I've brought the little angel-fish pin—badge of my Aquarium—and will keep it for you till you come, which I hope will be as soon as Miss Tewksbury can escort you. Come *very* soon!

We had 7 very lovely weeks in the island, & the lovable Miss Wallace was with us until recently. We made only one excursion to Spanish Point. Irene—one of my angel-fishes—drove me, & the others walked, & shoved Maude up the acclivities. You would hardly recognise Maude now. She has been closely clipped, & her pelt is shiny & smoothe, & looks like velvet.

Think—there isn't a solitary angel-fish in the house, Margaret. Francesca was to come to-day, but can't, because she has to go home to Georgia & get ready for Europe. Another was to have come yesterday to dine & stay all night, but she was called out of town. We telephoned Dorothy of New Jersey last night, but her mother cannot bring her until next Monday. Imagine this desolation—a house with not an angel-fish in it! Hurry up, dear!

I am inconsolable. Three days before we left Bermuda my shell was stolen from my watchchain. It grieves me deeply; but Mr. Ashcroft will hunt for another one—so that I can identify you when I see you, dear.

>With lots & lots of love.
>SLC
>Chief Slave of the Aquarium

DOROTHY STURGIS TO CLEMENS

>153 Beacon Street, Boston
>April 14th [1908]

My dear Mr. Clemens

I was so very, very sorry that we caught that horrid 5 o'clock train, and I wasn't able to dine with you![1]

I suppose you saw what they said in the newspapers about our being caught by that wave. The account in the Boston Herald was really very funny, and of course mostly incorrect!

We had a very comfortable trip out here, and arrived safely at our house shortly after ten.

I hope you got home safely, and that Mr. Ashcroft met you alright.

Please give my love to Miss Lyon, and tell her not to forget to send me those photographs she took of us on the steamer, and by the way do you want the pictures I took of you, if so I will send them to you as soon as they are printed.

>With ever so much love
>your newest angel fish
>Dorothy Sturgis

P.S. I would have written a much longer letter but I have so many lessons to do that I'm afraid I can't spend the time, but my next letter will
be longer.

DMS

1. See Clemens's Autobiographical Dictation of 17 April 1908.

CLEMENS TO MARGARET BLACKMER

[New York]
[15 April 1908]
Wednesday Morning

I have your letter of yesterday, & you are a very dear Margaret, &
have given us great pleasure. Now as I cipher it you are to go away with
your papa Thursday the 16th (to-morrow) & will return on or "about"
the 23d.

So I will look for you about the 23d. I am the honorary president of
the Children's Theatre, & on the 23d the children will give a performance in aid of one of the great charities. Ah, they are great, those
gifted children. Of course I shall be there (for I have to speak a few
words,) & it would be lovely if you could go there with Miss Lyon &
me. Can you? Will you?

Lovingly,
SLC
S
C. A̶. of the A.[1]

1. Clemens crossed out A (for Admiral) and substituted S. The acronym stands for one
of Clemen's epithets for himself, Chief Slave of the Aquarium.

CLEMENS TO DOROTHY QUICK

[New York]
[16 April 1908]
Thursday night

Friday—Saturday—Sunday—Monday—then you are here! Monday
afternoon. About half-past 2, I suppose. Well, I shall be on the look-

out, & powerful glad to see you. Shan't we have good times? I do most confidently guess so.

In Bermuda I bought a trinket for your Christmas. But I can't keep it that long, I'll give it to you now.

That reminds me that you are a member of my Aquarium Club, which consists of a few very choice school-girl angel-fishes & one slave. I am the slave.

I think you have the badge. But if you haven't, I'll get it for you.

Do remember me kindly to your mother & all the household, & don't forget that I love you, you dear little rascal.

SLC

DOROTHY QUICK TO CLEMENS

[Plainfield, N.J.]
[16 April 1908]

Dear Mr Clemens

I am very glad you are home and I am so glad I am to see you on Monday I will not be able to come Monday morning but will come on the one-nine train I will be so glad to see you   I am sorry not being able to be with you on Saturday but I really want to be with Grandpa and now I must close

With love to you and Miss Lyon

your loving
Dorothy

P.S. Grandpa is going away that is why I must be with him on Sunday
Dorothy

FROM AUTOBIOGRAPHICAL DICTATION, 17 APRIL 1908

After my wife's death, June 5, 1904, I experienced a long period of unrest and loneliness. Clara and Jean were busy with their studies and their labors, and I was washing about on a forlorn sea of banquets and speechmaking in high and holy causes—industries which furnished me intellectual cheer and entertainment, but got at my heart for an evening only, then left it dry and dusty. I had reached the grandpa stage of life; and what I lacked and what I needed, was grandchildren, but I didn't know it. By and by this knowledge came by accident, on a fortunate day, a golden day, and my heart has never been empty of grandchildren since. No, it is a treasure-place of little people whom I worship, and whose degraded and willing slave I am. In grandchildren I am the richest man that lives to-day; for I select my grandchildren, whereas all other grandfathers have to take them as they come, good, bad and indifferent.

The accident I refer to, was the advent of Dorothy Butes, 14 years old, who wanted to come and look at me.[1] Her mother brought her. There was never a lovelier child. English, with the English complexion; and simple, sincere, frank and straightforward, as became her time of life. This was more than two years ago. She came to see me every few weeks, until she returned to England eight months ago. Since then, we correspond.

My next prize was Frances Nunnally, school-girl, of Atlanta, Georgia, whom I call Francesca for short. I have already told what pleasant times we had together every day in London, last summer, returning calls. She was 16 then, a dear sweet grave little body, and very welcome in those English homes. She will pay me a visit six weeks hence, when she comes North with her parents Europe-bound. She is a faithful correspondent.

My third prize was Dorothy Quick—ten years and ten-twelfths of a year old when I captured her at sea last summer on the return-voyage from England. What a Dorothy it is! How many chapters have I already talked about her bright and booming and electrical ways, and her punctuationless literature and her adorably lawless spelling? Have I exhausted her as a text for talk? No. Nobody could do it. At least nobody who worships her as I worship her. She is eleven years and nearly eight-twelfths of a year old, now, and just a dear! She was to come to me as soon as I should get back from Bermuda, but she has an earlier grandpapa, and he is leaving for Europe next Monday morning, and naturally he had to have the last of her before sailing. Is she still her old self, and is her pen characteristically brisk and her spelling and punctuation undamaged by time and still my pride and delight? Yes:

Dear Mr. Clemens

I am very glad you are home and I am so glad I am to see you on Monday I will not be able to come Monday morning but will come on the one-nine train I will be so glad to see you I am sorry at not being able to be with you on Saturday but I really want to be with grandpa and now I must close.

With love to you

Your loving

Dorothy

P.S. Grandpa is going away that is why I must be with him on Sunday

Dorothy

Next is Margaret—Margaret Blackmer, New York, 12 years old last New Year's. She of the identification shell. Those shells were so frail and delicate that they could not endure exposure on a watch-chain, therefore we have put them safely and sacredly away and hung gold shells enameled with iridescent shell-colors on our watch-chains to represent them and do the identifying with. Margaret's father will bring her down from her school at Briarcliff on the Hudson six days hence to visit me—as I learn per her letter of five days ago—and then she will go with me to play at the Children's Theatre, where, as Honorary President of that admirable institution, I am to say a few words.[2]

Next is Irene—Irene Gerken, of 75th Street, New York, that beautiful and graceful and altogether wonderful child—I mean fairy—of 12 summers. To-morrow she will go to a matinee with me, and we are to play billiards the rest of the day. In Bermuda, last January, we played much billiards together, and a certain position of the balls is still known by her name there. When her ball backed itself against the cushion and became thereby nearly unusable, she was never embarrassed by that defect but always knew how to remedy it: she just moved it out to a handier place, without remark or apology and blandly fired away! Down there, now, when a ball lies glued to a cushion, gentlemen who have never seen that child lament and say,

"O hang it, here's another Irene!"

Next is Hellen Martin, of Montreal, Canada, a slim and bright and sweet little creature aged ten and a half years.

Next is Jean Spurr, aged 13 the 14th of last March, and of such is the kingdom of Heaven.

Next is Loraine Allen, nine and a half years old, with the voice of a flute and a face as like a flower as can be, and as graciously and enchantingly beautiful as ever any flower was.

Next is Helen Allen, aged 13, native of Bermuda, perfect in character, lovely in disposition, and a captivater at sight!

Next—and last, to date—is Dorothy Sturgis, aged 16, of Boston. This is the charming child mentioned in yesterday's chapter when I was talking about Lord Grey. On the voyage we were together at the stern watching the huge waves lift the ship skyward then drop her, most thrillingly H—alifax-ward, when one of them of vast bulk leaped over the taffrail and knocked us down and buried us under several tons of salt water. The papers, from one end of America to the other, made a perilous and thundersome event of it, but it wasn't that kind of a thing at all. Dorothy was not discomposed, nobody was hurt, we changed our clothes from the skin outward, and were on deck again in half an hour. In talking of Dorothy yesterday I referred to her as one of my "angel-fishes."

All the ten school-girls in the above list are my angel-fishes, and constitute my Club, whose name is "The Aquarium," and contains no creature but these angel-fishes and one slave. I am the slave. The Bermudian angel-fish, with its splendid blue decorations, is easily the most beautiful fish that swims, I think. So I thought I would call my ten pets angel-fishes, and their club the Aquarium.

The club's badge is the angel-fish's splendors reproduced in enamels and mounted for service as a lapelpin—at least that is where the girls wear it. I get these little pins in Bermuda; they are made in Norway.

A year or two ago I bought a lovely piece of landscape of 210 acres in the country near Redding, Connecticut, and John Howells, the son of his father, is building a villa there for me. We'll spend the coming summer in it. I have never been to that region, but the house is so lauded by Clara and Miss Lyon that I am becoming anxious to see it.

The billiard-room will have the legend "The Aquarium" over its door, for it is to be the Club's official headquarters. I have good photographs of all my fishes, and these will be framed and hung around the walls. There is an angel-fish bedroom—double-bedded—and I expect to have a fish and her mother in it as often as Providence will permit.

There's a letter from the little Montreal Hellen.[3] I will begin an answer now, and finish it later:

> I miss you, dear Hellen. I miss Bermuda too, but not so much as I miss you; for you were rare, and occasional, and select, and Ltd., whereas Bermuda's charms and graciousnesses were free and common and unrestricted,—like the rain, you know, which falls upon the just and the unjust alike; a thing which would not happen if I were superintending the rain's affairs. No, I would rain softly and sweetly upon the just, but whenever I caught a sample of the unjust out-doors I would drown him.

1. Oddly, even here Clemens avoids mention of Gertrude ("Marjorie") Natkin whom he met some eighteen months before Dorothy Butes, and to whom he wrote at least twenty-seven letters during the winter and spring of 1906.

2. Clemens became interested in the Children's Theatre of the Educational Alliance in the fall of 1907, and attended their benefit performance of *The Prince and the Pauper* on 19 November. Subsequently he became an honorary president of the organization and gave a curtain speech on 23 April 1908.

3. Hellen Martin. This is Clemens's only surviving letter to her.

HELLEN MARTIN TO CLEMENS

Montreal
[17 April 1908]

Dear Mr. Clemens

I wrote you a letter but was just to late for the mail for Bermuda. I hope you had a pleasant voyage coming back. My Brother Charlie who is at Boarding School, is coming back for the Easter Holidays. How are you feeling now? I am feeling fine. Lots of Love from

Your Loving Little friend
Hellen Martin

P.S. Wishing you a very Happy Easter. H.M.

Clemens to Dorothy Sturgis

[New York]
[19 April 1908]
Easter morning

Yes indeed, dear Miss Dorothy, I want the pictures you took; & I am hoping that Mr. Russell will not forget to send copies of those which he took of you & me, for I want good ones to frame & hang in the billiard room of the house I am building in the country—the said room's name being "The Aquarium" because it is to be the Aquarium's official headquarters.

It is 11 a.m. now, and as soon as Miss Lyon gets up I will remind her to send you the pictures she took of us on the steamer, when she gets up. She arrived late last night after a journey to Gloucester, where she secured a house for my daughter Jean.[1] She is probably tired out.

1 p.m. Miss Lyon is up, & I shall get up myself before long, as there is to be company at dinner. I am very glad she caught you on the telephone & delivered my affectionate greetings to you & got yours to me in return.

With a further consignment of love,

SLC

1. Jean Clemens had been living in various sanitoriums and continued to need medical supervision as well as supportive friendship. Isabel Lyon had just rented a house in Gloucester, Massachusetts for Jean and several friends to live in during the summer months. Contrary to Jean's desire, Clemens felt it best she not live at home.

DOROTHY STURGIS TO CLEMENS

[153 Beacon St., Boston]
April 23*rd* [1908]

Dear Mr. Clemens

I got my photographs the other day, but none of the ones I took of you came out at all so I won't send them.

When Miss Lyon was here in Boston I told her that I was going to send you an Easter present. It was a little sketch I drew while in St. George's, of the church on the hill which was started, but never finished. Mama said she thought that you would like it. Where I took it to be framed they said they would send it by Saturday, but I don't think they did, did they? I thought I'd better write and tell you who it was from as there was no card or anything with it.

Now that I have not got my own pictures of you, please tell Miss Lyon to be sure and send me hers. Give her lots and lots of love, and keep oceans for yourself.

Ever Lovingly
the newest arrival
DMS

CLEMENS TO DOROTHY QUICK

[21 Fifth Avenue]
[24 April 1908]
Thursday

I miss you so! I wish you were back, you dear little rascal.

When I found that your luggage could not be expressed until morning I asked Miss Lyon to telephone you so, right away, & no doubt she did so.

It is past midnight—we have been to the Children's Theatre, where you *must* go with us some day when you can be spared from home. You will like it, dear.

I thought you left your story with me, & I told Miss Lyon she might read it—but we couldn't find it, & she was so disappointed, & so was I. Won't you send it to me, dear heart? I will send it back as soon as she has read it.

I have been playing billiards alone for half an hour, but it is no fun, & there are no cats & no Dorothy, & the house is silent & asleep. I will follow suit now. With love good-bye, good-bye, good night!

SLC

CLEMENS TO HELEN ALLEN

21 Fifth Avenue
April 25/08

I miss you ever so much, you dear Helen. There's been a queer & constant reminder of you—salt in my hair—ever since that pleasant [ocean] bath until an hour ago when I washed it out with 5 separate and distinct soapings & scourings.

We had an enjoyable voyage—(though a little rough)—because I had a member of the Aquarium along, & also the Governor General. The Governor General (Gray) is just a love! There couldn't be a more winning and respect-compelling and human being at its best personality. And so the voyage was too short.

But I'm desolate now. My youngest daughter came yesterday, but she could only stay an hour or two, then hurry away. My other daughter (Clara) will arrive this evening. Meantime there's not an Angel-Fish on the place; the Aquarium is empty. Francesca (Atlanta, Ga) can't come till June. Dorothy (London) can't come any earlier. Margaret (up the Hudson at school) can't come till April 23d. Dorothy (New Jersey) can't come till next Monday. You can see, yourself, that things were looking gloomy for me—but my weather is improving, I'm glad to say. Irene has telephoned that she is coming Saturday morning. She will play billiards until luncheon & after that we will go to a matinee. Maybe her parents will allow her to stay over till Monday, then Dorothy will come.

The billiards room in the house we are building up country will be the official headquarters of the Aquarium. On the walls will be the framed photographs of the members, & over the door will be the sign "The Aquarium" in wood-carving. My daughter Jean will do the carving, & she is competent.

Good-bye, dear heart. Please remember me cordially to the others & at least all of that to yourself.

Lovingly,
SLC.

The people of the Sandwich Islands have offered me a mantel-piece, of native wood, for the new house. Isn't that nice? Miss Lyon & the architect have formulated the design, dimensions, etc.

CLEMENS TO DOROTHY STURGIS

21 Fifth Avenue
[late April 1908]

Dear Miss Dorothy, I thank you ever so much for the picture; I am very glad to have it—your mother was quite right about it. I did not know it was from you until your letter came. Miss Lyon thinks you think you told her you were going to send me an Easter present, but forgot to really say it.

It is generally agreed that Joe Jefferson's son's Rip Van Winkle is not as good as his father's was, & some folks say the like [about] Southern jr's Lord Dundreary as compared with his senior's rendition of the part —but *that* is [a] distinct mistake. Miss Lyon and I saw the piece this afternoon, & I laughed as I have not laughed before in 30 years—that is to say, not since I saw the elder Southern in the part for the last time a generation ago. When you have the opportunity, go & see that play.[1]

Miss Lyon sends you lots & lots of love, & so doth

SLC

1. Edward Hugh Southern's play *Lord Dundreary* was playing in New York at the time.

HELEN ALLEN TO CLEMENS

Bay House [Bermuda]
April 27th 1908
Monday

My dear Mr. Clemens,

I was afraid that possibly you had forgotten to write to me, so decided I would write you first, and tell you how much I have missed you, I shall always remember the lovely times we had together and particularly our fine swim that last day you were in Bermuda. When ever I use my camera I think of you, and how kind you were to help me get it. Please do write me soon. I remain always your loving and devoted "Angel-fish"

Helen Schuyler Allen

P.S. Please give my love to Miss Lyon.

H.S.A.

DOROTHY QUICK TO CLEMENS

[Plainfield, N.J.]
[27 April 1908]

Dear Mr Clemens
                    here is the story[1]

What would have happened. The guests were gone and Martin Chown sat by the fire it was almost out. Martin Chown was an old man no not old but he was not young he was 65 years old he was alone and his thoughts were sad they went back to the last Christmas where he had sat in the death chamber of his wife and how she had when his train of thoughts were suddenly interrupted by a figure clothed in white You are happier as it is it said so is she.

"No No interrupted the man"
You are said the spirit but I will show you what would have happened if she had lived Come Come

Martin Chown drew back.

Where was he to be taken but the spirit drew him forward do not be afraid come again. Martin Chown followed it. It led him to a room he looked and recognized the courtroom he was on the witness stand so was his wife

What does it mean he asked the spirit

it means that your wife would have loved someone else and gotten rid of you through the divorce court

Will she suceed he was about to ask when he looked up the spirit and the courtroom had vanished he was once more seated by the now dying fire there was no sign of the spirit

Martin Chown slowly arose it is better as it is he said slowly He had learned that it is best to be contented with what is ordained

I have missed you very very much (also the cats but not so much) the play went on very well everyone said I did very well thank Miss very much for sending the bag Mother would write but she is sick in bed with lots of love your loving

Dorothy

P.S. give lots of love to Miss Lyon

1. "Martin Chown," the story Clemens requested in his letter of 24 April.

CLEMENS TO DOROTHY QUICK

[New York]
April 28/08
Tuesday evening

Oh, you dear Dorothy, you have changed the story! You little rascal, you have put things in it that were not there before, & I want it *just as it was*. Be a good child, & send me the original manuscript—I will be sure & send it back to you.

Of course you did very well in the play—I knew you would.

Dear heart, can't you come up Saturday after next & play billiards and take lunch & go to a matinee & stay over till Monday? Can't you? Won't you? I hope so. Ask your mother, if you may come. I shan't be here long—only a month; then our new house in the country will be finished, & we'll go & live in it. And you must come there as soon as you can. There will be a bed in your room for your mother.

I haven't seen a cat since you went away until to-night—then Tammany came up to play billiards.

With lots of love
SLC

I like the story in its changed form, but I think I like the former form a little the best.

FRANCES NUNNALLY TO CLEMENS

St. Timothy's
Catonsville, Md.
April 30, 1908

Dear Mr. Clemens,—

While I was at home for my holidays, I started several times to write to you, but something always interrupted me, so I am going to try to write now. I had such a good time at home, that it was awfully hard when I had to come back to school. There is just six weeks to this term, though, and I think it will pass very quickly. When I come up to New York about the first or middle of June, I hope very much I can see you. Margaret Disosway told me when she came back to school that Mrs. Quick had taken her to call on you while she was in New York, and I surely wish I had been there.

I think we will sail for England on the "Minneapolis" on the sixth of June, but there may be some trouble about my leaving school before it is over. We have gotten our passage for that date and I don't know what we will do if they will not let me leave school early. They have always been very strict about that sort of thing here, though. Perhaps we can get passage on a later boat.

I want this letter to go off on the afternoon mail so I will stop.

With love,

Francesca

CLEMENS TO FRANCES NUNNALLY

21 Fifth Avenue

May 1/08

The way you are arranging things, you little rascal, what sort of glimpse of you am I going to get? Before the 6th of June we shall be living in the house I am building in the country. However, it isn't far away—only an hour & a half. When you arrive here I will come to town & see you—& then I hope you & your mother can run out to the villa with me & give me a visit.

If you should need to change your steamship-date, let me know, & I will put it into the hands of Ashcroft & Miss Lyon & save you the bother of attending to it.

It was a great pleasure to see Miss Margaret. I hope it isn't the last time. Francesca dear, is Atlanta vain of you two, or are you samples of just the ordinary average product of that place?

With love

SLC

DOROTHY STURGIS TO CLEMENS

153 Beacon Street [Boston]

May 2nd [1908]

My dear Mr. Clemens

How do you think I have spent my entire day to-day? Reading "The Prince and the Pauper". I always loved it, but now it has an added interest for me since I know its author!

Perhaps you remember that in your last letter to me you spoke of Sothern's Lord Dundreary. I saw it when it was here, and thought it was perfectly splendid, and just as funny as it could be!! But possibly a little too long drawn out in some places, such as the time when Lord Dundreary has that long conversation with the girl, whom [he] eventually marrys, just outside the house.

Papa went to New York last night on business, and I begged him to take me with him so that I could come and see you, but he remained hard hearted and refused to take me!

Give my love to Miss Lyon, but tell her I shan't love her any more if she does not send me those pictures of you pretty soon, because you must remember that I have no picture of you at all! On Easter mama gave me a beautiful Japanese silver picture frame, with the opening four inches in diameter, and I am hoping that a picture of you will fit that.

Ever your loving
Dorothy

CLEMENS TO DOROTHY QUICK

21 Fifth Avenue
May 4/08
Monday

You are just a dear, you little rascal! I shall be so glad to see you. I shall be downstairs waiting for you at 11:30 when you come.

It was lovely of you to send me the original MS of the story.

We certainly did have good times in Tuxedo, & I guess we will duplicate them in the new house in the country. We'll start the Author's League again, & you will dictate & I will be your emanensis.

Yes, Wednesday will be time enough to let me know whether you can come or not—but I hope you won't fail to come, dear heart.

I am watching out for the violets; it is very sweet of you to send them. With lots of love

SLC

CLEMENS TO DOROTHY QUICK

21 Fifth Avenue
May 8/08
Friday

(Joan of Arc's Day.)

Your letter came last night, dear, & brought me such a disappointment. I am so sorry you have a cold, but glad you are taking proper care of it. It would not be wise for you to make a journey in the draughty cars at such a time.

"If you want me I can come next week." If I *want* you! Can you imagine a time when I *don't* want you? As far as my understanding of it goes, I want you all the time. I hope you will get entirely over your cold, dear heart, & will come to me to-morrow week sound & well.

The violets came promptly, & the reason I did not write you to that effect was, that I wanted to tell you, & show them to you unwithered; for Claude undertook to keep them fresh, & he has done it. You dear sweet child, to send them to me.

SLC

CLEMENS TO DOROTHY STURGIS

21 Fifth Avenue
[9 May 1908]

Dear Miss Dorothy:

Why, bless your heart, your father isn't a bit necessary on a short journey like that. Use him for company, and leave the rest to us. We will meet you at the station, and take care of you; and when you return homeward we will put you on board your car. It is all easy, and handy, and safe—You see that it is, yourself. Next time you have a chance to come down, tell your train, and come right along. We will take you off your father's hands at the station, giving a receipt for you if required; and on your return we will deliver you unimpaired into his hands.

There, I've said it twice. That is because I wrote page 1 about a week ago, and didn't re-read it when I began page 2 at the bottom of page 1.

May 9. I have been waiting and waiting for the photographs to come from the developer before writing you. They never came until last night, and they were bad, when they *did* come. I enclose the only good one. The likeness of you is very good, but I wish you had washed your face before sitting. The picture ought to have been taken right after the wave-drench, then you would have been up to standard. The chair-back at your left is *very* good.

This picture will fit the frame your mother gave you, I think. You say you have no picture of me at all. Do you mean a solitaire? There's a plenty, but they are too large for the frame—but *they* don't belong in that frame, anyhow.

We are going to the police-parade, now. Good bye.
With the love of
S L C

P.S. Miss Lyon has brought copies of the two other pictures. I enclose them.

CLEMENS TO DOROTHY QUICK

21 Fifth Avenue
May 9/08

I hope the cold is well—I mean I hope *you* are well of the cold, you dear Dorothy. I had arranged to take you to the police-parade, but I took Miss Lyon in your place. Perhaps it was best that you were not there, for it was cloudy part of the time, & a little chilly. It was much the most splendid police-parade I have ever seen, either in Europe or America, & I am sure you would have enjoyed it.[1]

I took Ashcroft & Miss Lyon to the matinee, & the box was an unusually large & comfortable one, but I didn't like the piece. It was too frivolous & vaudevillish, & too much ballet & clothes and foolish songs. I got very tired of it, & was glad you were not there. We must find something better for next Saturday when you come. I miss you, & shall be so glad to see you, dear.

With lots of love

SLC

1. Clemens has enclosed a newspaper clipping, including a photograph of the distinguished guests on the reviewing stand. Sitting next to him were Cardinal Michael Logue, primate of Ireland, and Archbishop Farley of the New York diocese. Clemens has indicated, in pen, where Isabel Lyon is standing in the crowd behind him.

FRANCES NUNNALLY TO CLEMENS

St. Timothy's
Catonsville, Md.
May 10, 1908

Dear Mr. Clemens,—

Thank you very much for your kind offer to change our steamship passage for us, but we have already succeeded in getting very good accommodations on the "Minnetonka." So we shall sail on the thirteenth instead of on the sixth of June. By the present arrangements, I will only have about one day in New York before we sail, as I am not to leave here until the eleventh. I certainly hope I can see you before we leave. When do you expect to go to your new house? I know you will be glad to get there, in the country. I surely would love to make you a visit in your new home, but as I said, I will just have one day before we sail.

I am having to study awfully hard now, but in three weeks the worst part of my work will be over, and then it will not be anytime before school closes. Then I am sure my summer abroad will make up for all the hard work.

With love,
Francesca

CLEMENS TO DOROTHY QUICK

21 Fifth Avenue
[12 May 1908]
Tuesday Evening

You dear little Dorothy, it was fortunate that you escaped the pink-eye, for although a cold is bad, pinkeye is worse, & is a stubborn & painful malady.

I shall look for you Saturday morning with high anticipations. We've got a box for "Girls,"[1] & they say it is very good, & is clean & wholesome & hasn't any of that horrible ballet-dancing in it, such as we saw last Saturday.

Margaret Illington[2] has been trying to get into our Aquarium, & I wouldn't let her; but Sunday night she came here to dinner with her husband (Daniel Frohman), & she was dressed for 12 years, & had pink ribbons at the back of her neck & looked about 14 years old; so I admitted her as an angel-fish, & pinned the badge on her bosom. There's lots of lady-candidates, but I guess we won't let any more in, unless perhaps Billy Burke.

I've got something for you. It cost 10 cents. I took it away from Ashcroft.

I haven't seen the kittens lately, but Tammany came up Sunday night & jumped up on the table & helped us play billiards—uninvited.

With lots & lots of love

SLC

Dear heart, we must start the Author's League again.

1. *Girls* ran for sixty-four performances at Daly's Theater in New York and starred Laura Nelson Hall.
2. Margaret Illington was the wife of Daniel Frohman, manager of the Lyceum Theater and a friend of Clemens since 1886.

DOROTHY QUICK TO CLEMENS

[Plainfield, N.J.]
[12 May 1908]

My Dear Mr Clemens

I am almost well now but not quite. I am so glad you got the violets all right. It was so funny how I got this cold that I must tell you about it. I was in school Tuesday when suddenly my eye began to get red. & Miss Arnold (my teacher) said she was afraid I was going to have a pink eye and I had better go home which I did. I did not have pink eye but I got nervous; hence the cold. But I am all right now except a slight cough. How are the cats? "Oh dear! look at the time quarter of nine; I must go to bed." So I will say "good night" and close with lots & lots of love

I am
    Your very loving
      Dorothy

P.S. Please give Miss Lyon lots of love for me. Dorothy

HELEN ALLEN TO CLEMENS

Bay House   Bermuda
May 13th 1908
Wednesday

My dear Mr. Clemen's,

I was so glad to hear you hadn't forgotten me but that it was only the mail. How sorry I was to hear that Miss Lyon was ill and I am also glad to hear that she is better now. A dreadful thing happened the other night! Some dogs came and killed all my guinea pigs and rabbits, except one rabbit who hid itself away in the coal room.

There is to be a fancy dress dance at Government House on the 22nd of May. It is the Governor's little boys birthday and lots of children are asked and some of the cadets from the ships. Maxwell is going as an Indian Chief and I as Juliet, I went in this costume once before.

I have never met Irene, but I saw her with you while she was here and I must admit I envy her being with you in New York.

Mother and Daddy have not decided whether I am to go away this winter to school, but if I do not I am looking forward to seeing you here.

Will you please write to me again soon? because I shall love to here about all your plans and doings.

With lots of love for Miss. Lyon and yourself
   I remain
     Your "Bermuda angel-fish"
      Helen Schuyler Allen

DOROTHY STURGIS TO CLEMENS

53 Beacon St. [Boston]
[13 May 1908]

Dear Mr. Clemens

I'm just going to write you this letter to see how famous you are & not put any address on it. Do tell me if it reaches you![1]
DMS

Samuel Clemens
  21 5 Ave.
     N.Y.

I put this on so that if they don't know your address they will find it inside.

1. "It arrived promptly" was written in Clemens's hand on the page.

DOROTHY QUICK TO CLEMENS

[Plainfield, N.J.]
[14 May 1908]

My Dear Mr Clemens

I got your letter & will be so glad to come Saturday I may come in with grandma on an early train which will bring me to your house at 11 but if I come in with mother it will be half-past I am writing this letter in a great hurry so you must excuse it this is going to be a very very short letter as I want it to catch the first mail

With lots & lots of love I am your loving

Dorothy

CLEMENS TO DOROTHY STURGIS

21 Fifth Avenue
May 15/08

Dear Dorothy:

Yours of day-before-yesterday arrived this morning. It stopped over at Hartford for refreshments.

The newest photographs (and the best, we think) arrived from the photographer's yesterday evening, and Miss Lyon will mail one to you. The upper part of the figure, if judgmatically scissored out, will go into the 4 inch circle very well, if a part of the right arm be chopped off.

Land! I forgot all about the dancing lessons. I must attend to that.

Don't you mind about the "bother" and we shan't. All we need to know is about your trains, & we'll receive you and re-ship you, and take good care of you *between*. And there won't be any bother about it. Dorothy comes from New Jersey every now & then and stays two or three days (she is coming tomorrow), & we don't discover that there is any bother about it. Just you give us your trains, & leave the rest to us.

You remember the Waylands? They are just lovely. They come here to dinner every Sunday night. The Freemans too when they are in town.[1]

With lots of love,

SLC

1. Zoeth Freeman was Clemens's banker and became a director of the Mark Twain Company when it was founded in December 1908.

Dorothy Sturgis to Clemens

153 Beacon Street [Boston]
[17 May 1908]

Dear Mr. Clemens.

You are indeed a most noted personage if a letter will reach you without any address on it at all. But do tell me why it went to Hartford, did you ever live there?

I saw a lovely article about you in the Transcript the other day, headed

"Mark Twain-Nuisance[?] Senator Stewart tells how he wrote "Innocents Abroad" and frightened his landlady"! Was that true?! If so I didn't know that you were such a bad character, the description of you was truly awful, and not at all correct—now, except for the cigar. You wouldn't be you if you didn't have a cigar in your mouth or between your fingers.

Papa read aloud "The Brushwood Boy" to me last night for about the tenth or twelve time, I believe, & I love it more every time I read it.[1] Don't you think yourself that of all the short stories in the English language it is one of the most wonderfully worded, the most clearly expressed, and the most exquisitely thought out of any you have read? I certainly do. Did you ever come across a writer who could cover so large a space of time and introduce so many wonderful thoughts in so short a story.

Ever your loving Dorothy

1. Clemens knew Kipling, the author of "The Brushwood Boy," and visited with him during Clemens's trip to England in 1907.

DOROTHY STURGIS TO CLEMENS

153 Beacon Street [Boston]
[21 May 1908]

My Dear Mr. Clemens

I got the picture the other day, and it's a perfect beauty, not exactly four inches in size though, is it. I hate to spoil it by cutting it up, it's such a nice picture as it is.

Mama has gone up to Woodstock to spend a week or so, and I'm left all alone now, you see I only see Papa and my brother at breakfast and dinner, and not always there. But I'm doing all the housekeeping, and that's lots of fun.

Please give my love to Miss Lyon and thank her ever so much for taking all the trouble she has to send your various pictures out to me.

When you write next please tell me lots of news about yourself and Miss Lyon, and about what's happening in New York.

I spoke of The Brushwood Boy in my last letter to you, and that reminds me that I meant to ask you where Kipling is now, I have often wondered where he spends most of his time, and I have often longed to meet him, but I don't suppose I ever shall.

Lovingly Dorothy

CLEMENS TO DOROTHY STURGIS

21 Fifth Avenue
Sunday, May 24 [1908]

Dear Dorothy:

Indeed I would tell you lots of news if there were lots to tell, but there's *only some*. We shipped my daughter Clara to England a week ago, and she has just arrived there—so says her cablegram of this morning.[1]

Last Tuesday we shipped my daughter Jean to Eastern Point, Gloucester, Mass, where she has taken a house for the summer, and has two very charming companions who do for her what you are doing for your father and brother—keep house.[2] Miss Lyon found that place and secured it, but as Jean had never seen it we were in deep suspense and anxiety until we should hear from her, for it might not content her. But it is all right, now—she can't find adjectives enough to express her delight in it. I did not fully appreciate how cautious I had been, until her letter came and relieved me.

One of the angel-fishes is stopping over Sunday with us,[3] and she and I took the top of the electric stage this morning and traveled from our door to 90th Street, then down again to 55th where we entered the St. Regis and sat down to wait until church should break out. When the porter informed us, we crossed the street and mixed into the crowd issuing from a 5th Avenue church, and gained good and great reputation at no expense of fatigue or contributions. Everywhere you could hear people say in an awed and hushed voice, "How nice that young Clemens is—people think he doesn't go to church, but you can see he does." Then I whispered to the fish to look as if she had put 10 cents in the plate, and I put on a look indicating a dollar and a half—and you never saw such admiration as it excited. Many of the ladies swooned, from pure joy.

We joined every congregation between 55th and 28th, and by careful and delicate art convinced each and every of them that we had been partaken (sic) of *their* clerical feast. It has been a good lesson to this child: she will always know how to make an inexpensive good impression, Sundays, after this: and by and by it will have a splendid commercial value for her.

Kipling? I don't know where he is, now. England, no doubt. He winters in South Africa.

Good bye. With love—
SLC

1. Clara Clemens sailed for Europe on her first concert tour, returning home in September.

2. Jean Clemens and her companions, Marguerite Schmidt (Bebe) and Mildred Cowles, occupied the cottage at Gloucester, but it soon displeased them and they were sent to Berlin instead, along with Anna Sterritt, a maid hired by Clemens.

3. Probably Dorothy Quick, who wrote of a forthcoming visit in her letter of 14 May.

CLEMENS TO MARGARET BLACKMER

21 Fifth Avenue
May 25/08

Dear Margaret—

Did I tell you, when you visited me, that I had lost my half of the enameled shell in Bermuda? I've got it back again! Of course the real shell, the original shell, the fossil jetsam of the waves of Sandy Point, was the *valuable* shell, because of its odd & pretty associations (& I still possessed *that*), but I held the enameled one in very high regard because it was that original's official deputy & representative. I lost it off my watch chain at a dinner at the officer's mess at Prospect a day or two before we sailed, & now it has been found & handed to Major Graham by one of the servants. I shan't lose it again, dear.

One of my angel-fishes stayed over last Sunday with us, & another one stayed over yesterday with us. I wish you would do us that honor.

With love,
S.L.C.

DOROTHY QUICK TO CLEMENS

[Plainfield, N.J.]
[25 May 1908]

My dear Mr Clemens

I have intended writing every day since I left you to thank you for the lovely time I had with you   I haven't got my pony yet but we are looking all the time & may get one any day, it is very warm here today & if the weather keeps warm I suppose you'll be glad to get into the country yourself. My drawing class on pleasant days goes out to sketch from nature it is very nice but I don't like it very much   With lots of love hugs & kisses I am your very loving

                        Dorothy

HELEN ALLEN TO CLEMENS

                       Bay House [Bermuda]
                       [26 May 1908]

My dear Mr. Clemens,

The party at Government House was a perfect success, everybody looked their very best. I am going to send you some pictures taked of Max and myself just before we started and while we were there. We got there by 3:30 and went right down on one of the lower terraces and had our pictures taken and played musical chaires then had tea and after that the cotilion and just before we went home we fished for candies, we didn't get home until quite late, later than we expected.

Monday was a legal holiday and I went to a lovely picnic at St. David's Lighthouse. Tuesday I had a small tennis party. I am getting on beautifuly with my tennis but will not stop until I am not ashamed to play with anybody.

Dr. Herring told us that he saw you in New York and that you thought there was some hope of your coming down here this summer if so please let me know so that I will be able to be down to see you.

I will be delighted to get the pictures. With lots of love for Miss Lyons and yourself.

              Believe me as ever
                Your loving little "Angel-fish"
                Helen Schuyler Allen

DOROTHY STURGIS TO CLEMENS

153 Beacon Street [Boston]
[27 May 1908]

Dear Mr. Clemens

I got your letter the other day, and I never knew you had so many daughters before, but I'm glad you got them all "shipped" safely!

What are *your* summer plans? or haven't you got any? I don't know exactly what I am going to do except that in July and August I am going to a camp on Lake Asguam in New Hampshire, and in June I may go up to Woodstock and join Mama there.

I'm afraid I must stop now as I have lots of lessons to do.

Lovingly
Dorothy

Love to Miss Lyon!

CLEMENS TO CARLOTTA WELLES

21 Fifth Avenue
[29 May 1908]
Friday Night

Dear Charley, I am vexed to the last limit, & disappointed, & so sorry. If my secretary hadn't chanced to be out, it would not have happened, for she sees all strangers that come, whereas I see none of them. The butler took you for a stranger, & followed the law of the house, but if you had told him you were a friend he would have found me, for I was in my room. In fact he did find me, but I was asleep, & so he foolishly & criminally did not wake me. I hope you will not come as a stranger next time, & I also hope that there will be a next time.

Frances Nunnally is at school near Baltimore, & I shall see her here June 12th. She sails, Europe-bound, on the 13th. She & her mother visited me in Tuxedo Park last September, but it was only a glimpse, for they were flying homeward from Europe.

Mr. Ashcroft is well. He dined with us Wednesday, & spent the night.

The burden of city life is heavy upon me, but we go to the country for the summer June 15th. We have been delayed a month by an unfinished house.

I hope you will come again, & not as a stranger, Charley.

Affectionately, SL Clemens[1]

1. At the bottom of the letter Carlotta Welles (Briggs) later wrote this note: "This was my last letter from Mr. Clemens. I called at 21 Fifth Avenue around the first of June '08 just before going to Bryn Mawr where my sister was graduating. He sent this letter to Bryn Mawr. I have not got the envelope as someone begged to have it."

DOROTHY QUICK TO CLEMENS

[Plainfield, N.J.]

[30 May 1908]

My Dear Mr Clemens

My letter has not reached you are you have been sick. I am worried please let me know.

I'm very well and very very busy studying for examinations its awfully hard work. commencement is Tuesday June 9*th* I'm going to be there and expect to have lots of fun   Tell miss Lyon I send lots of love to her and hope she is well and now I must close

With lots and lots of love hoping youre not sick

I am

Your very loving

Dorothy

Please write

FROM CLEMENS'S NOTEBOOK

The Aquarium, (June 1908)[1]

Dorothy Butes (16) London, England (*Honorary*)	16
Dorothy Quick (11½) Plainfield, N.J.	12
Dorothy Harvey, (13.9) Deal Beach, N.J.	13
Dorothy Sturgis (16) 153 Beacon Street	16
Hellen Martin, (12) 1 Murray ave, Westmount, Montreal	12
Helen Schuyler Allen, (13) Bay House, Bermuda	13
Irene Gerken (13) 52 W. 75th street	13
Margaret Blackmer, (12) New York	12
Louise Paine (13) Redding, Conn	13
Frances Nunnally (17) Atlanta, Ga.	17
Margaret Illington	13
Jean Spurr,[2] (13) 129 Mt. Pleasant ave, Newark, N.J.	150
Marjorie Breckenridge, 15, Brooklyn	

The 12 children's ages foot up 165 years. Margaret Illington isn't a child, but she is charming enough to be one. She dressed for 12 & elected herself, & was accepted & invested with the badge of the Order (an enameled angel-fish pin).

1. This list (not strictly chronological) represents the complete membership of the Aquarium, including "honorary" angelfish Margaret Illington.
2. There is no record of correspondence between Jean Spurr and Clemens.

CLEMENS TO DOROTHY QUICK

21 Fifth Avenue
June 2/08

You dear little Dorothy, I am so glad to hear from you. No, I haven't been sick, I have been away, eight days, at Deal Beach, arranging a lot of matters with my publisher.[1] I am home now for a week, then I am going to Gloucester, Mass., to spend a few days with my daughter Jean, who has taken a house near there on the sea shore for the summer. After that I shall run back to New York & then up-country to the new house. It will be ready for us by the 15*th* or 20*th* of June, we think. By & by you & your mother must give us a visit there, when we get things well going. Miss Lyon & I will do our very best to make it pleasant for you. Promise me you will come, dear.

I hope you will have a splendid good time at Commencement. I expect to arrive at Gloucester about that date.

Clara is singing in London, & I judge by the cable-news that she is having a very satisfactory time.

Miss Lyon sends you lots of love, & I send you lots & lots of mine.

SLC

1. Deal Beach, New Jersey, was the home of his publisher, George Harvey, of Harper and Brothers.

Clemens to Dorothy Sturgis

21 Fifth Avenue
June 2 [1908]
Tuesday

Dear Dorothy:
I am just back this moment, and find yours of May 27. I have been down in New Jersey eight days, visiting around among my angel-fishes of that region, and have had a very good time indeed.

Oh yes, I have plans, but what disturbs me is, that they don't seem to fit in with yours very well. About next Monday (June 6) I expect to pass through Boston on a visit to my daughter Jean at Gloucester, Mass., and I was planning to stop over in Boston one or two hours, if the trains might permit, and run in to see you. But there are two maybe's —1, Maybe the trains will connect too closely; and 2, maybe you will be gone to Woodstock. Then there are some more maybes—thus: 3, maybe after I shall have spent a couple of days in Gloucester, the return trains may connect less closely in Boston; and 4, maybe you will be back from Woodstock by that time. And so I am going to hope for a glimpse of you in that Gloucester trip somewhere. Meantime I will wait and see what happens.

Lovingly,
SLC

CLEMENS TO FRANCES NUNNALLY

New York
June 3/08

Francesca dear, I am ciphering over the situation. The country-house is finished, & I shall move into it June 15th, by Miss Lyon's guess. So I am planning as thus:

Sunday, June 7, my last public engagement here.

Monday, June 8. To Boston.

Tuesday, 9th. To Gloucester, to visit my daughter Jean, who has taken a house on the sea near there.

Thursday, 11th. Back to New York, *to see you next day.*

That is my scheme. Tell me your hotel, dear, so that I can go & find you.

And make a note of my telephone address, for it is not in the book: *3907 Gramercy.*

With love
SLC

FRANCES NUNNALLY TO CLEMENS

St. Timothy's
Catonsville, Md.
June 4, 1908

Dear Mr. Clemens,—

Your letter came this morning and I am so glad you are going to be in New York when we sail. I was afraid you would have gone to your new house. Mother leaves Atlanta on the sixth and is going right to New York, as she has some shopping to do before we leave. Then Father is coming up and take me up on the eleventh. I shall reach New York on the afternoon of the eleventh and will be there until some time on the thirteenth, whenever the "Minnetonka" sails. We shall be at the Waldorf and I will telephone you when I get to New York. I certainly am glad I am going to have a chance to see you before I go. I wish you were going over again this summer. The picture you enclosed in your letter reminds me so much of last summer. It is awfully good, I think.

I want this letter to get off on the afternoon mail, so I will stop. Hoping to see you in about a week, I am

With love,
Francesca

DOROTHY QUICK TO CLEMENS

[Plainfield, N.J.]
June 5*th* 1908

My Dear Mr Clemens

I have a bad cold rose fever and Bronchitis together   its almost over now. We except to leave on Wednesday for Atlantic City   I have not gotten my pony and mother says that there is no use in getting one now as we are going away but get it in the fall and hire one whereever we go. I like that idea dont you? I have two rabbits. Billy and Dorothy (Dodo for short) they are two weeks old pure white with blue eyes. They're so lovely.

When we go away I shall let my friend Claire Kenworthy take care of them for me. She can have the products. You must be having a lovely time going everywhere. I hope you enjoy your visit with Miss Clemens I look forward to visiting you later on.

I hope you will like your new house when you see it. but, oh dear how late its getting and I must close with lots & lots of love your loving

Dorothy

P.S. Please give Miss Lyon my love

Dorothy

CLEMENS TO FRANCES NUNNALLY

21 Fifth Avenue

[6 June 1908]

You are a very dear & sweet Francesca to answer so promptly, & you so heavy-laden with work, you poor little chap! But soon you'll be at sea, & that will be fine & restful. I wish I could go with you.

I go away Monday the 8th, but shall plan to return Thursday fore-noon so as to be on deck & listening for your telephone message that afternoon. You & your parents must spare us a little of your time at our feed-trough, either at dinner that evening or at luncheon or dinner next day. I am going to count on that, dear heart.

With love,

SLC

CLEMENS TO DOROTHY STURGIS

[21 Fifth Avenue]

June 7/08

Dear Dorothy:

The Directors of the Children's Theatre are holding a business meet-ing down stairs, but as I am only Honorary President, I don't have to do any work & can therefore stay up here & answer Aquarium letters. Yours I cannot find; & so, as I don't know what state Woodstock is in I will send this to your Boston address.

I find I am not going to pass through Boston till the end of the month, because I can't get away from here earlier. I do hope you will be at home again by that time. I have to be in Portsmouth, N.H., June 30 for the Tom Bailey Aldrich Memorial dedication.[1]

I go visiting on Long Island tomorrow, but shall return on Friday to receive an angel-fish (the Georgian)[2] & her parents, who will dine with me & sail for Europe next day. Then I shall go back & finish the visit.

Yesterday we went to see "The Servant in the House" (oh, a noble play), and tonight I go dining out, to meet the author of it, whom I very much wish to know.[3]

I don't know how I have managed to mislay your letter. Such is not my custom—certainly it isn't as regards the letters of the Aquarium. I don't care for the others, they are Miss Lyon's affair.

Lovingly,

SLC

1. Clemens attended the Thomas Bailey Aldrich Memorial dedication on 30 June out of loyalty to his old friend, though he considered it folly and pretension to establish a museum for a man whose entire contribution to literature was "half a dozen small poems which are not surpassed in our language for exquisite grace and beauty and finish" (*MTA* 358).

2. Frances Nunnally.

3. Charles Rann Kennedy.

Clemens to Dorothy Quick

[21 Fifth Avenue]

[7 June 1908]

Sunday

You dear little rat, aren't you ever going to stop catching cold & struggling with bronchitis? I am so sorry for you. Wait till I get you up-country at "Innocence at Home"—then we'll set your health up![1]

Yes, I like the idea of waiting till fall to buy the pony. A hired one will answer quite well in the meantime.

I am glad you've got Billy & Dodo. In December they will be just right, & I will run down to see you & we will have them for dinner. I am like you, I just *love* rabbits.

I have been scheming to get down to your school-exercises day after tomorrow, but I failed, because of a string of business engagements which are going to keep me here for more than ten days yet. I would love to see you, dear.

Will it be safe to leave them with Claire Kenworthy? Do you know her well-enough? Is she good, & does she go to Sunday school? I think I wouldn't take any rash chances; because if she should eat them—however, maybe she can resist. I will hope so. She can eat the "products", & that will be all right, because they will belong to her.

Miss Lyon sends her love, & I send lots & lots of love, dear heart.

SLC

I reckon this will catch you before you get started toward Atlantic City. Tell me—what is your address there, & how long shall you stay?

1. This appears to be Clemens's first reference in a letter to the new name. According to Clara's book, *My Father, Mark Twain*, he made this change from Autobiography House to Innocence at Home on 3 June 1908.

DOROTHY QUICK TO CLEMENS

[Atlantic City, N.J.]
[11 June 1908]
Friday

My dear Mr Clemens

I received your letter just before I left I'm so sorry you could not have come out to commencement but I must confess I felt very much disappointed I wanted to show you my school and all my friends   Claire took the rabbits I think I can trust her

Dorothea Ofrdyttce[?] took my bird   Nellie Arnold my goldfish. so you see my pets are pretty well scattered around Plainfield

I wish you were here. It is lonely here and there is no crowd. I except to be here until July first and I expect Grandpa and Grandma will be back by then   My Rose fever is not very much better but I have scarsely been here long enough to be cured.

However, I slept through all of last night.

Which was a big improvement.

As I have been awake coughing all most every night for a whole week

I had a merry-go-round ride yesterday and got the brass ring Was'ant that exciting I wish you had been here to watch me catch it. it is almost an art. Please write to me very soon wont you.

With lots & lots of love to Miss Lyon & yourself and lots of hugs & kisses

Your loving
Dorothy

CLEMENS TO DOROTHY QUICK

[21 Fifth Avenue]
June 14/08
Sunday

I am so sorry, dear heart, that I could not come to Commencement, for I would have been so glad to see your school & meet your friends.

Miss Lyon is working very hard, these days, getting the new house up-country ready. Of course it requires a world of labor to get a new house in shape. She has been at it night & day, the past week, & has gotten all the furniture & the orchestrelle & a billiard table in, at least, & says the house will be ready for me next Thursday. I shan't be able to leave here till Thursday afternoon—then I'll go. I am sure I shall like the house, from all accounts. I think you will like it too, when you come to pay me a visit.

You careless child ! How do [you] know you can trust Claire & Dorothea & Nellie? As for me, *I* never expect to see those rabbits nor that bird nor that goldfish again. I wish *now* I had gone to Plainfield while they were still alive.

I wish you wouldn't be sick so much, dear. You seem to be always traveling from one malady to another, & it grieves me. Get *well*, dear! & *stay* well! Won't you?

I am glad you got the brass ring—I think you did well.

Miss Lyon sends you lots of love, & so do I—multiplied by 6.

SLC

CLEMENS TO DOROTHY STURGIS

[21 Fifth Avenue]
June 14, 1908
Sunday

Dear Dorothy:

Charles Rann Kennedy is the author of "The Servant in the House".
His wife, who was the Chief figure in "Everyman", plays in it, & so does
his niece, a girl of 18 or 19. It is a wonderful play & a wonderful cast.

The reason I didn't know where Woodstock is, was because I knew it
used to be in another state and had moved, but I didn't know what state
it had moved to until your last letter came.

Yesterday morning I shipped the Georgian member of the Aquarium
to Europe, with her parents: but they will visit me at "Innocence at
Home" (the house I have built near Redding, Conn.) the 21st or 22nd
of September, & I hope you can come at that time, too, & have ven-
tured to enter you upon the list accordingly. The house is about ready
now, & I shall go up there next Thursday, if nothing happens to defeat
Miss Lyon's calculations. I haven't seen it yet.

Yes indeed, I wish I could come to Woodstock, but I know I can't
manage it. I'm too old to skirmish around like an angel-fish.

Yours, with love,
SLC

CHAPTER FOUR

Innocence at Home

19 June 1908 – 5 November 1908

SAMUEL CLEMENS took very little interest in the building and decorating of Autobiography House, the details of which he was happy to leave in the hands of his architect, John Howells, son of William Dean Howells, and his secretary, Isabel Lyon. In fact, he was inclined to mutter, while the house was under construction, "the country house I need is a cemetery" (*MCMT* 458). It had seemed appropriate to call the place Autobiography House since it was paid for with Clemens's royalties on the twenty-five installments from his autobiography that George Harvey published in the *North American Review*. As the move approached, however, Clemens changed the name to Innocence at Home, a name he later said was especially appropriate for the many angelfish he hoped to entertain there. The house was designed in the style of an Italian villa, dramatically set on a hilltop and surrounded by 248 acres of rolling Connecticut countryside. In addition to an abundance of bedrooms, reception rooms, and staff quarters, the house contained a billiard room (Club headquarters), a glassed-in loggia, broad terraces, and a garden pergola surrounded by classical columns and cedars.

When Clemens arrived at the Redding rail station, he was greeted by a crowd of townspeople. Carriages decorated with flowers formed something of a parade, transporting Clemens, his well-wishers, and curious onlookers the three miles to the gates of his new home. The house and its grounds seemed to him perfect in every detail. That night more townsfolk and some neighbors stopped by to set off fireworks in the garden and give welcome to their celebrated new neighbor. Afterward, because the billiard table was already in place, Paine and Clemens played until after midnight. Before retiring that night he wrote to Dorothy Quick, inviting her to come for a visit. He also announced his intention to have at least one angelfish under his roof all the time. " 'Innocence at Home' is the right name for this house, because it describes me, & describes the Aquarium Club," he added, indicating the importance of the angelfish in his plans for permanent holiday (19 June 1908). The next day Dorothy Harvey and Louise Paine, his first two angelfish visitors at Innocence, arrived for a week's stay.

Clemens's delight in the new house continued throughout the summer, and his close circle of staff and friends tried to occupy him with a succession of guests, including angelfish, and other activities. One such activity was the planning of a Mark Twain library to be located in Redding, further indication of the permanency of his residence there. After many years of travel and rented houses, he had his own home once again, and at last a home befitting the wealth he was accumulating during his last years.

Young Harry and Mary Rogers were among his early visitors. Mary gave him a guestbook, the pages of which filled rapidly. Other visitors included Ida Tarbell; David Munro, an editor for *Harper's Weekly*; Helen Keller; Lord Northcliffe, the publisher of the London *Daily Mail*; and Howells, who was eager to see his son's handiwork. In fact, Clemens had twenty-one visitors within the first seven weeks, according to his guest book, some of whom stayed at Innocence for a week, as was Clemens's preference. Although he left Redding for several occasions during the summer, such as the dedications of the Thomas Bailey Aldrich Memorial Museum in Portsmouth, New Hampshire, and of City College in New York, he felt surprisingly homesick during his time away. It seemed, no doubt, the perfect setting for permanent retirement; as he told Howells, "I have retired from labor for good, I have discharged my stenographer, & have entered upon a holiday whose other end is in the cemetery" (*MTHL* 833).

This was not to suggest a pall had settled over Clemens in his first summer at Innocence at Home; quite the contrary seems to have been the case. On 9 July Dorothy Quick arrived for a week's stay, and to their previous games of billiards and hearts they added charades. In her published reminiscence Dorothy described one game of charades in which Clemens, Louise Paine, and she were partners and had to act out the word *mosquitoes*. "For the first syllable SLC wound a marvelous yellow scarf turban-fashion around his head and draped a large piece of Indian embroidery over his shoulders. . . . Suddenly he pretended to hear the call to prayer. He threw his two arms upward to where the supposed caller of the faithful was. Then, just as any true worshipper of the East, he spread his prayer rug on the floor and knelt in the direction of Mecca and said his prayers to Allah" (*EMT* 191–92).

Dorothy had been fonder of 21 Fifth Avenue than Clemens, but, she recalled, he was so anxious for her to like Innocence at Home, and so infectiously happy there, that she could not help falling in love with the big house. On pleasant summer evenings, after coffee on the terrace, actors and audience would stroll down to the pergola for their charades, sitting on the marble benches and using the Greek columns as part of their backdrop. Dorothy recalled acting out *dogmatic* with Clemens in this setting. After the audience had guessed *dog* and *mat* Clemens portrayed a "slightly inebriated gentleman," weaving in and out of the stone columns. As Dorothy described the moment, "The moon had turned his hair to pure silver and cast an unearthly glamour over the very earthy man he was acting" (*EMT* 193).

As the summer wore on, most of the angelfish paid Clemens at least one visit in the new surroundings. In September, before the girls were drawn back to their schools, Clemens was visited by Dorothy Quick, Dorothy Harvey, Louise Paine, Marjorie Breckenridge, Dorothy Sturgis, Frances Nunnally, and Margaret Blackmer. Stimulated by this enriched environment of schoolgirls, Clemens developed the "rules and regulations" of the Aquarium, the full text of which follows shortly after this introduction. It reads like a set of field notes and was written primarily for Clemens's own amusement. The rules appear to have been completed for the great surge of September angelfish visits. Clemens changed his own title from curator to admiral. The rules set out the qualifications for membership, which Clemens stuck to, except in the case of Margaret Illington, who was older but on all other counts deserved membership, he argued. Otherwise, they are filled with hyperbole, such as the notion that the house, which was begun before he even formed the Aquarium Club, was built for the "comfort and accommodation of the Aquarium." Membership had its potential perils, too, with a detailed code of conduct and of criminal proceedings. An angelfish could be tried for that vague crime of "conduct unbecoming her high state," and the Club's admiral and author of its rules was also their judge. As might almost be expected, conspiracies were indirectly encouraged by the rules, but the punishments for all angelfish crimes were lighthearted and designed to amuse.

In addition to the games and antics there were lengthy luncheons during which Clemens would tell stories and sometimes read from his own works. There were also pleasant rambles through the surrounding countryside. During such walks, Dorothy Quick recalls, Clemens would talk to her as one writer to another. One such bit of writer's advice she committed to memory: "Always remember, Dorothy, to catch the attention of your reader in the opening paragraph. Once you've caught your fish, you're sure to land him unless you do something foolish later on and let him get away" (*EMT* 196–97).

On 8 September Clara Clemens returned home from her European singing tour to inspect the new family residence and the young ladies who had swum into her father's life. From some of Clara's later comments and actions it is clear she was no great admirer of the angelfish. Within two months of her arrival home she convinced Clemens that Innocence at Home was an inappropriate name for his house and that it should be changed to Stormfield. Clara's interference in her father's antics and pleasures was nothing new, of course, and Clemens was a past master of deception; he may have felt a change in name was less objectionable than a change in habit. It is impossible to know how severely Clara intended to damage the kite of her father's angelfish holiday, but, as this chapter makes clear, soon after her arrival the Clemens household stopped saving letters from angelfish. It is obvious from Clemens's letter file that correspondence and occasional angelfish visits continued, but with Clara's return the giddy summer of Samuel Clemens's Aquarium was coming to a close.

Two other events complicated Clemens's angelfish activities. On 18 September two men broke into the kitchen at Innocence at Home. Isabel Lyon was the first to hear noises and came down to investigate, surprising the thieves as they were bagging the silver. Claude Benchotte, the butler, fired at the retreating burglars, and they dropped the silver. They were captured several hours later by the sheriff, accompanied by Clara's friend Will Wark and another family friend, H. A. Lounsbury. Clemens found the episode most exciting, as if another diversion staged for his entertainment and reflection, and his letters to the angelfish made mention of the event for weeks afterward. He told Dorothy Quick that he awakened to the sounds of the butler's shots, but "thought some champagne was being opened and promptly sank back into his slumbers" (*EMT* 201). When the trial came up in Danbury, Connecticut, Clemens was on hand to give testimony and afterward posed for photographs with a pistol in hand, a contrast indeed to his immaculate white outfit. Dorothy Sturgis arrived the day after the robbery, and she and Clemens enjoyed composing a notice to the next burglars, which appears in this chapter with his correspondence of 18 September. The incident had quite the opposite effect on Clara, who moved permanently to New York, and on the household staff, all of whom quit, with the exception of the ever-faithful Isabel Lyon and Ralph Ashcroft. The other event that briefly soured Clemens's autumn was the death of Tammany, the Aquarium's "mascat," and "the finest cat and the handsomest in America" (5 November 1908). Since Tammany was an officer of the Aquarium, Clemens called on all M.A.'s (members of the Aquarium) to wear black hair ribbons in mourning. However, he ended his letter to Margaret Blackmer with the lighthearted epitaph: "Requies Cat in Pace" (1 November 1908).

CLEMENS TO DOROTHY QUICK

Innocence at Home
Redding, Connecticut
19 June 1908

Oh, this will never do! You are having altogether too good a time, you little rascal (because I am not in it.) Still, I'm glad. I mustn't break into it now, but I'll have to do it before long; you & your mother will have to pay me a visit here. I want you; & I want my other angel-fishes. I must have a couple of them under this roof all the time, from now until January. There will be 2 under it to-morrow, to stay a week, I hope.[1]

The billiard room, downstairs, is the Aquarium's official headquarters. Their framed photographs are being hung around its walls.

"Innocence at Home" is the right name for this house, because it describes me, & describes the Aquarium Club. What do you think, dear?

I was never in this beautiful region until yesterday evening. Miss Lyon & the architect built & furnished the house without any help or advice from me, & the result is entirely to my satisfaction. It is charmingly quiet here. The house stands alone, with nothing in sight but woodsy hills, & rolling country.

We brought Tammany along.

With lots & lots of love

SLC

1. Dorothy Harvey and Louise Paine.

CLEMENS TO MARGARET BLACKMER

Innocence at Home
June 20/08

Dear Margaret, I thank you for inviting me to the musicale. I would have been there sure, if I had received the message in time.

Do you know, I lost my shell! The enameled one. I missed it from my chain a day or two before I sailed from Bermuda. I was so grieved about it! I didn't tell you, when you visited me, because I hoped to be able to find a duplicate of it before I should see you again. And I was careful not to strike a histrionic attitude & exclaim.

"Why, you look almost exactly like a little Margaret of mine! Maybe you *are* that Margaret. I think not—I am afraid not—No, it is some other Margaret. If it was mine, she could produce the duplicate of this shell."

I couldn't say it, for I hadn't any shell.

But I've got it now! The officers dined me at Prospect just before I sailed, & I lost the shell there, though I always had supposed it was stolen at the hotel. A waiter found it & the Major of the regiment has sent it to me. It was put into my hand when I stepped into this new country-house of mine for the first time! day before yesterday—a good omen!

Two angel-fishes arrived this afternoon, to stay a week, & we shall have good times. After dinner they took billiard-lessons until their bed-time, half past 8. We took a long discovery-walk thro' the woods first. I hope you will come & see me here one of these days.

With love and good wishes.

SLC

Mr. Ashcroft is coming tomorrow.

CLEMENS TO FRANCES NUNNALLY

Innocence at Home
June 20/08
Saturday

You dear little fish, I suppose you are arriving in England today. I had a cable from Clara 4 days ago, announcing a successful recital. I hope you & your mother will see her, but I don't know her address— except J. P. Morgan & Co., bankers.

I have seen the house at last, & have been in it two days, now. You & your mother will like it when you step into it about the 20th of next

September—to stay as long as you can. It is altogether satisfactory & requires no change.

Half of my fishes are framed & are decorating the wall of the billiard room, on the ground floor, which is the Official Headquarters of the Aquarium, & the other half will be there presently. Your Atlanta picture & the London picture of the two of us are there.

I am so sorry I took the New York house for another year. If I hadn't done that, I would never go back to New York again. Here there is nothing in sight between the horizons but woods & hills; & the stillness & serenity bring peace to the soul.

Good-bye, dear. With kind regards to your mother, & love to you—

SLC

[P.S.] Two fishes will arrive at mid-afternoon—to stay a week, I hope —Dorothy Harvey & Louise Paine; also Dorothy's governess.

CLEMENS TO DOROTHY QUICK

> Innocence at Home
> Redding, Connecticut
> 28 June 1908
> Sunday

Dorothy dear, bring with you a doll about 8 inches long—Paine's little daughter Frances[1] will fetch a doll when she comes up the hill to visit you, & you & she can have a fine domestic time together.

With lots of love

SLC

Frances is a doll enthusiast.

1. Frances Paine is probably a younger sister to angelfish Louise Paine.

ALBERT B. PAINE TO DOROTHY QUICK

Hotel Touraine, Boston
June 29/08

Dear Dorothy:

Mr. Clemens asks me to write a line to you to say that we expect to leave here Thursday morning (8 am), for Redding, Mr. Clemens's new home. We shall reach South Norwalk in time to catch the same train that you would take, if you left N.Y. (Grand Central Station) at 12:03. Mr. Clemens hopes that you will do this & bring your mother along, as it will be quite hard for him to come to the Grand Central, as was his first plan, and as Miss Lyon has no doubt written you. Now, if for any reason you cannot take the 12:00 train, or if your mother can't come through with you, then please write just as soon as you get this and say just what you can do. You can write to Mr. Clemens at this hotel & he will get it, if you write at once and put on a special stamp.

I shall also telegraph you tonight that I have written you about coming. Of course this letter takes the place of anything that Miss Lyon may have written or telephoned you, as we left her this morning early & did not change our plans until we got started.

Remember, the train that leaves the Grand Central at 12:03 for So Norwalk will meet our train there—that is we will be waiting for you, there & all go to Redding together, & your mother is to bring you & spend a day or two, if she can.

Yours truly,
A B Paine

ALBERT B. PAINE TO DOROTHY QUICK

Hotel Touraine
June 29/08[1]

Dear Dorothy:

Mr. Clemens has changed his mind about his return from Boston & asks me to say that he will leave here at Eight o'clock Thursday morning & will reach South Norwalk in time to meet the train that leaves New York at 12:03 (noon). He hopes you will take that train, with your mother & come to S. Norwalk where you will change & take the Redding train. I am with Mr. Clemens and we will be on the platform waiting for you & then we will all go up to Redding together—

I wrote a letter a while ago, like this, to you, but I'm afraid I forgot to put on the name of your hotel, so am writing again. I have also sent a telegram to you to "wait for a letter."

Remember, you are to take the 12:03 train from the Grand Central, for Redding, via, South Norwalk, Conn. & we will meet you at the latter place, & your mother is to come for a day or two, if she can spare the time.

Write as soon as you get this & put on a spl stamp. Write to Mr. Clemens, here c/o Touraine.

Yours truly,
A B Paine

1. Sent together with the preceding letter in one envelope.

CLEMENS TO DOROTHY STURGIS

Innocence at Home
[July 1908]
Sunday noon

Dear Dorothy,

I was not in Boston much, but I slept there 3 nights at the Touraine. I went to your house the first day—not really expecting to find any one there, but hoping to be pleasantly mistaken as to that.

The weather is divine here, to-day & I wish we had some angelfishes with us to enjoy it. We have had visits from two, & another is coming day after to-morrow. Meantime Mr. Paine comes every day & plays billiards, & Ashcroft comes up for weekends. I may stay here all the winter, but I suppose I shall keep the New York house. But I shan't be there much. This place is pleasanter.

Cohasset, if I remember rightly, is in Michigan—or maybe India, or around those places somewhere. I will inquire, or send this letter to Beacon street when I finish it to-morrow.

The billiard room in this house is Aquarium headquarters, & on its walls hang the framed photographs of 6 of the 12 members—yours among the 6; but it is not a good picture at all, & I think you must send me a better one. I shall soon have all the 12. However, it can very well wait until you come here. In time I hope to have all the beloved dozen photographed here on the premises.

Ten Days Later
It has long been my impression that this letter went to the mail at the time it was written, but that was a mistake. It got mislaid, and has turned up by accident this morning.

To-day is Tuesday. Can't you come next Saturday, Dorothy & give us a few days? I hope you can. Miss Marjorie Clinton,[1] a highly valued friend of ours will arrive at 6 that evening, & Ashcroft our favorite male friend will come by that or an earlier train. It isn't a hard journey for you, you are so young. You leave Boston at 8 a.m. (there's a Pullman car) and in 4 hours you reach South Norwalk. There you descend & cross under the tracks and take a train which is *waiting* and ready for you. It fetches you to Redding in half an hour, & Miss Lyon or I will be waiting for you there with a carriage. The drive is a half-hour, over a country road. Do come, dear, and telegraph or telephone us.

With lots of love,
SLC

1. Marjorie Clinton was a friend and neighbor of Mary Rogers in New York. She occasionally visited Clemens both in Tuxedo Park and in Redding.

CLEMENS TO DOROTHY QUICK

Innocence at Home
July 2/08

You dear Dorothy, I got your latest letter in Boston last night, & was ever & ever so glad that you & your mother can come to us here on *next Wednesday, July 8.* You will be very welcome.

And now I must tell you *the one & only train to come by:* it leaves the Grand Central at

4.15 p.m.
& comes straight to Redding
without change of cars

It has a Pullman car, but one must apply for seats a day or two beforehand.

Miss Lyon expects to be in New York the 8th, & she will come up in that train.

I hope your mother will spare you to us a whole week, as she did in Tuxedo that time. *When* she sees this place she will realize that it will be healthy for you.

I'll be glad when you come!

Lovingly
SLC

CLEMENS TO MARGARET BLACKMER

Innocence at Home
July 7/08

I was wondering what was become of you, you dear little angel-fish, & was very glad to find out by your letter, which came an hour or two ago. I hoped and believed I should hear from you before very long. My fishes are good & faithful correspondents. There are 12 of them, & two days seldom go by without a letter from one or another of them. Yesterday I answered letters from Dorothy Harvey, Dorothy Quick &

Dorothy Sturgis. I watch the mails, for [the] Aquarium is one of my life's chiefest interests.

The fishes are as good as they can be, & they come and see me whenever they can. The first to come, when I opened this new house among the hills and the woods, were Dorothy Harvey & Louise Paine; they stayed a week & said they enjoyed it. I know *I* did.

Dorothy Quick will arrive with her mother day after tomorrow & stay a week. Irene Gerken expects to come before long; Francesca Nunnally will come when she lands from Europe Sept. 21; Helen Allen, (Bermuda), is coming in December, & her mother too, I hope. And I hope you & your mother will come when you return home. The English member (Dorothy Butes) expects to come over before the summer is ended. The others are coming as opportunity offers.

I like the new house so well that I am likely to remain here all the winter. We are on high ground & it is always cool, for we get all the breezes. All about are richly wooded hills, & only half a dozen houses in sight. There are no sounds but the singing of the birds, so it is very quiet & peaceful.

We spend our days in the loggia, which opens out from the living-room & has 8 tall arches & they frame the scenery & make 8 pictures of it. It is tilepaved, & the fishes play diablo & other violent games in it. I think I will call it the Fish-Market, for I built it for the fishes.

The billiard-room is Aquarium headquarters, the angel-fishes are in command there. Their framed photographs hang on the walls, & yours looks very sweet there.

Half a mile from the house there is a deep little gorge spanned by an antique stone bridge with a single arch under it. I am going to stop up the arch & make the water flow over the bridge & make a cataract, to be called the Aquarium cataract. The arrested water will make a fine pool above the bridge & the children can skate there in winter. My house is named "Innocence at Home" & it is the angel-fishes that are to furnish the innocence, though the public don't know that. It isn't the public's affair. Please remember me to your mother.

With lots of love to you dear.

SLC

Dorothy Harvey and Clemens on the front steps, Stormfield, Summer 1908. (Courtesy, The Mark Twain Project, The Bancroft Library)

Clemens to Dorothy Butes

[25 July 1908]

Miss Dorothy Butes
Steamer Celtic.
Goodbye you dear child, and a happy voyage.[1]
  S.L. Clemens

1. At a later date Isabel Lyon added the following note to her copy of the letter: "The King was heart sick to have Dorothy sail away for England" (MTP 8058‡).

Clemens to Dorothy Quick

Innocence at Home
[26 July 1908]
Sunday

Dorothy dear, I miss you. It seems a long time since you were here. Louise has been here once, for a few minutes, and we have had a five minutes' glimpse of Frances; Frances went back home to her father's house the day you went away.

We have not been lonely, for we have had company almost all the time, & Mr. Paine has come whenever he could, to play billiards.

Mr. and Mrs. Freeman & Mr. Ashcroft are here now. On Friday Paine and I played 37 games of 10-point caroms and I beat 24 of them. Yesterday Freeman and Ashcroft and I played 62 games of 3-handed hearts. Freeman got 285 hearts, Ash got 295 and I got 223. It was great fun, my dear. On Friday night & last night we played billiards from 9.35 till past midnight, & I shall do the same to-night.

They're all at luncheon now. We have spent the whole forenoon in the loggia reading & talking & enjoying the wonderful day—with Ashcroft at the orchestrelle much of the time.

"Hearts" will begin in ten minutes from now. So I will go down stairs & be ready.

I send lots & lots of love to you & my kindest regards to your mother. I think we had good times, those days.[1]

Lovingly
SLC

1. A reference to Dorothy's visit, earlier in the month.

CLEMENS TO FRANCES NUNNALLY

Innocence at Home
Redding, Connecticut
July 29/08

Dear Francesca—

Your letter arrived to-day, with picture of Interlaken.[1] What an architectural transformation! There's nothing of the former Interlaken left but the jüngfraü.

I am sorry you did not catch my daughter in; & she was sorry, too.[2] She was more fortunate with Dorothy Butes, who found her at home.

You said Sept. 12, & will reach New York the 20th. So I shall keep the succeeding days open & the guest-room ready for you & your mother up to the 26th, when a couple of Bermuda friends will arrive. I hope you will occupy the room those several days. I wish I could invite your father, too, but there is only one other good guest-room & it will not be furnished until October, when we give up the New York house.

This place is easier to reach than Tuxedo, there being no river to cross. You will not mind the journey of one hour & 43 minutes. Good train. Pullman car.

With a good deal of Love to you, Dear, & kindest regards to your mother.

SLC

1. A town near one of Switzerland's highest mountains, the Jungfrau. Clemens refers to changes in Interlaken since his last visit, probably in 1891.
2. Clara Clemens was on a recital tour in Europe.

Dorothy Harvey, Clemens, and Louise Paine in the "Fish-Market,"
Stormfield, Summer 1908. (Courtesy, The Mark Twain Project,
The Bancroft Library)

THE AQUARIUM
Issued By
THE ADMIRAL

INNOCENCE AT HOME
REDDING, CONN.
SUMMER-TIME 1908

Qualifications for Membership
Sincerity, good disposition, intelligence, & school-girl age.

Secrets of the Order
Members of the Aquarium are forbidden to divulge its affairs to any
but their parents & guardians.

N. B.
This is the only copy of these Rules & Regulations. They must be
read to each Member when opportunity shall permit, but they must not
be printed or otherwise copied.

Note
I have built this house largely, indeed almost chiefly, for the comfort & accommodation of the Aquarium. Its members will always be
welcome under its roof.

The Name
Its Aquarium name is "Innocence at Home," & it is not misnamed,
for I know the Fishes well, and am aware that they can furnish the
innocence necessary to make the name good.

Private Headquarters
The Billiard Room is the Aquarium's Private Headquarters. Members may exclude non-members from that room at any time they choose,
& for as long as they choose. They may stop a game whenever they
please & put the players out. The power to exercise these privileges is
lodged not only in the Members as a whole, but may be used by a single
Fish if she shall desire to do so.

Neither the Admiral nor the Officers and Servants of the Aquarium are immune from this rule.

The Fish-Market

This is the *Loggia*, which projects from the Western end of the house. It is open to the scenery & the breezes, by grace of its high & wide arches, & forasmuch as its piers support a second-story wing, it is sheltered from sun and rain. It is large, & cleanly tiled, & is the Aquarium's play-&-exercise quarters when the weather is not of a sort to invite the children to the wood, & hills.

The Niche

This is in one of the piers & will contain a vase of flowers at times, & at other times an Angel-Fish who has been tried & found guilty of conduct unbecoming her high estate. The Court may sentence her to remain in the Niche of Repentance for a period of not less than two minutes nor more than ten. While under sentence she must live on bread & water.

The Criminal Court

This is the spacious room which opens upon the Fish-Market. Here accused Members will be tried for conduct unbecoming an Angel-Fish. The Admiral will sit as Judge, & the prosecution & defence will be conducted by the Official Legal Staff of the Aquarium.

All prisoners shall be granted trial by jury.

None may sit upon the jury except Members.

The jury shall consist of not fewer than one Member nor more than three.

Any Member refusing to sit upon the jury shall be fined. The Judge alone may name the fine, & he alone may collect it.

Non-Members cannot act as witnesses.

Conspiracies

The right to conspire is restricted to the Membership. Conspiracies cannot be concocted in the house; nor anywhere upon the estate except in the gorge below the Aquarium Cataract in the daytime, nor anywhere at night except in the privacy of the Pergola at the foot of the grounds below the northern front of the house.

Members desiring to conspire must give notice to the Admiral & tell him what it is about.

Except when the proposed conspiracy is against the Admiral himself; in that case notice must be given to the Official Legal Staff.

Persons intruding upon a lawfully arranged conspiracy with a view to obstructing it, will be tried in the Criminal Court.

Portraits

The only important decoration of the Billiard Room is the framed photographs of the Membership. Portraits of non-members are not permitted there.

The Badge

The official Badge of the Order is a small angel-fish pin. It bears the splendid colors of that beautiful inhabitant of the West Indian waters, exactly imitated in enamels. Members wear it upon the left breast, usually. The Admiral is obliged to furnish this pin to every Member without charge, & he is also obliged to replace lost ones on the same terms. Members need only give him notice.

Membership

Members are created by appointment. By the Admiral.

None above school-girl age is admitted.

But, once a Member, always a Member—for life.

Margaret Ellington Frohman, a choice & valued Member, is beyond school-girl age, but with opportunity the Admiral will be able to explain her case & justify it.

M.A.

Members of the Aquarium are entitled to put M.A. after their names.

Non-members can be admitted only by pass, signed by the Admiral. They are not privileged to take part in the proceedings.

Bribery

Attempts to bribe the Court or Jury, by either members or non-members, will be subjected to such punishment as the Judge in his discretion prescribe.

Dress

At all trials the Judge, the Mother Superior, the Chatelaine & Staff must appear in their official robes.

Spectators must wear evening dress.

Members must wear their badge and their head-ribbons.

Ceremonial

Proceedings cannot begin until the Chatelaine shall have made proclamation that the Court is now open & ready for business.

Order of Appointment

There are 12 Members, & the names of the same are here set down in the order of their appointment, with the ages which they had reached at the time of appointment.

Dorothy Butes, 14, England. (honorary)

Frances Nunnally, 16, Georgia.

Dorothy Quick, 10 & 10 months, New Jersey.

Margaret Blackmer, 12, New York.

Irene Gerken, 12, New York.

Helen Allen, 13, Bermuda.

Hellen Martin, 13, Canada.

Jean Spurr, 13, New Jersey.

Dorothy Sturgis, 16, Massachusetts.

Margaret Illington, New York.

Dorothy Harvey, 13, New Jersey.

Louise Paine, 13, Connecticut

Marjorie Breckenridge, 15

Honorary Members

Members who fail to write the Admiral during an unbroken period of 3 months do not cease to be Members, but are retired from the Active list & banished to the roll of Honorary Members with reproaches!

Conspicuously charming unmarried ladies above school-girl age may be appointed to this degree. But the members in occupation must at no time exceed 6.

The Board
Admiral of the Aquarium
S.L. *Clemens*
Mother Superior, Miss *Clara Clemens*
Legal Staff, Dan Frohman

The Admiral is a Member, but gets no salary; the others are paid, but not Members,

The foregoing Constitution, Rules & other particulars are respectfully submitted to the Aquarium, for approval or dissent, by

S.L. Clemens
Admiral

CLEMENS TO HELEN ALLEN

[Redding, Conn.]
[Summer 1908]

We have good times here in this soundless solitude on the hilltop. The moment I saw the house I was glad I built it, and now I am gladder & gladder all the time. I was not dreaming of living here except in the summer-time—that was before I saw this region & the house, you see—but that is all changed now; I shall stay here winter & summer both and not go back to New York at all. My child, it's as tranquil & contenting as Bermuda. You will be very welcome here, dear.

CLEMENS TO MARGARET BLACKMER

Redding, Connecticut
[Summer 1908?]

I'm already making mistakes. When I was in New York, six weeks ago, I was on a corner of Fifth Avenue and I saw a small girl—not a big one—start across from the opposite corner, and I exclaimed to myself joyfully, "That is certainly my Margaret!" so I rushed to meet her. But

Louise Paine and Clemens in the angelfish headquarters, the billiard room, Stormfield, Summer 1908. (Courtesy, The Mark Twain Project, The Bancroft Library)

as she came nearer I began to doubt, and said to myself, "It's a Margaret—that is plain enough—but I am afraid it is somebody else's." So when I was passing her I held my shell so she couldn't help but see it. Dear, she only glanced at it and passed on! I wondered if she could have overlooked it. It seemed best to find out; so I turned and followed and caught up with her, and said, deferentially, "Dear Miss, I already know your first name by the look of you, but would you mind telling me your other one?" She was vexed and said pretty sharply, "It's Douglas, if you're so anxious to know. I know *your* name by your looks and I'd advise you to shut yourself up with your pen and ink and write some more rubbish. I am surprised that they allow you to run at large. You are likely to get run over by a baby-carriage any time. Run along now and don't let the cows bite you."

What an idea! There aren't any cows in Fifth Avenue. But I didn't smile; I didn't let on to perceive how uncultured she was. She was from the country, of course, and didn't know what a comical blunder she was making.

CLEMENS TO DOROTHY STURGIS

Innocence at Home
Aug. 3/08

Dear Dorothy:

Good! Then you will be very welcome in September, & your journey from Boston will not be a heavy one. We will tell you how to come, & what trains to take.

And so this is hoping you can come September 18th, & stay till Sept. 25th. Francesca M.A. (Member of the Aquarium) will arrive Sept. 20 or 21st from England. Other guests will arrive on the 26th.

I enclose a photo made a few days ago, in the loggia (where I am writing this). The cat is "Tammany," the pride of the place. You will notice that I have become extraordinarily humpshouldered. The doctors say it will never diminish, but will increase. They say it is due to bad circulation, lack of exercise, & excessive smoking. I do not care. It is good enough shape, & I like it.

Lovingly
SLC

CLEMENS TO DOROTHY QUICK

Innocence At Home
10 Aug 1908
Monday

Dorothy dear I have been to New York. It was a week ago. I was gone two days, in that sweltering weather, & it brought on a bilious attack. We have no such weather here. I shan't make any more summer trips.

I am sorry about the rabbits, but you can get some more. You still have your bird, so you are not out of luck altogether. I have only Tammany & her kittens, & Miss Lyon & Mr. Ashcroft. But they are all good company. Yesterday we played hearts several hours—at least 3 of us did. I got 116; Miss Lyon got 185, & Mr. Ashcroft 208. Ashcroft plays the orchestrelle for me a great deal; & he has improved so much that if I am out in the loggia & don't see him I think it is Miss Lyon. And he plays good billiards now. Not as good as Col. Harvey or Mr. Paine, but better than formerly. Col. Harvey has been here, & David Munro of the North American Review, & we had very good times; Miss Ida Tarbell & Miss Jennette Gilder drove over & lunched with them.[1] Also we have had the Whitmores, and in a day or two John B. Staunchfield & his wife & daughter are coming, & after they go the Freemans are to come for a few days. But Ashcroft is going away tomorrow & I am sorry. I have seen Louise but little; she has been away on several visits: and I have had only a glimpse or two of Frances. Miss Lyon goes to New York to-day, to send up my daughter's furniture & piano—then the house will be complete & nothing more to do.

I miss you Dorothy dear, I wish you were here. Please give my kindest regards to your mother & my love to yourself.

SLC
Curator of the Aquarium

1. Both were Redding neighbors of Clemens. He had known Ida Tarbell since at least 1904, when he had arranged for her to interview H. H. Rogers for her history of the Standard Oil Corporation, which was published serially in *McClures Magazine* the same year.

CLEMENS TO DOROTHY QUICK

[Innocence at Home]
Aug. 12/08

Dorothy dear, I wrote you a number of days ago, & mailed it to Epping, but I don't think you'll get it, because I couldn't make sure of the address you gave me. If it is Dow, you should write it like this: DOW—not like this: Dow (which is the way you wrote it). Don't ever again write a proper name in any but CAPITALS—do you hear?

But you'll never get this, so why should I go on writing?

With lots of love
SLC

CLEMENS TO MARGARET BLACKMER

Innocence at Home
Aug. 13/08

To Margaret Blackmer, M.A.
(Member of the Aquarium, you understand)

It's a charming letter, you cunning little angel-fish! and glad I was to get it. My fishes find many ways to entertain themselves: You with the Indians & the circus; Irene with sea-bathing; Helen of Montreal with climbing mountains in Scotland; Helen of Bermuda with regatta —races on stormy seas; Boston—Dorothy with foot-races & swimming-races in her school-camp away up toward the North Pole—& she wins them, too. The others are scattered far & wide, but I shall hear from all of them presently & know what they are at, for they are not going to neglect me; they are too dear & faithful for that. I answered letters from 3 of them yesterday; & this morning I have your letter & one from Irene.

I shall be so glad to welcome you & your mother here, when you get back home. You will arrive September 16th, & now will write me on the 17th, won't you? & you & I will arrange that visit.

Good bye, dear, with lots of love,

SLC

Curator of the Aquarium

CLEMENS TO DOROTHY STURGIS

Innocence At Home
August 15/08
Sunday

Dear Dorothy

Good! You will be very welcome.

To-day, in a lovely place in the woods a mile and half from here we visited a fine swimming-pool a hundred yards long, twenty wide and 26 feet deep—water as clear as crystal, with a perpendicular rock jumping-off place 15 feet high—densely wooded shores all around. You get to it by an obscure path leading from the distant wagon-road. It is an ideal bathing-place. I thought of you, but you can't use it, because there is no bath-house. But you shall go & look at it—& grieve because you can't get into it. If I had it on my land there'd be a bath-house.

With love and best wishes,

SLC

DOROTHY QUICK TO CLEMENS

Hampton Beach, N.H.
Sept 2nd 1908

My dear Mr Clemens.

I wrote to you from Epping telling you I had changed my address but as I have not heard from you I have decided my writing was so bad you

Dorothy Harvey and Clemens, Stormfield, Summer 1908.
(Courtesy, The Mark Twain Project, The Bancroft Library)

could'ant make it out yesterday I was 12 years old and I had a beautiful birthday   Mother and my aunt Syda took me to Rye Beach in the
afternoon to see Ben Greet in an outdoor performance of "As you Like
it" It was really wonderful right out in the woods with the sea roaring
in the distance I wish you had been with me you would have liked it
and I would have loved to have you. Then I returned and had a party
and in the evening we went to see Olivette, The Opera of the casino at
Hampton beach about fifteen minutes on the car from here so today I
am rather tired and glad it is stormy so I can rest   We expect to remain
here until Sept 15 school opens the 17 or 19th   I dont know which it
has been to cold here to go in bathing but it is beautiful on the beach
last Wed we had a terrible storm and mother said she had never seen
such a wild and beautiful sea before but she loves it and I dont. I liked
it at Epping and Redding much better I shall even be glad to get back
to Plainfield and all my friends will you give my love to Francis and
Miss Lyon and keep lots & lots for yourself.

> your loving
> Dorothy

Clemens to Dorothy Quick

> Innocence At Home
> Sept. 3/08
> Thursday

   Dorothy dear, I have been over-busy with guests, for a time, & I
guess you are back home before this. There isn't much news to report.
We lunched with the Paines day before yesterday & saw Louise, but
Frances has gone back to her school in Rochester. Louise is soon going
away to school on Long Island. We had a kind of house-warming three
or four days ago, and the people of the country side came, about 300,
young & old, & boys & girls, & we had a very pleasant afternoon. The
Waylands have been here several days, & went away today. Some more
guests are coming tomorrow & next day, to stay over Sunday, & on the
10th my daughter Clara will arrive from Europe. Jean will sail for Ger-

many toward the end of this month.[1] There will be some more friends coming in the meantime—two young girls & an elderly couple.

I hope you and your mother have had a pleasant summer, & that you are well rested-up & ready for school & glad to begin again.

Miss Lyon has nearly emptied the New York house, & so this one looks more furnished & less naked than it did.

With lots of love.

SLC

1. Jean Clemens sailed for Germany on 26 September 1908, accompanied by her friend Marguerite Schmidt and hired maid Anna Sterritt. She was assigned to the care of Professor Hofarath von Reuvers of Berlin, who was convinced he could cure her epilepsy.

FRANCES NUNNALLY TO CLEMENS

Brown's Hotel, London
Sept. 4, 1908

Dear Mr. Clemens,—

Thank you so much for the invitation you have given Mother and I to come visit you at "Innocence at Home." We should like very much to come up and spend the day with you any day that it is convenient before the twenty-sixth. I am very sorry we cannot spend more time with you, as we are very anxious to see you, but there are so many things to be attended to in New York before I go back to school and we will not have quite ten days. I shall let you know as soon as I arrive at the Waldorf, and then if you will tell us when it suits you best, we should love to come up for a day.

We left Paris a little over a week ago and came directly here. We met a great many friends in Paris and so I enjoyed my visit there, but I don't like the city itself nearly as much as London. One of the pleasantest days we had, was out at Versailles, where there is so much of beauty and interest to be seen. We made another excursion out to Chantilly, but I think we should have gone there before we went to Versailles. Our hotel was quite near the Louvre, so we went in there several times, but after all that, I don't think we have seen half of the things in that enormous place. We enjoyed the pictures more than any other part of the museum, but we spent a good while looking at the beautiful "Venus de Milo."

After about ten days we crossed a very rough channel and came to London, where it has been raining incessantly. Just a week from tomorrow we sail and I shall be very glad to see the "Minneapolis" again, though I don't like to think that it is carrying me back to school.

Lovingly,

Francesca

CLEMENS TO MARGARET BLACKMER

Innocence At Home

Sept. 18/08

You dear little Margaret! I am so glad to hear from you. Yesterday, in the billiard-room I said to Mr. Paine, "There's Margaret, hanging on the wall, & I know by some instinct that within 3 days I shall hear from her"—and it has come true.

I have not been away from this house since I arrived here just 3 months ago; but I am going to New York Sept. 25, (Friday), arriving toward 1 p.m., & shall walk over from the Grand Central to the Woman's Club, 9 East 46th Street & call upon you and your mother. The rest of the day and evening I shall spend with my youngest daughter at the Martha Washington Hotel & then see her off to Germany next morning.

I have had a most pleasant 3 months here, with delightful guests coming & going, some staying a day or two & some a week. A while ago Louise Paine, M.A. & Dorothy Harvey M.A. were here together 6 or 7 days; Dorothy Quick, M.A. and her mother gave us 6 days; Marjorie Breckinridge M.A. left here last Monday; at 7 this evening Dorothy Sturgis M.A. and maid will arrive, and will remain until the 25th; on the 26th Miss Wallace (you remember her?) will reach New York from Europe, & she and Mr. Ashcroft will come home with me the next morning (Sunday) in the 9 a.m. train, which reaches Redding in about an hour & forty minutes.

And as soon as we can arrange the date, you & your mother must come. I hope you will like this place, & I am sure you will.

Yes indeed, dear heart, you can have any book of mine you want.

My favorites are: Joan of Arc; Prince and Pauper; Huck Finn; Tom Sawyer. I will take them to you on the 25th.

I hope you will have your shell with you, for you have been away a long time, & without it I should be almost certain to mistake you for somebody else.

With lots of love

SLC
(Curator)

Burglars in the house after midnight this morning. They are on their way to jail this afternoon. We are buying a couple of bulldogs & hoping they will call again.

CLEMENS TO FRANCES NUNNALLY

Innocence At Home
Sept. 18/08

Francesca dear, you are wearing these shoes, now, & in less than a half a week you & your mother will arrive, & run up here, according to schedule. You will be very very very welcome. I hope your father can come too. Will you please ask him? Expresses leave the Grand Central for Redding at 9 am & 4:15 pm on all days but Saturdays, & come through in an hour & forty minutes.

Will you telephone Miss Lyon or me & tell us your train, so that we can meet you at the Redding station, which is about 20 minutes by country road from this house.

With love,

SLC
C. A. (Curator of the Aquarium.)

CLEMENS TO DOROTHY QUICK

Innocence At Home
Sept. 18/08

Dorothy dear, the post cards have just arrived, & I judge you are reaching Plainfield to-day. You have had a long holiday, & I guess by your letters that you have had a healthful & delightful good time. So have we. Very pleasant guests right along, all the time. Among them a member of the Aquarium, (Marjorie Breckinridge M.A.) who left here last Monday. This evening Dorothy Sturgis M.A. will arrive, & remain until the 25th; & not long after that date I shall expect Margaret Blackmer M.A. & her mother to come. Yes indeed, it has been a most delightful summer for us.

With lots of love

SLC

(C.A.) Curator of the Aquarium

Burglars broke in after midnight this morning. But they were caught afterward, & are on their way to jail this afternoon.

Note from Francesca Nunnally M.A., England. She & her mother are due here next monday for a short visit.

[Innocence at Home]
[18 September 1908]

NOTICE

TO THE NEXT BURGLAR.[1]

There is nothing but plated ware
in this house, now and henceforth.
You will find it in that brass thing
in the dining-room over in
the corner by the basket of kittens.
If you want the basket, put the
kittens in the brass thing. Do not
make a noise—it disturbs the family.

NOTICE.

To the next Burglar.

There is nothing but plated ware in this house, now and henceforth. You will find it in that brass thing in the dining-room over in the corner by the basket of kittens. If you want the basket, put the kittens in the brass thing. Do not make a noise — it disturbs the family. You will find rubbers in the front hall, by that thing which has the umbrellas in it, chiffonier, I think they call it, or pergola, or something like that. Please close the door when you go away!

Very truly yours

S. L. Clemens

You will find rubbers in the front
hall, by that thing which has the
umbrellas in it, chiffonier, I think they
call it, or pergola, or something like that.
      Please close the door when you go away!
                              Very truly yours
                              S.L. Clemens
                              Dorothy Sturgis

THE HOUSE THAT TWAIN BUILT

This is the House that Twain built.
This is the silver that lay in the House that Twain built.
This is the burglar that got the silver that lay in the house that Twain
   built.
This is the Lyon that scairt the burglar that got the silver, etc.

1. Dorothy Sturgis arrived on the day of the early-morning break-in and assisted
Clemens in the wording of this notice, which suggests the cavalier attitude Clemens took
toward the episode. Illustrations accompanied the notice and its postscript.

CLEMENS TO MARJORIE BRECKENRIDGE

Innocence At Home
[September] 19/08[1]

Marjorie dear, we all thank your mother ever so much for her invitation, but meantime I have been accepting an invitation to a matinee on
the 26th & was waiting for the tickets to come, so that I could send a
couple to you and your mother & ask you to come to that matinée. The
tickets have just arrived & I enclose two. Do come if you can, for they
say Billie Burke is just irresistible in this piece.[2] Indeed you must, must,
must come! At 2 p.m., Saturday, Sept. 26 you will find Miss Lyon & me
waiting for you at the door of the Lyceum Theatre, 45th St. between
Broadway & 6th Avenue. But if by chance we should be delayed, don't

wait for us but go into the box & wait for us there. You won't have to wait ten minutes.

Dorothy Sturgis M.A. arrived yesterday evening. She will stay till the 25th. We've been playing billiards this morning. On Tuesday Francesca M.A. will arrive from Europe but can stay with us only a day. Margaret Blackmur M.A. is coming before long, with her mother. They reached New York day before yesterday from the Pacific. After luncheon Dorothy, Miss Lyon, Ashcroft & I will drive down & call at the house of the Sheriff & inquire. He was shot by one of the burglars in the scuffle early yesterday morning.

Miss Lyon & I walked down (by way of the old bridge) to your house day before yesterday & climbed those cliffs that fence your clearing. It is to be repeated tomorrow. I found your porch a comfortable & restful & welcome place after that violent climb. We returned home by a perfectly charming woodland trail that I hadn't known of before. We will exploit it when you come. Good-by, dear, with lots of love—

SLC

1. Clemens's letter gives the date as April 1908, but his reference to the 18 September robbery fixes the date in September. Furthermore, he could not have met Marjorie Breckenridge until he moved to Redding. Marjorie and her parents had a summer house overlooking the brook and gorge Clemens refers to so often in the angel-fish letters. Their house was but a short walk from Innocence at Home.

2. Billie Burke was starring in *Love Watches*, which opened at the Lyceum Theater on 27 August.

Margaret Blackmer to Clemens

[telegram]

[New York]
Sept. 20 1908

To: S.L. Clemens
So Glad they did not steal you

Margaret Blackmer M.A.

CLEMENS TO LOUISE PAINE

Redding, Connecticut
Sept. 30/08

Dear Louise,

I was very glad to hear from you. Your father brought back the plated ware to-day, & I have forgiven him, for he did not know it was plated or he would have not taken it. He thought it was silver: that was the only reason he took it, he said so himself.[1] One is not blameable for mistakes, we all make them. A mistake is not a crime, it is only a miscarriage of judgment.

Your father & mother & Mr. & Mrs. Verbeck have just gone. We had a very pleasant hour or two together.

We had two fishes & some other nice guests up to yesterday. When they all went away, & Miss Lyon & my daughter Clara with them. And so I am to be alone now several days; then on Friday we shall have another angel-fish & her mother, & Mr. Ashcroft.

My daughter Jean sailed for Germany yesterday, & is now in mid-ocean. I had a wireless message from her a few minutes ago saying she is well & is having a comfortable voyage.

Your father is coming to play billiards with me to-morrow—then I shan't be lonesome.

With love & all good wishes.
SLC
Curator of the Aquarium

1. Clemens is teasing Louise, whose father, Albert Bigelow Paine, had nothing to do with the robbery or the discovery of the stolen silver.

CLEMENS TO DOROTHY STURGIS

Redding, Connecticut

September 30, 1908

You dear delightful Annieanlouise! You cannot realize how much we all miss you, nor what a contenting charm your presence was, nor how it pervaded this house like a fragrance, & refreshed its mouldy and antique atmosphere with "the unbought grace of youth." I wish you were back again. However, if wishing could do any good, you would be *already* back. It was lovely of your mother to let us have you, & I hope & trust she will let us have you again soon. Will she? Pray say she will.

Yes, we played billiards that night, & Benares beat me by one point; (that is, by two of his points, which is one of mine.) Yesterday Miss Lyon failed to find a comrade for me, so Benares came up in the 4:15, & after dinner he played the Erlkönig twice for me, then we played billiards until 10:30. He made 150 points while I made 280: so he beat me again, and worse than before. He was to have stayed here with me until tomorrow, but he is gone; Miss Lyon telephoned him while we were at breakfast, & he left by the 10:31, half an hour before your letter came. And so, all day today, & all day tomorrow & all day next day there isn't going to be *anybody* here but *me*, and I don't count, as personal society. *These* aren't the "bes' g.d. days" for me, for sure.

Mr. Lounsbury[1] has just this minute been in, with a "find". It is the stolen plated ware. The burglars hid it behind a rock almost in front of that farm house which he says you called beautiful. I do not remember which one that was. The finding was an accident, & happened early this morning.

Yesterday morning, after the rainstorm I went down to the gorge to see the results. You can't think what a cataract was raging past the Brushwood Boy's seat! But it was a double stream, & needed some practised experts to dam one of them & concentrate the waters in a single volume.

"And say we shall always be true."

That was lovely, & just perfect, until you took it back on the postscript. Why did you do it, unless the sentiment was a jest? I don't want it to be a jest. Come Annieanlouise dear, you mustn't say it was a sarcasm: I wouldn't have you say that for anything. In my belief it wasn't a jest when you wrote it, because I think it goes without saying that if it had been, it would have stopped in your thought & you wouldn't have written it. I am going to believe that the postscript was a momentary afterthought, & you underestimated the force of it. Isn't this solution correct?

1. H. A. Lounsbury lived nearby and was in charge of the construction of Clemens's house. He and Will Wark also assisted the sheriff in capturing the burglars.

CLEMENS TO MARGARET BLACKMER

Innocence At Home
Oct. 6/08

You dear Margaret, I went to your room an hour ago on my way to breakfast, to call you—then I remembered. I had to go down all alone. I should have been much better satisfied if I had had your company. To look at you a person would think you couldn't take up much room, but you do; this place seems pretty empty without you.

We went down to the gorge toward sunset yesterday afternoon & sat a good while on the rocks that border the bridge—where we hulled the nuts. Then Ashcroft went down on the upper side, where we gathered chestnuts, you remember, & when he was tripping his way to the entrance of the tunnel he found the chocolate & the letter on the ground. You see, I threw them there & forgot about it.

A beautiful little bird has just flown into the kitchen. The cook brought him to me, & he was not at all afraid. She is taking him down into the woods below the pergola to keep Tammany's family from getting hold of him.

Oct. 7. Your letter came yesterday, & was very welcome. Do the kittens miss you? Indeed they do. Why, even the rocks, & the trees & the flowers miss you. Yes, & the landscape, too. It doesn't think as much of

Frances Nunnally and Clemens, Stormfield, 1908. (Reproduced by permission of The Huntington Library, San Marino, California)

itself as it did when you were a part of it, & I shall not be satisfied with *it* until you are a part of it again. It is pathetically doing its very best to make up for your loss with other splendors, but it doesn't succeed— doesn't with *me*, dear, for sure.

I am not quite certain of your school-address, so I am waiting till I hear from you again.

Oct. 8. You've been gone so long, now, that I suppose I wouldn't know you if I met you. But fortunately there's the shell! By that I should know you in a minute; for there's only the one shell.

Day before yesterday Ashcot and I found a new trail, & a long one. First it goes down the road to Miss Lyon's; then takes the old road to the left (the one we drove over to the Branchfield station when you & your mother went away); by & by you turn sharply to the left again & prowl through deep woods over an old grass-grown road which curves gradually leftward & at last comes out on the road that goes down past the red barns & the gorge. You cross our bridge there & go up past the mound toward our hickory trees, & up the slope to the top, & there you are! with the kitchen-end of the house in sight—& in two minutes more you are at home. It is a splendid long oval tramp, you see, with quails whizzing up all about you & the deep woods rich with autumn colors. Next time you come, dear, we'll try it, nicht wahr?

As soon as Helen is old enough to travel you must bring her here every little while & teach her to like the place, for your sake & mine. Will you, dear? And her brother, too. I know I shall love the children; in truth I love them already, & often think of them.

Noon, 8th. I got up at 9:30 & went down stairs. The woods were so beautiful from my bedroom window, all drenched with sunshine & purpled with shadows, that I *had* to go down & observe them from the loggia arches.

The servants came to bid me good-bye, at 11. They gave notice a week or ten days ago, still frightened to death about that burglary. All of them are gone, except the two outside men (Harry and the Italian general-utility-man). Our two old-time Italian servants will arrive from New York at 5 this afternoon. The man is a good cook & his wife is expert in chamber-work. We shall get some natives from the farm houses in a few days, & bother no more with city servants. Meantime we are quite comfortable & perfectly satisfied. Tomorrow Ashpan[1] will arrive with the captain of one of the great Cunard liners & his body-servant, for over Sunday, & also my daughter Clara will arrive with her aunt.[2] Ashhopper & Miss Lyon & I will dress up in aprons & gorgeous Chinese jackets & east-Indian turbans & wait on the table & have lots of fun; & if we could only have you here, in your dainty blue costume to pass the cocktails around in the library the whole scheme would be just perfect! I wish we had you, you little witch!

Friday, Oct 9. I have a lovely letter from your mother this morning, & I gather from it that one of these days you are going to invite me again to visit the school. That is very pleasant, dear heart, I shall be sure to accept.

Do you like romances? Very well, here is one. About next Tuesday or Wednesday a Missouri sweetheart of mine is coming here from Missouri to visit me—the very first sweetheart I ever had. It was 68 years ago. She was 5 years old, and I the same.[3] I had an apple, & fell in love with her & gave her the core. I remember it perfectly well & exactly the place where it happened, & what kind of a day it was. She figures in "Tom Sawyer" as "Becky Thatcher." Or maybe in "Huck Finn"—anyway it's in one of those books. She is bringing one of her grand-daughters with her—a grown-up young lady, I guess.

It is noon, now. I think I will get up. There is no hurry about finishing this letter; I will mail this much of it today, & then go on with it a paragraph per day till I get it done some time or other. You are busy & I musn't tax you; but whenever you've got any love for me, save it up till there's enough of it to fill a few lines, then find a chance when you've a minute to two to spare, & send it along.

Distributed along through this letter I'm sending you *my* love—not all of it, but such of it as I've found room for.

SLC, Curator

1. "Ashhopper" and "Ashpan" were among Clemens's nicknames for Ralph Ashcroft.

2. Captain Dow of the *Coronia* visited for the weekend; Clara Clemens had returned home from Europe on his ship.

3. Clemens refers here to Laura Hawkins (Frazer), his first Missouri sweetheart. She did pay him a visit and received a Mark Twain photograph inscribed, "To Laura Frazer, with the love of her earliest sweetheart."

CLEMENS TO MARGARET BLACKMER

Stormfield[1]
[7 October 1908]
Sunday, 10 p.m.

You dear Margaret I clear forgot to show you the enclosed letter from a most charming human being, chaplain of a battleship whereon Miss Lyon & I spent a jovial day in Bermudian waters. I was going to ask you to let me send your love along with mine to his "dear girl friend" in England; and so I ask you now—but only as a formality, because I have already *done* it.

He wrote Miss Lyon too, still she wants *this* letter also, & I am glad, because in returning it you will have to send me a line & tell me what *your* idea is of what you owe me. *I* think it's 14.

An hour after we got back to the house Mr. Starr telephoned to say all his photographs (the colored ones) had come to nothing in the developing except one, & he was wildly delighted over that one because it was letter perfect. It was the one with you beside me. That makes me very well satisfied indeed.

It was lovely of your mother to come to us when she had so little time, & we thank her for it ever so much. Tell her that both you & she will need a whole week here to brace up in after tropical Bermuda & I hope she will cut a week out of the month's vacation & give it to us.

I *think* it's 14. I am not perfectly sure; it may be 15.

Remember me with warm regards to your mother—and tell her what I've been saying.

We have had cards & billiards, & now I've gone to bed. I miss you, dear; I wish you were back. I send you my love.

SLC

P.S. I remember now. It's 16.

Next Morning. 8 a.m.

Before breakfast. I have been downstairs on a flying trip, & what do you think? I found Danbury sitting on the billiard table looking up at your picture & crying; the tears running down his cheeks—oh, ever so pitiful to see. It was because he scratched your hands; & now he was sorry when it was too late.

1. The first appearance of the Stormfield letterhead, reflecting the change of name from Innocence at Home to Stormfield.

CLEMENS TO MARJORIE BRECKENRIDGE

Innocence At Home
October 7, 1908

Dear Marjorie:

Indeed you are right: this region is beautiful now: every day adds new & richer tints & shades to the splendor of its autumn glories. I wish you were here to prowl the woods & the glen with me.

Those three fishes have been here, and they all liked the place and greatly admired the Gorge. Margaret & her mother went away day before yesterday, the others on the 28th Sept.

So Dear, the score remains. Not a woman in the house has had a good night's sleep unpersecuted by ghastly dreams since the burglary 19 days ago. My daughter Clara has the shudders every time she thinks of that night, & so does Miss Lyon.

Miss Lyon is now in New York for a day or two, & Mr. Ashcroft went away this morning. So I am a solitary. I don't like being a solitary. However, it isn't for long: Miss Lyon will return this evening, & Mr. Ashcroft tomorrow!

With my kindest regards to your parents, & lots of love to you, dear.

SLC

Clemens to Dorothy Quick

Innocence At Home
Oct. 7/08

How are you getting along, dear heart? The women-folks in this house are not getting along well at-all. Their sleep is broken, & is pestered with dreadful dreams every night—dreams about burglars. Catherine says she has the same dream nightly, in which a swarm of masked burglars are riddling her with bullets. It fetches her out of her slumbers with a shriek.[1]

We've built a garage. It was necessary, for the Sunday morning train is taken off, & actors cannot come to us now, save by motor car. They can fetch it by train to South Norwalk, & motor the rest of the way in less than an hour.

We are putting glass in the arches of the loggia now, & turning it into a winter parlor, so that we can sit there with our knitting & watch the snowstorms.

We have plenty of cats & kittens, now—all descendants of the incomparable Tammany.

With lots of love to you, dear,

SLC

1. With the exception of Isabel Lyon and Ralph Ashcroft, the entire staff quit soon after the burglary and had to be replaced with local help plus two experienced servants from 21 Fifth Avenue.

Clemens to Frances Nunnally

Innocence At Home
Oct. 10, [1908]
Saturday, 10 a.m.

I have had a fine time worrying about you, you dear little rascal! It didn't begin until you had been gone seven days—then it swiftly made up for lost time! By yesterday, morning—after a vacant mail—I was perfectly sure you were sick or had met with an accident. Miss Lyon said no, you were only very busy with school-work, & would write presently. But it did not convince me, for I am like any other mother, I suppose, when her imagination gets alarmed. I said "try the telephone the first thing in the morning & see if Francesca *is* well." And so she did. She brought up the news a little while ago, before I was dressed, & if she had been a man I would have hugged her.[1]

Monday, Oct. 12—noon.

I find it no sin to be still lying in bed, for we have been having very diligent times entertaining ourselves Friday evening, Saturday & Sunday. Ashcroft & Capt. Dow of the Coronia (Clara's ship) arrived Saturday afternoon. Clara followed in a later train, & Mr. Wark[2] in a still later one! Our old servants were all gone, & in their places we had only our two Italians from the New York house with a new & untrained butler (a native youth of the neighborhood,) & with Clara's maid & the Captain's table-steward to join these forces. But no matter, we got along ever so well with the "simple life," & had a good time. Oh, you should know the captain! The loveliest darlingest Irishman that ever was. We were all photographed many times, yesterday, in singles, couples & groups—which reminds me! When you came to dinner with the beautiful pink bows on the back of your head I wanted them, to hang up over your picture in my room when it comes from the developer in New York, but I resisted the temptation to steal them. Now for that resistance you ought to give them to me. I mean, when you are done with them, don't throw them away, but remember me & send them. Will you? And in return I'll send you a book—"Anne of Green Gables." It came two days after you went away, & I was to read it & give it to Francis Wilson: but I was at once so taken with it that I thought I would send it to you & get another copy for him. I think Anne is a very pleasant child to know, & that the literary quality of the book is fine. You may not have time to read it, & in that case you mustn't: but don't waste it, dear—give it to some other girl, who appreciates good literature.

Your letter arrived an hour ago, & was very welcome; and so you are forgiven, now, for alarming me. But don't you do it again! Next time, I will go straight down to Catonsville & preach you a sermon. Francesca, you will have a long holiday at Easter—won't you spend it here? Miss Lyon & I will gladly go to Catonsville & fetch you. Don't make any other arrangement, please.

Lovingly
The Curator

P.S. I know you are busy, & I don't want to overtax you greatly, but indeed you *must* send me a line now & then. Do you hear?

No there have been no more conspiracies & I have warned Ashcroft that *he* musn't conspire again, for he isn't a Member.

P.P.S. I am going to plant 12 Aquarium cedars—but I'll tell you about it some time when there's more room on my paper.

1. A line designed for a laugh, no doubt, but also reinforcing Clemens's concern that there be no suggestion of anything beyond a friendly and professional relationship with Isabel Lyon. In the spring of 1907 Clemens was accused of keeping Isabel Lyon as a mistress, an accusation for which there is no supporting evidence.

2. Wark was Clara Clemens's accompanist for a time, and at least one paper (New York *World*, 7 September 1908) rumored that they were engaged, although it seems most unlikely. Their friendship waned soon after the date of this letter.

CLEMENS TO MARGARET BLACKMER

Redding, Connecticut
[11 October 1908]
Wednesday

Oh you Dear Margaret you are coming up with Ashcroft, & I'm just as glad! He will go to your school & fetch you. Then by the 5 p.m. train, Sunday he will take you back or rather, *I* will take you back to your school & we will let him accompany us & see that we don't get lost. I have to go to Deal Beach Monday afternoon or Tuesday morning; so I mean to go down on Sunday & take you home, then wait over in New York till Monday afternoon or Tuesday morning, according as Col. Harvey shall elect.[1]

I haven't eaten all the hickory nuts, I'm saving some for you; & at noon to-day I found a good chestnutting place. I think, on the main road below our bridge. We will exploit it when you come, & see if it will pay us for our trouble.

We are all to help open the Mark Twain Library about an hour from now. It won't be a very formidable ceremony.[2]

Love to you, dear!
The Admiral

P.S. That is according to the new By-law, which transforms The Curator into the Admiral and requires the members to say "Admiral, do so & so," instead of "Mr. Clemens, do so & so." Don't you forget it, Dear. I added that By-law last night. Curator isn't a large enough title for me.

(S.L.C.)

1. Clemens went to Deal Beach, New Jersey, to visit George Harvey and to discuss a plan that would extend copyright protection to his earlier works.

2. Clemens gave a large collection of his surplus books to the town of Redding to be used as the nucleus for a public library. An unused chapel, which could be seen from his house, was obtained for the library. Clemens was elected president of the Mark Twain Library of Redding and delivered a brief address at the opening ceremony. Dorothy Quick and Louise Paine were visiting Clemens at the time; they dressed up in Japanese kimonos and carried paper parasols at the dedication.

CLEMENS TO MARGARET BLACKMER

[Redding, Conn.]
[24–29 October 1908]

Dear heart, you wouldn't let me go to the gorge that Monday morning & recover the lost section of the cup, & now—oh dear, the place is all covered deep with fallen leaves. So soon as we got back from New York we went to the gorge, & Ashcroft & Miss Lyon shoveled the leaves away & hunted a long time, but there was no result, & I was so sorry. I ought to have made you stay back, that day. While I went down &

got it; but you were a disobedient angel-fish & you *wouldn't* stay back. You'll have to be tried for this.

Send me a kiss. No, *bring* it.

Lovingly,

S.L.C. *Curator*

(*Continued*)

Four or 5 days later—Oct. 29.

The glass windows are in the arches now, & the loggia makes a most cosy & comfortable parlor. It was snug & pleasant in there this morning during a driving rainstorm, with the kittens roughing around.

The kittens are fine—Amanda & Amanci. Do you remember Billiards? Billiards is the tame big brother. A remarkable cat, for he isn't prejudiced against water. The other day Ashcroft dipped him in the fountain to see how he would like it. He didn't object at all & didn't try to scramble out. When we went off walking down toward the springhouse he followed; & when we came back Ashcroft set him in the fountain & took his hand away & Billiards sat there quite contented. I suppose such a cat as that is worth three or four thousand dollars.

The Mark Twain library is getting along very nicely. I am required to give a reading or a talk for the benefit of its treasury during the month of November. You are invited. I invite you. You'll be the only complimentary ticket. The performance will take place here in the house. Miss Lyon & Lounsbury & the other officers will select a date presently.[1]

Ashcroft & I had a delightful time at your school, & we wish to thank the Misses Tewksbury cordially through you.

I went down to Deal Beach the next day & was there until Friday noon with Dorothy Harvey M.A. Friday was her 14th birthday.

(*Continued. night*) Come back,

Dear, it is too lonesome here without you. To-day there is no company. At least none except between-trains company. Miss Newcomb has been with us a week, but she went away this morning. We are telephoning Miss Margery Clinton, & we hope she will join Miss Lyon, & Ashcroft on board the 3.32 train tomorrow & come up. You see how lonely you make it by going away from here, you little rascal.

Very lovingly
SLC

1. Albert Bigelow Paine recalled that Clemens placed a notice on the billiard room mantel, requiring each male guest to contribute a dollar to the Library Building Fund. In Clemens's own words, "Every male guest who comes to my house will have to contribute a dollar or go away without his baggage" (MTAD, 4 October 1908).

CLEMENS TO FRANCES NUNNALLY

Redding, Connecticut
[24–31 October 1908]
Sat.

Yes, keep the Easter holiday in mind, you dear Francesca, & don't let any of those mates of yours persuade you to go home with them. No, come here! And persuade your mother to come with you; she will be needing a change from the Georgian gentle climate by that time.

Come, dear, let's make a bargain—like this: if your mother can't come with you, I will send Miss Lyon for you: then, later, I will go down & see you graduate. That will be one journey for me, & I am just old enough & rickety enough to dread two journeys. I do dearly want to be there when you graduate; & I am not going to miss it for any light matter.

The first shadow has fallen upon the Aquarium—Margaret Illington is very sick. I am speaking for all the members, & sending her their sympathy & good wishes.

Some of those photographs came out so-so. Two of you are better than any of the others, but not so good as they ought to be. I will enclose copies. The best one is to be enlarged for my room. That is the one I want the ribbon-bows for—please don't fail to send them when you are done with them, dear.

Monday, 26th. Now if you are—however, I am interrupted.

Tuesday, 27th. Interrupted.

28th. It was a very very pleasant interruption. It was the mail, & brought the pink ribbons. Thank you, dear, ever so much. They will make a charming decoration for the enlarged picture.

Thursday 29th. The glass is in the arches now. There is steam heat. So the loggia makes a cosy winter-parlor, with plenty of chance for sunshine. Miss Lyon is going to put a couple of powerful reflector-lamps in there for night-service—then seen from all the distances, the glare will make the place look like a light-house. At night, with a light in every window & no foliage to intervene, & viewed from that white church over on the Ridge, the house already looks like a factory that's running over-time to fill rush-orders. Conde the painter lives over there & he says it's the cheerfulest object under these skies on a gloomy night.

A new fact in natural history; some cats *do* like water. Ashcroft dipped Sinbad in the fountain, & he manifestly liked it. He made no objection, & presently came back for another dip—& got it, & looked pleased & grateful.

Lovingly
SLC

Oct. 31 I haven't finished this letter yet, but Ashcroft wants to play billiards; so I will start it along, & finish it another time.

With Very much love
SLC

CLEMENS TO DOROTHY STURGIS

Redding, Conn.
October 27, 1908

Dear Annieanlouise,

When you wrote last you had been indulging in a good many gay activities, & manifestly enjoying them. Go on with it—it is wholesome. I have lately been gay myself—partly upon compulsion. Business. Flying around. I did not get entirely over the fatigue of it until last night. I was in New York, Boston, Deal Beach, & Irvington—& kept late hours part of the time. I mean to sit at home, now, all the winter, & be quiet.

We've got the burglar alarm in, & nobody in the house is nervous now, or loses any sleep. And the arches of the loggia are snugly filled with glass, and we occupy that place a good part of the day, because it is so cozy & so deluged with light. It is equipped for steam heat—a fact which we discovered by accident. The pipes come up under the floor.

The heart-game begun early in September still goes on, & the record is kept. Benares' score is 1385 hearts, mine is 1418, and Miss Lyon's is closing up on 1600. So the game stood today when Benares left in the last train for New York. He is well, & is getting very fat.

It is a good book you sent me, but your annotations are better still. Thank you very much.

Margaret (of the shell) was here several days. Benares & Miss Lyon brought her up from her school, & Benares and I took her back to it, & had a very enjoyable time there.

Paine was here yesterday for billiards, & Sinbad assisted the game for half an hour and was killingly entertaining.

With a great deal of love,
The Major

Ten minutes later. I went to the billiard room a moment ago to get a picture of Tammany which you have not seen, & there I found some friends of your—the Kittens. The two Omars are slumbering on the sofa, and Sindbad is asleep in his pocket in the billiard table—the same one you saw him in. We put him there just when Benares was leaving.

Tammany's part of the photograph is good, but the rest of it is bad; and not only bad but unflattering, which is a crime.

You are very busy these days, I know, but please don't be too busy to write me.

Lovingly, The Major

CLEMENS TO MARGERY ———

[Redding, Conn.]
Oct. 30/08

Dear Miss Margery:[1]

Good, you're coming! Well, I am glad. Even *dern* glad, as Pontius Pilate used to say. I think it was Pontius; at any rate it was the one that wrote Paradise Lost, & was eventually burned by the church for falling down the mountain & breaking the tables of stone. I never cared for him, although an ancestor. He ought to have known he was in no condition to carry things down a mountain & everybody looking at him.

With love & thanks
S.L.C.

1. This letter could have been written to Margaret Blackmer, Margaret Illington, or Marjorie Breckenridge, and certainly resembles an angelfish letter. The letter may also have been written to Marjorie Clinton, whose anticipated visit he mentions in his 24 October letter to Margaret Blackmer. The letter is written in Isabel Lyon's hand.

CLEMENS TO DOROTHY HARVEY

Redding, Connecticut
Oct. 30/08

Dear Dorothy,[1] you have been 14 so long now, that it no longer seems strange & bizarre & impossible & unthinkable, but has settled down into a calm & logical & to-be-expected & uninflammable fact. It is very odd, to watch 14 & see it perform; see it appear a vague speck on the horizon; see it get larger & a little larger & a little larger, & nearer & nearer & then suddenly swell up & occupy all space for an instant & go

crashing & thrashing & thundering by; & the very next moment there's
nothing in sight but some whirling leaves & dust—& lo & behold you
are 14! in 5 minutes that dust settles down, & you recognize that you
don't really feel any more different than you did before. You have been
14 exactly a week, now, Oct. 30, & already you are perfectly used to
it. It is like being a mother a week: feels as if one had always been a
mother. I remember it very well.

I am feeling better this morning, & the physicians & nurses think
there is hope. The most alarming difficulty was that I could get no
sleep, during the whole of four consecutive nights and days. It was on
account of my Cabinet. I felt that if I should be elected, I ought to be
able to name my Cabinet at once, so that they could go to practising
& be competent for work as soon as confirmed. I decided upon your
father for Secretary of State; Mr Duneka for Public Printer & Major
Leigh for Librarian of Congress: but in trying to select the right people
for the other places, I lost my sleep & my mind, & those places are
vacant yet.[2]

This may all be premature, I know that. There is not the slightest
likelihood that I shall be elected, yet experience has long ago taught
me that it is always best to look sharply out for the unexpected & be
prepared for it, because *that* is the thing that happens—not the other
thing. It logically follows, then, that it is the *most* unexpected thing
that happens. Very well, you will see that. I will have this Cabinet all
coopered up & ready.

I had a most lovely time down there. I wish I could have those free-
gratis-for-nothing-voyages-&-nothing-to-do-but-look-at-you every
day. I should grow fat and satisfactory.

France has 207,000 sq. m.; Oregon, 194,000; Texas, 265,000; & each
of them farming 2000 a year. The picayune was a silver coin worth 6¼
cents in America & 3 in England & its origin was Spanish. I know some
other things besides these, but these are the bulk of my education.

Will you ask your father if he thinks Howells would do for War?

Very lovingly S.L.C.

P.S. I am ever so glad the pin pleases you; for, selecting pins is pure
guesswork with me & can easily result clumsily.

1. Daughter of George Harvey. He had visited the Harveys at Deal Beach, New Jersey, the previous week. The letter is in Ralph Ashcroft's hand, presumably dictated by Clemens.

2. Clemens refers to the upcoming 1908 presidential election (won by William Howard Taft over William Jennings Bryan). Clemens offers imaginary cabinet posts to Harvey, Harpers treasurer Frederick Leigh, and Harpers editor Frederick Duneka.

CLEMENS TO MARGARET BLACKMER

[Redding, Conn.]
Nov. 1/08

You sweet Margaret, I have been trying to get Ashcroft shot & I went to Police Commissioner General Bingham about it, but he was full of objections & lame excuses & said it would make too much talk. I have known Bingham ever since he was our military attaché at the German Court 18 years ago, & yet the very first time I ask a little favor of him he hunts up excuses.

Do you know what Ashcroft did? I will tell you. When he and I were walking down Fifth Avenue that next day, I stopped at a Jeweler's to get "1908" engraved on my shell & I sat down to wait. But Ashcroft said: "Never mind waiting, let them send it to the hotel." It made the blood run cold down my spine. Do you see what he had in his malicious mind? He thought you might be in town & he hoped I might meet you on the street. Then what would happen? Of course I would spring at you joyfully & say: "Oh, you dear Margaret!" Then you would say coldly & haughtily: "I beg your pardon, I do not know you, sir." "But dear heart, I am Clemens, old Mr. Clemens, of Redding, you know." You would answer, sarcastically: "Indeed? Then perhaps you carry about you a certain shell, a duplicate of *this* one."

Then I would begin to cry & you would say:

"Now, go away, shameless imposter, & molest me no more, or I will give you into custody."

You see? That is what Ashcroft was hoping & expecting would happen. But I saw through him & defeated him. I stayed right there till I got my shell back, engraved. He saw he was caught & he was the most ashamed person on this planet. Bingham disappointed me, but no matter, there are other ways of getting Ashcroft shot. He will see.

DIED

By violence, in the depths of the forest, victim of enemies unknown—

TAMMANY

The most beautiful of her race, admired, beloved & now lamented, by all who knew her.

She leaves behind her, inconsolable, two children by her first marriage, BILLIARDS & BABYLON, & three grandchildren by her second espousals. AMANDA, ANNANCI and SINBAD.

REQUIES CAT IN PACE

(S.L.C.)[1]

---

1. In Ralph Ashcroft's hand, presumably dictated by Clemens.

CLEMENS TO FRANCES NUNNALLY

[Redding, Conn.]
Sunday, Nov. 1/08

Francesca dear, dont you be alarmed at my writing you so continuously; it puts no obligation upon you. At least, no very burdensome one. You have to spare me ten lines when you are writing your other letters —that is all—but don't you forget to do that, & don't you neglect it, do you hear?

An hour ago, at noon, I was drifting about the ground-floor noting the enchantments; the brilliant sun was working upon this & that & the other object possessing color; a glowing copper vase on the black mantel, with yellow berries drooping from it; a splash of intense white light upon a many-hued rug, the rest of the rug lying subdued & soft & mellow in shadow; a blaze of mingled gold & crimson flaming in that darling billiard room fender, observed down the intervening be-rugged hall from in front of the library fireplace, in a shaft of sunlight from the front door glorifying one-half of a bowl of pink flowers mid-way up the hall, the rest of the mass dimmed to a vague flush by a deep shadow; a burning touch of sun upon the center of a vase of red flowers on the dining table, which the dream image of the flowers reflected like a miniature sunset cloud in the polished dark-wood of the table—& so on & so on and then I glanced down the terraces to the columned "pagoda" & lo & behold I had an idea! That group of beautiful cedars down there settles the question. They are thrones! They are sacred to the Aquarium now,—no others need apply. Nature placed them there. Nature grouped them about the columns, no man's defiling hands assisted. They are fine, they are delicate, they are shapely, they are graceful, symmetrical, beautiful, & without flaw or blemish —like my fishes. They will always be under my eye, & I will subtly nourish them with my worship & my affection. If I should plant trees they might die and wound me; but these will still be green & lovely & full-flushed with life when I have been dead a century.

It was the luckiest idea! One after the other the fishes will come, and each will choose her tree & stand up against it & be photographed & will put her name on her tree, & keep record of the date in a book. If I had only thought of all this when you were here! But never mind, you are coming.[1]

1. The letter is in Ralph Ashcroft's hand.

CLEMENS TO LOUISE PAINE

Redding, Connecticut
[4 November 1908]

Dear Louise:

I don't expect this to reach you, for your habit is to violate the first law of correspondence, which is, repeat your address in every letter.

Tammany is dead. I am very sorry. She was the most beautiful cat on this western bulge of the globe, and perhaps the most gifted. She leaves behind her, inconsolable, two children by her first marriage—Billiards and Babylon; and three grandchildren by her second—Amanda, Annanci and Sinbad. She met her death by violence, at the hands of a dog. She was found dead in the early dawn, under my windows, whither she had apparently dragged herself from a predacious excursion, for she had with her a field mouse that had suffered death by murder.

She was buried by Miss Lyon with the honors due her official rank —for by appointment she was Mascot to the Aquarium, and brought it good luck as long as she lived. She took great interest in the M.A.'s, and went to the billiard room every day to look at their pictures.

Requies Cat in Pace

As a token of respect and regret, it is requested that each M.A. wear black head ribbons during one hour on the 30th of this month— Tammany's birthday.

Lovingly
S.L.C.

CLEMENS TO DOROTHY QUICK

Redding, Connecticut
Nov. 5/08

Dear heart, I said last night "I will write a letter in the Morning & give a certain Dorothy a scolding & inquire what has become of her." So you have spoken up just in time to save yourself!

Yes, No. 21 is rented & occupied. We shan't leave Redding any more, winter or summer. We like it here better & better all the time.

Dear, I haven't heard of the second robbery. If it was only books of mine that were stolen & not Bibles, I am glad, for the robbers will read those books & become good citizens & valuable men—but they wouldn't need Bibles.

It is a pity you lost the cat, but I can sympathise with you, for we have ourselves suffered a heavy loss in that line. Tammany is dead. Killed by a dog, we think, when she was out hunting. She was the finest cat & the handsomest in America. Moreover, she was an officer of the Aquarium.

I appointed her myself. She was the Aquarium's Mascat, & brought it good luck as long as she lived. Miss Lyon buried her with the honors due her rank.

In token of respect for her memory & regret for her loss it is requested that each M.A. shall wear black head-ribbons during one hour on the 30th of this month—Tammany's birthday. See that you obey.

With lots of love, dear Dorothy,

SLC

CHAPTER FIVE

Stormfield

29 November 1908 – 21 April 1910

AT CLARA CLEMENS'S INSISTENCE the name of the Redding, Connecticut, house was changed from Innocence at Home to Stormfield in October 1908. In addition to a new name, Clemens had to get used to a new household staff, with the exception of Lyon and Ashcroft, hired to replace those who quit after the 18 September burglary. Even though Clara would no longer stay at Stormfield more than a few days at a time, she came out for frequent visits. New York was far more convenient for the pursuit of both her singing career and her growing interest in pianist Ossip Gabrilowitsch.

The household was alternately amused and alarmed when family friend Robert Collier announced that he was giving Clemens a baby elephant for Christmas. A ton of hay and a "trainer" arrived soon afterward. The promised elephant turned out to be wicker, to the relief of everyone except Clemens. Through the Christmas season things remained reasonably cheerful at Stormfield, although tensions and animosities were developing just beneath the surface.

When Dorothy Quick heard that Innocence at Home had been turned into Stormfield, she thought the new name sounded chilly and foreboding, especially for such a big house set off by itself on a windy hilltop several miles from town. The new name was, in fact, a prophecy as well as a foreboding, for, as Dorothy described it years later, "It became a house of storm and stress, tragedy and tears" (*EMT* 205).

By the early winter of 1908 the Aquarium Club had begun to decline. The number of Clemens's letters to his angelfish diminished, and he no longer pleaded for visits. In contrast to the one hundred or more letters he wrote to them in 1908, there are but twenty-five known letters from Clemens to angelfish during all of 1909, and very few surviving letters in reply. Half the angelfish swam from his Aquarium altogether, and no new "fish" were caught to take their places. Not only were there fewer letters but also significant changes in mood and content. Clemens frequently complained about his poor health, urged his angelfish to stop growing up, and muttered about their boyfriends. In these final letters he begins to sound, for the first time, like an old man admonishing his granddaughters to fold their wings and "quiet down." When he is not complaining about the "lawless" qualities he loved but a year earlier, his letters are still warm and affectionate, though missing the exuberance so often present during the previous years.

Indeed, it would have been difficult to create the old mood, given the changed circumstances of Clemens's life. During the fall of 1908 Clara began to wage war on Clemens's secretary and house manager, Isabel Lyon, and his business manager, Ralph Ashcroft, both of whom she accused of embezzling his money. Lyon and Ashcroft were among his close and loyal friends, and Clemens had great confidence in them as employees, entrusting them with complete power of attorney over the financial aspects of both his professional and domestic affairs. For her affectionate as well as efficient attention to nearly all aspects of Clemens's life, Lyon was paid the absurdly small salary of fifty dollars a month. She obviously considered herself as much a member of the family as an employee. Clemens ignored the battle as long as he could but eventually sided with his daughter and her slight, inconclusive evidence that Lyon and Ashcroft were out to swindle him of his fortune. The pair did not allay his growing fears when they married each other in March 1909. Clemens gave Isabel Lyon her notice in mid-April, and she left Stormfield for good a few days later. However, once Clara had convinced her father of wrongdoing in his household, mere dismissal was not enough. Clemens had given Lyon the Lobster Pot, a small cottage on the Stormfield property, as a gift, and now insisted she return it to him along with the sum that had been spent on its decorating, or he would take her to court. He accused her not only of embezzling his money but also of guzzling down his scotch. He called her "an old, old virgin and juiceless" woman who flaunted herself about the place hoping he would marry her. As the conflict grew in vituperation, it also became public knowledge. Reports of charges and countercharges appeared in the New York papers, the editors of which must have enjoyed writing headlines such as "Mark Twain Must Explain." Clemens seems to have been both anxious to do battle yet also appalled at the chaos that had been created out of his happy retirement. In late May he commented, "This house has gone to hell, and I'm going to get out of it" (*MTGF* 227).

He did not leave, of course, but continued to press the attack, with able assistance from Clara and a raft of attorneys and accountants, until a thoroughly bullied and terrified Isabel Lyon signed over the deed to the Lobster Pot and agreed to make the demanded cash payment. Although it is difficult to separate facts from fantasies among the surviving records, Hamlin Hill concludes that "all three Clemenses were illogical and lacking in compassion; and Clara's and Jean's harassment of the defenseless and high-strung secretary and her mother was needlessly vicious" (*MTGF* 231).

Meanwhile, what had happened to that almost-forgotten innocence at home? By the time the Stormfield household had returned to some sort of equanimity and calm, the summer was over and the angelfish with whom Clemens still corresponded were back in school. Whereas the angelfish had been Clemens's "chief delight" during 1908, the venomous purging of Lyon and Ashcroft was his chief preoccupation during 1909.

For all the loss and unhappiness 1909 produced, two events must have given Clemens particular happiness: Jean Clemens's arrival home and Clara's wedding. Jean moved to Stormfield on 26 April 1909, having never seen the Italianate mansion before, and she continued to live there until her death. During the months that followed, Clemens discovered, unexpectedly, her strength of character, kindness, and good judgment. Clara and Ossip Gabrilowitsch gave a recital for 525 guests to benefit the Mark Twain Library on 21 September, and they decided that night to marry. It all happened quickly; Clara and Ossip married on 6 October and left for an extended trip to Germany on 12 October. Clemens may well have looked on the wedding and rapid departure with mixed feelings. Clara had precipitated the disruption of his household and the loss of two former employees and friends, causing Clemens great unhappiness. Now she was leaving for Europe.

A month later, on 18 November Clemens and his one remaining soldier from the old guard, Albert Paine, sailed for Bermuda. They stayed in the home of United States consul to Bermuda, William H. Allen, and, more important, the home of angelfish Helen Allen. While there Clemens wrote to another angelfish, Frances Nunnally, that he had retreated to Bermuda to drive away "the dyspeptic pain" in his breast and his furious memories of "Miss Lyon and Ashcroft, that pair of professional traitors and forgers" (14 December 1909). Except for anginal chest pain and lingering bitterness, he found Bermuda as agreeable as always and pleasantly occupied himself with rides and card games with Helen Allen.

The final blow of 1909 came but a few days after Clemens's return home to be with Jean during the Christmas holidays. Jean, who had long suffered from epilepsy, drowned in her bathtub on Christmas Eve morning during a seizure. Clemens was, of course, greatly shocked by the death, and probably never quite recovered. He was so overcome by grief and angina pains that he could neither attend the funeral service nor make the trip to Elmira, New York, to bury her beside her mother and sister. Instead, he wrote an elegy titled "The Death of Jean."

With Clara in Germany, Jean dead, and no one nearby except his biographer, Clemens felt lonely and envied Jean that she had beat him to the grave. Soon after the funeral Clemens returned to Bermuda, vowing never again to live at Stormfield, that formerly sunny home now filled with such bitter and desolate memories. He wrote to angelfish Margaret Blackmer that "Jean was set free from the swindle of this life." He added, "My ship has gone down, but my raft has landed me in the Islands of the Blest, and I am as happy as any other shipwrecked sailor ever was" (26 January 1910‡).

His last visit to Bermuda was again spent as a guest of the Allen family. Clemens wiled away many happy hours with both Helen Allen and his old angelfish pal, Dorothy Quick, on one occasion introducing them to Woodrow Wilson, then president of Princeton University. But Dorothy could not stay long, and Clemens became increasingly fascinated with Helen Allen. Pages of his Bermuda notebook are filled with descriptions of her "winning and sweet nature," which was also "tempered by outbursts resembling the wrath of God." This was no doubt a frustrating situation for Clemens, having to endure frequent pyrotechnics as the Allens scolded Helen and she lashed back, returning "insult for insult." Since he felt he could not talk freely with either Helen or her parents, he turned to his notebook and the writing of the Helen Allen manuscripts for solace.

Clemens's angina attacks became both more frequent and more severe, causing the Allens sufficient alarm to notify Albert Paine, suggesting he come to Bermuda to take Clemens home. Even on shipboard and in failing health, Clemens continued to write about Helen Allen, expressing surprising jealousy over her boyfriend Arthur and wishing he "could trade places with [her] Teddy" (HAM 2). His writing ends in a pathetic plea to Helen to protect the "diamond" of her innocence and to be "cautious, watchful, wary" (HAM 2). On this note Clemens concluded his years of correspondence with and writing about his angelfish. He died a week later, at Stormfield, on 21 April 1910.

CLEMENS TO MARGARET BLACKMER

Stormfield
Redding, Connecticut
[29 November 1908]

You "suppose" I had a happy Thanksgiving, do you? You don't suppose anything of the kind, you dear little rascal. You know very well I wouldn't have a happy Thanksgiving & you not here.

But it was just sweet of you to send me the flowers. They are lasting very well; they haven't lost their freshness yet.

We've been telephoning, last night, & I am hoping we are going to capture you next Friday. But we have to wait & see if your mother will consent. Mr. Howells is coming, & he is just a love (but you mustn't flirt with him;) & Colonel Harvey is coming; if there is a spare bed I hope your mother will come, too.

With Love

SLC

CLEMENS TO MARJORIE BRECKENRIDGE

Stormfield

December 1, 1908

Dear Marjorie:

You see I have followed your suggestion—so the house has two names: "Innocence at Home" for the Aquarium girls, and "Stormfield" for the general public.

Those poor burglars have gone to jail. I haven't anything against them, I bear them no malice & put no blame upon them, for it is only circumstances & environment that make burglars, therefore anybody is liable to be one. I don't quite know how I have managed to escape myself. Yes I do: my circumstances & environment protected me. Whenever a man is not a burglar, that is the only reason—there is no other.

If your turned ankle afflicted you only a fortnight, you are fortunate. Don't turn it again—it is a bad business; sometimes it hangs on & pesters a person a couple of years; I have had that experience.

Three days ago I walked down to your cabin with a guest. It was in good shape. There was a bow & some fishing tackle on the porch, and the wood-pile had not been robbed.

Although the beginnings of winter are here & the trees are more or less bare, the landscape is still astonishingly beautiful; indeed we can't swear that it has ever lost any of its beauty at any time; what it loses in one way it seems to amply make up in another.

Love to you, & a Merry Christmas, & the best of health and prosperity.

SLC

CLEMENS TO DOROTHY STURGIS

Stormfield
[6 December 1908]
Sunday

Dear Annieanlouise:

A week ago I drifted over the 73-year frontier safely & entered my
second childhood in good shape. It was like passing a milestone in
the Dark—I couldn't notice that anything was happening. It is very
different at 50 & at 70. And again at a hundred, of course.

We have had a good many guests since the burglar days, but not an
actress. I was too slow. October came, all of a sudden, & brought a
time-table change which effectually put up the bars against the profession. There was but one who was free—Margaret Illington. Free by
Disaster, emancipated by broken health. It looks as if the stage is going
to lose her, but I hope it will not happen.

I was in New York day before yesterday, & was to have stayed with
the Rogerses, but at the last moment Mrs. Rogers was taken ill, and
Mrs. Benjamin also (surgical operation); so I stayed with other friends.
I saw Benjamin, & he said Mr. Rogers would probably go to Bermuda soon.

Your fellow-visitors of Sept. 18 have been tried, sentenced, & sent to
jail—one of them for 4 years, the other for 9—this latter for burglary
and shooting with intent to kill.[1] The terms were light because they
pleaded guilty. I had a letter from the murderous one three days ago.
He is clearly a merciless devil, a bloody-minded devil, but softly senti-
mental, just the same, for he is a German. In his lament he says, *"ich
träume in des lebens Blütezeit*[?]*."*[2] (He is about 43.)

With lots of love,
Major

1. Dorothy Sturgis arrived at Clemens's house on 18 September, just hours after the burglary had taken place. One of the two burglars, perhaps the one who wrote to Clemens, later published his biography, titled *In the Clutch of Circumstance: My Own Story* and subtitled "The Mark Twain Burglar's Story of His Life" (D. Appleton and Co., 1922).

2. The German translates: "I dream about a new (better) life."

CLEMENS TO FRANCES NUNNALLY

Stormfield

Dec. 9/08

They will celebrate John Milton this afternoon in New York; & now, when it is too late, I wish I had accepted—which I didn't, because I was sure I hadn't anything to say about John that I dearly & particularly wanted to say. But it is different, now: all of a sudden I am full of things I want to say about him; full of things I want to put into Howells's mouth & then refute them & handle Howells without gloves for saying them. I mourn, I mourn, you dear sweet Francesca, I mourn! for now that is going to be a solemn & sombre function, & I would have lifted some of that cloud from it & let in the sunshine.[1]

Yes, I mourn: for Howells will be the only red Oxford there in all that pack of black gowns, & will have that splendid conspicuousness all to himself: whereas if I could only be there I would get in front of him where nobody could see him, & do all the showing-off myself.

There'll be a full complement of week-enders arriving here day after tomorrow: Howells, Col. Harvey, Ashcroft, & Margaret Blackmer & her mother. If you were coming too, I should be very glad; I would give you my room & I would sleep on the couch in Clara's parlor, or in her chickencoop outside of her windows. Then you could select your tree, down at the pergola. No member of the now sacred group has been consecrated yet—all the 12 stand nameless, for there's been no angel-fish on the premises since I devoted that cluster to the Aquarium. Margaret will be the first to choose a tree.

The framed enlargement hangs in the billiard room now, & looks really good, though not as good as its neighbor the Atlanta picture, which is incomparable; it is the finest triumph of photographing in the house.

No indeed, I shan't forget about your graduation; & also I shall keep you reminded of Easter.

An hour later. The morning mail is in. The Colonel is caught out & can't come this week: he has to speak at a dinner to Carnegie. I had told him he must be sure to come or Howells would get off at Syracuse or Peoria or somewhere around there & get lost, but he says Howells is 72 & *must* learn to take care of himself before he gets old.

Note from Howells. He can't come till Saturday, then he will stay till Wednesday, if permitted. He does not believe there is a Lexington avenue station, but will take a taxicab & hunt for it & see. I know he is going to get lost, & we shall never see him again.

Good-bye you dear Francesca
SLC

1. The event was the three hundredth anniversary of John Milton's birth, celebrated at the Church of the Ascension in New York on 9 December 1908. The rector, Percy Grant, provided the sermon, and Howells and others presented readings and tributes.

CLEMENS TO DOROTHY QUICK

Stormfield
Dec. 10/08

I am sorry, Dorothy dear, that your old bird died, but glad you've got a fresh one. I know it is a pretty one, for by your description of it I recognize it as a bird I am very well acquainted with. It is a chicken hawk, & is one of the finest of the feathered singers. I used to have one. When it was not catching chickens & cats it would sit around & sing by the hour, & was a delight to everybody on the place. I hope you will get the other one all in good time.

Irene's bird is dead. It was a beautiful creature. She got it in Bermuda when we were there a year ago. That is one of the main troubles about pets: one gets very fond of them then they die & break your heart.

I'm not going to Bermuda this season. I have now spent 6 summer months here, and shall stay here right along until winter comes. That will be about next July I reckon, the way things look.

Miss Lyon sends her love, & I send lots & lots of love.

SLC

CLEMENS TO DOROTHY QUICK

21 Fifth Avenue
Dec. 10/08

I am very sorry you didn't see Peter Pan, you dear child, but you will see it yet. Meantime you can hunt up something else when you come.

Saturday after next? Can't you come then—& stay over till Monday? We hope you can; & that is why I am writing now, at sleep-time, instead of waiting till tomorrow, when I am going to be busy & could be prevented.

I've been all over the Jewish technical School to-day, I have seen 400 girls, 14 to 16 years old, at work in the class-rooms, at all sorts of handicrafts. I think it's a wonderful school. I wonder if we can match it anywhere. The pupils do not have to pay anything.

They make fine gowns there, at half the price the big stores charge. Miss Lyon & my daughter are going there to drive a bargain.

The girls that make the clothes get all the money, the school takes none of it. They could make clothes for you & your mother, Dorothy. The school-term is a year and a half: then the girls are able to earn their living in many commercial ways. Some of the graduates earn $1500 a year; 700 of them earn an average of $600 a year, which is an aggregate of about $400,000. But for their gratuitous training, they couldn't earn the half of it. Every one of them has to learn how to cook and make beds, etc.

Oh, it's very late!

Good-night, dear, & sleep well!

SLC

CLEMENS TO DOROTHY STURGIS

[postcard] [1]

> Stormfield
> Dec. 26/08

Dear Annieanlouise:

All the 12 were heard from yesterday except you and one other. The missing pair were heard from to-day, & the tale is complete & I am glad.

That is a perfectly lovely work of art—& done with your left hand. I am sure—the same that wrought the notice to the burglars which Mrs. Doubleday is using in an illustration, in color, in her article description of "Stormfield."

The happiest of happy New Year's to you!
> With the love of
> the Major

1. Postcard photo shows Clemens in window with a pipe, flanked by Ralph Ashcroft (Benares) and Miss Lyon, with the following caption:
Miss L.: If you could only repent!
C.: I can't, and I won't.
Benares.: Try. Do try.
C.: I won't. I feel ready to cry because I didn't do it some more.

CLEMENS TO FRANCES NUNNALLY

> Stormfield
> Dec. 29/08

Go it, dear! Go to all the dances & teas & luncheons, & all the other wholesome dissipations that offer—they are the due of your youth. I used to do like that, myself, in the early part of the last century.

Benares sails for England to-day, on some business of mine. We shall miss him.[1]

Billie Burke spent last Sunday & part of Monday here, & was her charmingest self. We've had lots of delightful company lately, & lots

244 MARK TWAIN'S AQUARIUM

more are coming. But not you, you rascal!—& it's a pity, *I* think.

Margaret, M.A. has been here, with her mother. They are in Bermuda now.

"Stormfield?" I made the change lately. That's its public name; the other is its official name, for my fishes; & is restricted to the Aquarium.

You are a Democrat, perhaps. No matter; when the President-elect comes you must shake hands with him for me, & give him my very best wishes. I am a Mugwump (the only one left, perhaps), but I like him ever so much & am glad he was elected, for he will make a good President. He lets on to like me, & I think he does.[2]

1. As an officer in the Plasmon Milk Products Company, of which Clemens was president and a substantial investor, Ashcroft sailed for England on company business.

2. William Howard Taft was the president-elect. The Mugwumps were Republicans who refused to support their party's 1884 presidential candidate, James G. Blaine, and threw their weight behind Democratic candidate Grover Cleveland.

CLEMENS TO GERTRUDE NATKIN

[Redding, Conn.]
Dec, 31/08

It is the last day of the year, Marjorie dear, & I hope the incoming one will bring you happiness & prosperity to your full content—with the like to follow as time moves on.

SLC

CLEMENS TO DOROTHY QUICK

[postcard][1]

Stormfield
Jan. 2/09

Happy New Year!

It is a very nice poem, Dorothy dear; that is my opinion, & Miss Lyon's, too.

We had a very pleasant xmas in spite of Robert Collier's elephant. Miss Lyon & Mr. Ashcroft were horribly worried about the elephant for several days and nights, trying to think what to do with him. Then he came, & the worry ceased. It was a very successful joke.

Lovingly,
SLC

1. Postcard with photograph of Clemens's house, titled "Innocence at Home," Mark Twain's Residence, Redding, Connecticut, with *Mark Twain's Residence* crossed out and *Stormfield* written in.

CLEMENS TO MARGARET BLACKMER

Stormfield
Jan. 3/09
Sunday Noon

I wonder where you are, you dear little rascal. Yesterday your welcome message by wireless came, & I took it to mean that you had instructed the Bermudian to send it from sea, but had remained in Bermuda yourself; so I cabled New Year greetings to you at once; but last night the cable-office telegraphed from Bermuda that you had sailed. That *was* a surprise! for we thought you were going to make a long stay in the Islands. Well, I am glad to have you back, on any terms. I hope you & the rest of the family whom you control have had a pleasant time & have been advantaged by your outing.

I've got the colored photograph of you & me & it is perfect. All the colors are exactly reproduced. Yes, & the pose is easy & natural & unconscious—not a detail of it could be bettered, I think.

Miss Lyon & I are going to arrive at Robert Collier (752 Park Avenue) at noon the 20th of this month & remain there the 21 & 22nd & perhaps till the 3.32 the afternoon of the 23d. Be sure you come there & see us if you come to town. And you must telephone before hand, dear heart. It would be lovely to have a glimpse of you.

Major General Sir Ralph Ashcroft, Lord Bishop of Benares, has gone to England on business for me & we do miss him so!

Billie Burke has been here to spend a weekend, & she was charming. You must do the same everytime there's a chance; & your mother too. Will you greet her affectionately for me, & thank her for her letter?

Gabrilowitsch is here, & Miss Ethel Newcomb—professional pianist; also my Daughter, professional singer. Music? Bless your heart it's going all the time, night & day!

Isn't this bed of mine pretty large? Sometimes it is, but now it isn't; it's full of cats, & they are all over on my side. I must get a shovel & clear them out.

Good-bye dear. Make my best compliments to Madame & the Misses Tewksbury.

Lovingly
SLC

Clemens to Dorothy Sturgis

Stormfield
Sunday, January 31, 1909

My dear Annieanlouise,

I have been in New York ten days, visiting friends, & got back home with some guests yesterday evening by the light of the fresh snow, no lanterns being needed and none displayed either at the front door or in the loggia. So the days are really lengthening, & I *am* so glad!

Mr. Rogers had a birthday, night before last, (69) & a family dinner-party—a pretty large one, for it is a big family when they all get together. He was a happy man, for the last rail of his railroad was laid down & spiked that morning—a road just twice as long (lacking 6 miles) as the distance from New York to Boston: & he has built the bulk of it since the panic began & all large enterprises were hampered, crippled, & thrown into confusion. A stately achievement for a man of his age. The first through train will leave Norfolk tomorrow for the terminus, 446 miles west'ard.

Benares went to England for me a month or more ago, & is on the ocean, now, homeward bound & aware that there's trouble awaiting him when he arrives at this house on the evening of the 6th of February: for I sent a message by him to the English angel-fish, & he has confessed, himself, by letter to Miss Lyon, that he utilized that opportunity to flirt with her. I think he *hunts* for trouble. The last time Margaret was here we took her home to her school at Irvington-on-Hudson, & they flirted all the way, in the most mutinous disregard of my authority.

The burglar notice is to appear in "Country Life in America", but I don't know the date. The article is by that gifted & charming lady Mrs. Doubleday, who writes the books about the birds.

1 p.m. I think I will get up, now, & talk with the guests while they feed.

Affectionately,
The Major

CLEMENS TO MARGARET BLACKMER

Stormfield
Feb. 5/09

Good! I've heard from you at last. Often & often, on the last week or so, I have said to myself, "What *can* have become of my Margaret?" Yesterday I said to Miss Lyon "I mean to take paper & pen & give her a scolding." She took no notice of it in words, but her unbelieving face said, "If Margaret waits till *you* scold her she'll have to wait a good while." I suppose it's true. In fact I know it is. On paper, anyway. Next time I'll take to the telephone.

Meantime I'll tell you what is the fact: You may always leave me letterless 3 weeks & I won't complain—*then* if you don't write me, dear heart, something will happen! *It will happen at the end of this month if I don't hear from you, you busy little scamp.*

You've been having very industrious good times, dear, & you are entirely excusable for not writing me.

We went down to New York 16 days ago; (Jan. 20) & we were going up to see you on the 23d, but Miss Lyon had to return home. I was ever so disappointed. She didn't get back to New York. The doctor put her to bed & she has never been out of it since.[1]

We had a wireless from Benares yesterday, saying his ship would reach New York tomorrow (Saturday) in time for him to take the 3.32 for Stormfield. I wish you were coming with him. No—it wouldn't do, you would get to flirting with him; & if I were not along he couldn't protect himself.

Look at the handwriting of this enclosed letter. When I saw the superscription I was so glad! And then I found it wasn't from you, after all. But dear me the resemblance *is* strong. Burn it, dear—I've answered it.

Yes, I'll give your love to Miss Lyon & Ashcroft, because you have been good & have given me more than you give to them.

Spring's a-coming! Then you'll come, too, & your mother. And the Misses Tewksbury, too, I hope.

How are the cats? Oh, well, you ought to see Danbury! (I've forgotten the name you knew him by.) He is the handsomest creature afloat. And so wise, & so thoughtful. Night before last he made a spring & landed on the table & hit a ball a swipe with his paw just as Mr. Payne was delivering a shot. It lost Payne the game, & he *was* so aggravated! He got no chance to win another.

With lots of love, you dear child

SLC

1. Isabel Lyon had suffered a mental and physical breakdown, most probably caused by overwork and the tension of coexisting with Clara, who saw Lyon as a rival for her father's attention. On 23 February Lyon went to Hartford for further recuperation at her mother's house, and while there announced her plans to marry Ralph Ashcroft. While she was absent from Stormfield, Clara began the investigation of her bookkeeping that led to her dismissal.

CLEMENS TO FRANCES NUNNALLY

Stormfield
Feb. 9/09

You dear Francesca, I find your last (Jan. 11) in my letter-drawer, marked "not yet answered." I remember, now—I answered it in imagi-

nation & stopped with that; just (as) a person winds his watch in imagination, with the result that presently the *watch* stops.

Soon afterward I went to New York & stayed 8 days. I thought I might
never go again, & so I might best make a long stay.

Miss Lyon is sick abed these two or three weeks. It is a sort of nervous
break-down, attributable to too much work & care. But she is mending.

Ashcroft has been to England for me, & has just arrived back. He
saw a number of your acquaintances & mine. Also he went to the
English angel-fish's house to carry a message from me, & she answered the door-bell herself. He asked—in his punishable way—"Are
you Dorothy?" and she answered "Yes—are you Mr. Ashcroft?" We do
not know how she was able to make that guess. He dined with her &
her parents, & they all went to the theatre.

Dr. Quintard has been here to-day, with a friend: Clara & Gabrilowitsch came yesterday, Ashcroft will arrive again to-night, & Martin
Littleton & his wife will come for over Sunday. We have had 141 guests
since the end of June—& very very good times. You talk as if maybe
you can't come at Easter, & it makes me ever so sorry. Your parents
have the first claim, but I am not going to stop hoping yet awhile.

I hear Ashcrofts wheels a-churning along; I'll run down & welcome
him. Good-bye, dear heart, with lots of love.

SLC

The plumber is coming Feb. 23d; a girl you would greatly like. She
isn't a M.A., but is not without good qualities, nevertheless. She is official plumber of Stormfield, by her own request, but doesn't know how
to plumb. Name, Margery Clinton.

CLEMENS TO FRANCES NUNNALLY

Stormfield
Feb. 17/09

Oh, you sweet Francesca, what a charming Valentine it is! Dear me
but you are beautiful, you little rascal! We all think it is just a shade,
or maybe *part* of a shade, more beautiful than the exquisite Atlanta

picture of you. Am I to put all the pictures of you out of sight except this one? Is that your idea? It isn't going to happen. I'll merely change them around from time to time. At present the London picture of you & me is on my dressing-table, here in my bed-room, & the Atlanta gem & the enlarged picture of you & me standing with the pergola-pillars for a background hang in the billiard room. For a time I will keep the new one with me until it is framed, then transfer it & let it glorify the Aquarium—or the "Tank," as we sometimes call it.

It came in the mail an hour ago, & Ashcroft brought it to me as soon as he had finished his breakfast. It nearly took my breath away. He has just left for New York. He is to get it framed, & bring it back when he comes day after tomorrow for the week-end. The inscription is to be cut out & countersunk in the picture-mat. I am strenuously at work on an article taking sides in the Bacon-Shakespeare controversy,[1] but I can't possibly resume until I've thanked you for this lovely reproduction of your lovely self.

By my calculation you will be snatched up & married by some daring young adventurer within a twelvemonth, & if he is up to standard he will get my blessing—otherwise, bricks in place of it. Fetch him here & let me look him over & make up my mind as to whether I'll have him in the family or not. Beatrice will fetch *her* young person up, next month, for judgment. She confided to me very privately a fortnight ago, that she possesses such a person. She is twenty, & I have known her 16 years. See that *you* give me early notice, too. It is my right.

My, you ought to see the place this morning! The sun is brilliant, there's a wind blowing, the tall grasses & shrubs are bowing & scraping, every blade is strung with ice-beads, every bead is white, or blue, or green, or yellow, or red; and so from every window you see a wide & flashing & fiery splendor of diamonds, emeralds, rubies, & all the other imperial jewels you can name or think of. Alas, alas, alas, & you not here!

Most lovingly, you dear child

SLC

1. Between January and March 1909 Clemens worked on his manuscript *Is Shakespeare Dead?*, in which he disputed the authorship of Shakespeare's plays. Clemens

quoted extensively from a manuscript by George Greenwood, without credit, and no one close to him was enthusiastic about the project. Harpers was obliged to publish it, according to the terms of their contract.

CLEMENS TO MARGARET BLACKMER

Stormfield
Feb. 20/09

Attention, you dear little tyke!

You will have a long vacation at Easter: can't you & your mother spend it with us? I do hope so. When Ashcroft-Benares goes to New York Tuesday, I want him to catch your mother on the telephone & discuss the matter with her.

With lots of love,

SLC

CLEMENS TO DOROTHY QUICK

Stormfield
March 3/09

Well, dear, so you are going abroad in June. It's the very best month for it, & you will have a good time. If I were 60 years younger I would pack my grip & go along with you. Louise Paine, M.A. went abroad a fortnight ago—her first trip, & she was wild with delight. She went with her father, who is my biographer, & they will go over the ground I traveled in the "Innocents Abroad" 42 years ago, & make notes.

Dorothy Butes, M.A. is *coming* abroad (to visit me—she's a Londoner) next August. Francesca M.A., is going abroad in June. Helen Martin, M.A., will go abroad in May; Dorothy Harvey, M.A. has already gone abroad. It's a frisk-about lot, my angel-fishes. I can't keep enough of them in the Tank to make a show.

Miss Lyon has been sick abed several weeks, and has gone to Hartford to have a good long uninterrupted rest with her kin. Indeed she needs it. We have had guests all the time & she has overworked herself.

Good-bye & good times to you dear.
With lots of love

SLC

CLEMENS TO DOROTHY STURGIS

Stormfield
March 3, 1909

Dear Annieanlouise:

Of course I would have answered your invitation immediately, one way or the other, as courtesy & custom require, but there wasn't time, because your dance was to take place the evening of the 19th, and I didn't get your letter until 6 p.m., the 19th, so I knew you would not be expecting me. But I couldn't have gone anyway, because railway travel kills me dead, & I have to avoid it; & indeed always do avoid it when it isn't a life-&-death matter. I had a life-&-death matter on hand in New York at that time—an old, old, mouldy, and long-forgotten stand-over engagement for February 20th which I wasn't ever expecting to be called upon to fulfill. So I went down on the 20th—and got stranded and didn't get back for 8 days.

I was greatly interested in what you said about those wonderful little foreigners whose schools you & your father visited, for I had friendly pleasant contact and acquaintanceship with a good many of their blood on the East Side, through being President of the Children's Educational Theatre the past two or three years, & I have a vast admiration of them. I think we turn out some excellent little actors & musicians there —little folk whose English is faultless, yet I don't suppose they can spell their own names without wrecking the alphabet, & of course neither they nor anyone else can pronounce them. Certainly not without prayer for strength and guidance beforehand.

You must not forget to let me know when you are starting South in the Spring, for we want a visit out of you then. I am housekeeper, these past 2 weeks, and am winning credit for my work in that line. I have had 3 young-lady guests, & can get a recommendation from them. Also, I had my daughter here 4 days, & can get one from her. A good one, too —the *best* kind: that is to say, she is coming back day after tomorrow to endure it again. Benares helps me over the weekends, and is learning.

Miss Lyon went to Hartford a fortnight ago, by the doctor's orders, to be with her kin and have an extended and uninterrupted rest. She had been sick, abed for several weeks, and was near to a nervous breakdown. She is improving, now.

Nein, ich fahre nicht nach Bermuda;[1] I prefer Stormfield, in all weathers.

Very affectionately,
The Major

1. The German translates: "No, I am not going to Bermuda."

CLEMENS TO DOROTHY QUICK

[postcard]

Stormfield
[5, 31 March 1909]

Dorothy dear have I sent you this before? The likenesses are very good I think.[1]

March 31

Dear Me, I wrote that 3 or 4 weeks ago, & I must have been called away, as I did not finish it. I have now found it in my table drawer with two *other* unfinished letters, written the same week. I give you my word, dear heart, that I had not been thinking.

I am just leaving, now, for Virginia, with Ashcroft, to be gone a week or ten days.

With lots of love.

SLC

1. The postcard photograph shows Clemens and Ralph Ashcroft looking out an open window, with a profile of Isabel Lyon standing outside but next to the window. Clemens

looks as if he has been caught at one of his pranks by a rather sober Lyon and Ashcroft. The following dialogue appears on the front of the card in Clemens's hand:

L: If you *could* only repent.

C: Alas, I can't And *won't.*

A: Try. Do try.

C: I won't. I feel ready to cry because I didn't do it some more.

Clemens fired both Lyon and Ashcroft within the next few weeks.

AUTOBIOGRAPHICAL DICTATION, 10 MARCH 1909

Miss Lyon came into the billiard room an hour ago, where I was busying myself in the freedom of a dressing-gown, in perfecting myself in a new wonder-compelling shot which I discovered by accident last night—perfecting myself in it with the idea of playing it in a casual and indifferent way before Ashcroft when he comes to-night; also with the idea that when, after he has seen the shot executed, and shall proclaim that notwithstanding this successful execution of it, the shot is impossible and can never be made again; also, with the further intention on my part of assuring him that I have never seen the shot attempted until now, but that I believe I can achieve it again. So I was practicing as I say, and when Miss Lyon came in I had made myself so capable in it that I could make it four times out of five, and was already entirely sure of astonishing Ashcroft this evening. We drifted into an incident of a few weeks ago, where I called at the private school in New York to see one of my little angel-fishes, Irene, and was refused permission to see her. The austere old virgin to whom the school belongs informing me it was against the rules for her young girls to receive visitors during school hours. My vanity was badly hurt, my dignity had been trampled under foot; I had been treated just like an ordinary human being, instead of as clay of the salt of the earth, and I could not endure it. I got a letter right away, as soon as I was back in Stormfield, from Irene, saying that her special teacher, Miss Brown, was ashamed of the fact that I had been treated just as the rules required ordinary visitors to be treated, but if she had known it was I she would have dismissed her class immediately, and I could have had Irene into my taxicab and carted her off to her home.

This incident naturally brought up another. In '93, when the charming Carey; the bright Carey, the lovely Carey, the incomparable Carey, was still with us in the land of the living, and was still occupying his long-time post on the staff of the Century Magazine, he came along the hall one day, that leads to the editorial rooms, and here in the dingy twilight he found a venerable and profoundly-revered and illustrious citizen of the United States waiting for admission. Carey's banks overflowed, and he poured out a flood of apologies, and escorted that citizen at once to the editorial sanctum. Then he went to his own place, and sent for the boy. The boy conceded that the great citizen had been waiting there a good while; also, the boy defended himself quite competently by saying he had only obeyed the rule of the house. Carey stormed at him, and said:

"The rule of the house! A child ought to know, and if a child doesn't know, then somebody ought to inform the child that there was never yet in the world a rule that can be or ought to be enforced upon all occasions. There must always come a time, in the life of any rule, when the occasion rises away above the rule, and automatically abolishes it. At these rare times the person in charge must remember that a part of his duty is to now exercise his discretion, and let the rule go."

Meantime Carey had ranged three large lithograph portraits alongside each other—Washington, Lincoln and Shakespeare—and he said to the boy:

"Now, impress these faces on your memory; burn them into your memory, so that they will stay there forever. Now then, if either of these gentlemen should ever call, and want to see the editor of this magazine, suspend the rule instantly, and take him to the sanctum."

CLEMENS TO FRANCES NUNNALLY

Stormfield
March 28/09
Sunday

Dear Heart, where are you going to be—well, about the 10th or 12th of April? Because at that time I shall be publishing a booklet. Shall I send it to Atlanta, or to St. Timothy's?

Next Thursday, April 1st, I am going down to Norfolk, Va., by steamer, & shall sail thence for New York on Monday the 5th. Mr. Rogers will be celebrating the opening of his big railroad Saturday night, the 3d—no, Norfolk will be celebrating *him* with a banquet, that night. It's the merchants & other business men. I have not asked for any privileges, but in their kindness they have volunteered them without the asking, & I am most sincerely thankful: I am allowed to stay away until the banquet is over & the speeches begin: 10 p.m. & am not required to come in black clothes. I cannot endure long banquets —the fatigue too great, & as for black clothes, my aversion for them is incurable.

I note your promise to bring him here for inspection & possible approval. Don't forget it. It took me only two days to size-up Beatrice's young man & accept him. Now then, go carefully, don't be rash. When you find yourself inclining toward a candidate, banish *him* from your presence & banish the *thought* of him from your mind, until you & your parents have had plenty of time to talk him over & arrive at a decision. It is the only wise way. You'll not take him; nor his successor, either; nor his successor's successor; but you will take No. 4 or No. 5, & be glad you let the others go. And so shall I. I reckon there's a young fellow creeping into your mind now. *Throw him out*—& follow the above prescription. It's a hundred to one he isn't the right one. You are the very dearest sweetest Francesca there *is*; & you are not to waste yourself.

Lovingly
SLC

CLEMENS TO FRANCES NUNNALLY

Stormfield
April 29/09
4.30 pm

Snowing hard.

No, it has just stopped. But it did snow hard, from 1 until a minute ago—4.30. Only the third snow of the winter—if one may call it by that large name.

You are a very dear Francesca, & you are a very sweet Francesca; but all the same you don't give me any *dates*. Why are you so abstemious about dates? I am under command to be at Margaret's school to see a play, along about the end of May, but I can't get the *date* out of that child. And you don't tell me when I am to be at St. Timothy's. Give some particulars, dear. Come!

I rather expect to go to Baltimore all by myself. I shall get lost, I know it well.

1. Tell me on what date I must reach Baltimore—leaving Hoboken, or Jersey City, or one of those places about 1 p.m.

2. Tell me what hotel to anchor in, in Baltimore.

3. Tell me how to get to Catonsville, from Baltimore, & what time o'day to start.

4. Tell me how to get to St. Timothy's after I *get* to Catonsville.

Now you dear indolent child, sit down & answer me these questions. *You* don't want me to go astray & get eaten by the cows. You would always regret it. Are there many cows? and what kind are they?

I have needed & used the afghan you made for me almost constantly for these past 6 months. I was expecting to pack it away, now, but I see that idea was premature.

> Lovingly
> SLC

5. Dear heart, one more: what is the name of the hotel in Catonsville? There's 5 questions. Answer *all* of them!—do you hear?

I've been reading about myself in Harper's Monthly for May, & I do feel that some people can write most truthfully.

Clemens to Frances Nunnally

> Stormfield
> May 18/09

Certainly, you dear sweet Francesca, you've answered every question to perfection, & I applaud! And so I have registered my itinerary —thus:[1]

June 8.   Go to New York.
June 9.   Go to Baltimore (Belvedere)
June 10. Taxicab at 10 a.m. for St. T's.
           Exercises to begin about 11.
           During the exercises I am to talk to the girls.
           Luncheon.
           Taxicab to the Belvedere.

I shall certainly carry out this program if nothing of an insurmountable character intervenes to prevent it, Dear heart. I would not disappoint you for any avoidable thing.

Don't let Miss Carter take the trouble to invite me; it isn't in the slightest degree necessary. I am coming as your auxiliary grandfather, & so the formalities are not requisite.

With lots of love,

SLC

---

1. The itinerary is for Clemens's trip to Maryland to address Frances Nunnally's graduation class from St. Timothy's School.

CLEMENS TO MARJORIE BRECKENRIDGE

[postcard]

[Redding, Conn.]
May 26, 1909

To Marjorie:
The summer is clothed in all its splendors, Marjorie dear, & it is beautiful here now. I have to go away & leave it for a while, but shall be back the middle of June, & by that time I hope you will be housed in that shady nook in the glen.
With love and good wishes

SLC

CLEMENS TO DOROTHY QUICK

Stormfield
May 26/09

Well, you dear Dorothy, where is the picture? You said you were having it taken and would send one to me—don't you remember?

I suppose you are glad the summer has come; & certainly *I* am. But I must lose some of it, for I am getting ready to go away, & shall not return until the middle of June.

I hope you are well of your bronchitis by this time, & that you will be careful & not bring on another attack; for I know a great deal about that disease by experience, & if one wants to be sick or *must* be sick, it is best [to] try something else.

Dinner-time! & I am not hungry.

With lots of love,

SLC

CLEMENS TO DOROTHY QUICK

[postcard]

"Stormfield"
June 4/09

Dorothy dear, it is too bad, but I shall be in Baltimore from the 8th to the 12th. This is an engagement I made with Francesca several months ago—she graduates on the 10th of June.

It is a nice photo—thank you, dear, with lots of love—

SLC

CLEMENS TO FRANCES NUNNALLY

Stormfield

June 7/09

Yes indeed, you dear Francesca, I shall be proud to be a member of the Epsilon Theta Psi & wear the pin at Commencement—& thence-forth.

Albert Bigelow Paine & I will go to New York tomorrow morning & to Baltimore the next afternoon. Maybe you will be at the hotel when we arrive. I hope so. And maybe the entire four of us can go down to Catonsville together next morning. What do you think, dear.

Lovingly

SLC

CLEMENS TO FRANCES NUNNALLY

Stormfield

June 18/09

Well, no, you dear Francesca. I have not been in good shape lately, but the doctor will come up from New York tomorrow & see if he can mend me up.

Don't you forget, dear, that when you go to West Point you & your brothers must come & see us if you find you can manage it.

I had a very delightful time at your school, & remember it with great pleasure. If I were not so inadequate in age & sex I would go there and take a term or two.

Remember me most kindly to your mother, please. And with great love to you, dear heart,

SLC

Clemens to Marjorie Breckenridge

[postcard]

Stormfield
July 6 [1909]

Dear Marjorie—

I am very glad you are back again. I would come & see you, but the doctor does not allow me to walk so far, & I don't drive because I don't enjoy it. So you must come & see *me*. I am oldest, anyway, you know.

Lovingly   SLC

Clemens to Dorothy Quick

[postcard]

[Redding, Conn.]
July 11/09

Dorothy dear, I've been intending to write this a good while, but I am on the sick list & can't very well do things. I went to Baltimore, June 8, & the journey & the weather together broke me down. I haven't had a well day since. Lately I keep my room almost all the time, & I don't like the confinement much. A journey to New York last August gave me my first setback, but I soon got over that one. I shall get over this one by & by, but not right away. The old saw says "go it while you're young"—& that is what I advise you to do, dear.

With lots of love

SLC

Clemens to Frances Nunnally

Stormfield
[15 July 1909]

I can answer your question definitely, now, Francesca Dear. It is heart-disease. Not the best kind, but good enough for the purpose. It is decided that I have what is technically termed a "tobacco" heart.[1] This will move even the wise to laugh at me, for in my vanity I have often bragged that tobacco couldn't hurt me. Privately & between you & me, I am well aware that I ought to laugh at *myself*—& would if I were a really honest person.

However the victory over me is not much of a victory after all, for it has taken 63 years to build this disease. I was immune *that* long, anyway.

So, as I have said, this is not the best form of it. The best form is the one that plucks the life out of you suddenly, as by a lightning-stroke; whereas this one is slow & tedious & procrastinating, & you have to wait & wait & wait till you get run over by a freight train before you can get rid of yourself. Meantime it subjects you to many many many inconveniences. For instance, you can make no journeys, even short ones; you must spend about 20 of the 24 hours in your room—& mainly in bed; you must smoke only 4 times a day instead of 40; & finally, you must do very little work. If you neglect any one of these things, the blood-pressure increases & the pains come. It is the pains that persuade you to behave yourself—nothing else could do it. Every day when the pains come, you reform; you reform right away, & you do not misbehave again for hours & hours.

Are there any compensations? Plenty of them. As a rule the pains come only about twice a day; & the rest of the day is comfortable, & also agreeable. Idleness is my occupation; life is become a continuous holiday; a pleasant one, too, on the whole.

At West Point you were "interested in seeing all the buildings." *Buildings*? That isn't any way to spell Cadets. Go straight back to St. Timothy's & start over again.

With lots of love,

SLC

1. "Tobacco heart" is a term sometimes used to describe a rapid, irregular pulse caused by excessive use of tobacco. The chest pains Clemens complains of are anginal, caused by coronary artery disease, from which he suffered intermittently until his death.

CLEMENS TO FRANCES NUNNALLY

Stormfield
Aug. 27/09[1]

Yes, I got the letter, dearheart, but I have been pestered so much with the pain in my breast that I haven't had energy enough to write or to make any other exertion. This condition of things makes a dull life for me, for I can't have company. Because I am of no use to a guest: I can't walk, I can't drive, & I am down stairs only 4 hours in the 24— from 4:30 p.m. to 8:30. All this is because the least exertion, the least fatigue, brings the pain.[2]

So you see I stick to my room & *read.* I do a plenty of reading, & of course there is a heap of entertainment in that.

Well, what a time you *are* having! You haven't been off your feet long enough to take a nap since the 10th of June. If I were as pretty a girl as you are, & as sweet, *I* should be flying around just like that, & being worshipped. I wish I *was* a pretty girl. However, it is no use to try; we all have our limitations.

Keep it up, dear! it's what youth is for. Keep on writing me, honey; I'll answer.

SLC

1. Clemens dated this letter "Aug 27/07." The postmark, however, dates it as 1909.
2. Clemens's doctors had diagnosed his chest pains as angina pectoris.

FRANCES NUNNALLY TO CLEMENS

[postcard][1]

[Waterbury, Conn.]
September 5, 1909

Dear Mr. Clemens,

We are touring in a motor car all through New England and the White Mts. We are taking what is called the "Ideal Tour" which lasts two weeks. I will write soon and tell you all about it.

With love
Francesca

1. A note on the front of the card reads: "We are spending the night here and tomorrow night will be in Lenox."

Clemens to Dorothy Quick

[postcard]

[Redding, Conn.]
Sept. 10/09

Dear Dorothy:

I am glad to hear you are enjoying yourself. I am still a prisoner in the house these past 3 months, with no prospect of getting out for a long time to come. But I guess it's all right. Infirmities & disabilities are quite proper to old age. Have a good time while you are young, dear!

With lots of love

SLC

Clemens to Margaret Blackmer

Stormfield
Sept. 15/09

You thoughtless little rascal why didn't you tell me where you were going to be, *now*? You are gone from Lake Placid by this time, & this letter won't ever reach you.

Yes, Greenwich is not far from Redding, but I don't suppose I can go there, because the doctors say I must not make any journeys, even short ones. So, you see, if it chances that I can't go to you, you will have to come to *me*. Are you agreed?

You are very busy, as usual like all of my fishes. But I'm not. Except in the matter of reading & smoking—which is not really business at all, but pastime. However, there's two hours of billiards every afternoon, with Mr. Paine.

I dreadfully want to see you, dear. When is it going to be? I want to see you, but I shan't know you, you are growing so fast.

Good-bye & take care of yourself.
With lots of love—

                                                    SLC

CLEMENS TO FRANCES NUNNALLY

                                          Stormfield
                                          Sept. 27/09

Francesca dear, you are certainly a scandalous little rascal! I suppose
you have been within a mile of this house half a dozen times, lately, &
yet you wouldn't come & see a person. However, you have put in your
time better, & so I forgive you.

If I were well enough I would be in New York now, looking at the
show—that is, *you.*

I don't know whether you are ever going to get home or not, but if
you ever do, let me know, so that I may cease to be uneasy about you.
Fold your wings & quiet down! You are the only aeroplane of the lot
that doesn't have to keep coming down all the time to get some more
gasolene.

With lots of love dearheart, & kindest regards to your father &
mother.

                                                    SLC

CLEMENS TO MARJORIE BRECKENRIDGE

                                          Stormfield
                                          [Fall 1909]
                                          Wednesday

I can't, Marjorie dear, my activities are pretty definitely suspended. I
can't drive, I can't walk, I am a prisoner. I am as well as anybody—as
long as I keep still; but the least little exertion gives me such a bitter
pain in the chest that I could enjoy it more than anything in the world
if somebody else had it.

You must look in on me, Marjorie, & if I get over this before you go away, I'll pay back.

Affectionately

SLC

CLEMENS TO MARGARET BLACKMER

Stormfield
Nov. 18/09

I don't seem to remember you, dear. At first I thought it might be Margaret-of-the-Shell, but doubts intruded, because I knew *she* wouldn't be a whole year getting ready to write me. However, you will be sure to see her, for she goes to your school; & when you see her & make her acquaintance, you will find her very sweet & lovely. And will you be so good as to tell her day after tomorrow, I am expecting to be back before the middle of December. Also that by that time I shall hope to be well enough to run down to Greenwich & see her.

And please give her a great deal of love from

SLC

CLEMENS TO DOROTHY QUICK

Stormfield
Nov. 18/09

Dorothy dear, I haven't been well for the past 5 months, & so I haven't stirred from home; but now I've got to make a trip, by the doctor's orders. I don't want to. But I must obey, I suppose. I sail for Bermuda day after tomorrow, with my Secretary Mr. Paine for company. Perhaps we shall be back by the middle of December—we can't tell, yet.

I wonder how big you are by *this* time! I suppose you have grown clear out of recognition. I wish I could have a glimpse of you one of these days—& I hope I can.

With lots of love

SLC

CLEMENS TO HELEN ALLEN

[inscription] [1]

25 November 1909

Helen Dear. This story was told me by Captain Stormfield and is probably all true for he had been a sailor 65 years and could not lie . . . love.

S.L. Clemens

1. Inscribed in shorthand in a copy of *Extract from Captain Stormfield's Visit to Heaven*, which Clemens presented as a gift to Helen Allen.

CLEMENS TO FRANCES NUNNALLY

Hamilton-Bermuda
Dec. 14/09

Francesca dear, I received your last just before I left home & was glad to see you were carrying on as joyously & as turbulently as ever. I hope there has been no abatement, & that there won't be any while you are young.

I reached here a month ago & had hardly registered at the hotel when an angel-fish arrived with her mother & took me to their home by the sea, & I have been their grateful & contented guest ever since.[1] They have promised to give me a good long visit in the autumn before the school at Larchmont opens (the fish is going to it.)

I have driven two or three hours every afternoon with my hosts, after school hours, over these fine roads, in this fine air, with the brilliant blues of the sea always in sight, & have thus driven the dyspeptic pain in my breast almost entirely away. Also the furious thoughts about Miss Lyon & Ashcroft, that pair of professional traitors & forgers.[2]

We (Paine & I—he is my secretary) sail for home next Saturday (20th) & reach New York 22nd.

Dear heart, you must come & see me by & by. You said you would, you dear Francesca.

With lots of love
SLC

Helen Allen and Clemens, Bermuda, 1908.
(Courtesy, The Mark Twain Project, The Bancroft Library)

1. Helen Allen and her parents.

2. Clemens fired Lyon and Ashcroft the previous spring, but the controversy dragged on until September 1909. This is his first mention of the schism to an angelfish, and of the extent to which it may have exacerbated his angina condition.

GERTRUDE NATKIN TO CLEMENS

[card]

[New York]

[December 1909]

I want to wish you a very bright and happy New Year and hope that with its coming it will bring you health & happiness

Marjorie

CLEMENS TO FRANCES NUNNALLY

[postcard]

Bermuda

[17 December 1909]

Love and Merry Christmas to Francesca M.A.

SLC

CLEMENS TO DOROTHY QUICK

[postcard] [1]

[Bermuda]

[21 December 1909]

Merry Xmas to Dorothy
SLC

1. Oddly enough, Clemens used here an earlier postcard that pictures him at Stormfield with Lyon and Ashcroft.

CLEMENS TO HELEN ALLEN

[inscription] [1]

[Bermuda]

[1910]

To Helen Schuyler Allen with the apologies *from* the author for offering her a book which exposes the fact (page 15) that the First Man introduced slang into the world, & thus tacitly, by his high authority, made its use legitimate forever.

    1. Inscribed in a copy of *Extracts From Adam's Diary.*

CLEMENS TO MARGARET BLACKMER

[card] [1]

Hamilton, Bermuda

[17 January 1910]

To all friends who have expressed sympathy for me in my bereavement I offer my sincerest gratitude

S.L. Clemens

I shall answer, by & by, you dear Margaret [2]

    1. A printed bereavement card sent after the death of Clemens's daughter Jean.
    2. Clemens added this note by hand.

CLEMENS TO MARGARET

Hamilton, Bermuda

Jan. 26/10

You Dear Margaret! [1]

    I am so glad to know you are happy! for I love you so. Some are born for one thing, some for another; but you were especially born to love and be loved, and be happy—and so things are with you now as they ought to be.

I fled to Bermuda when the disaster fell—the *double* disaster, for Clara was gone into permanent exile 13 days before Jean was set free from the swindle of this life. Stormfield was a desolation. Its charm all gone and I could not stay there.

My ship has gone down, but my raft has landed me in the Islands of the Blest, and I am as happy as any other shipwrecked sailor ever was. I shan't go "home" till. . . . oh, by and bye. I don't know when—There's no hurry. Hurry? Why, there's no hurry about *anything*, suddenly the hurry has all gone out of my life.

Bless your dear heart. I love you so!

S L C

1. The recipient of this letter is uncertain. Since Clemens also wrote to Margaret Blackmer on this same date, it is possibly Margaret Illington.

Clemens to Margaret Blackmer

Hamilton [Bermuda]
Jan. 26/10

Dear Margaret—

So you have reached Rosemary Hall at last. I know it must be recently, or you would have run up to see me at Stormfield.

I suppose I shan't see Stormfield again very soon. I have no sorrowful associations with Bermuda, so I expect to spend a good deal of my time here in future. I am not in any hurry to go back to America.

You & my Bermuda angel-fish are about the same age, & a couple of years ago about the same stature, & could have been weighed in the grocer's balances—but *now*!

Well, now it's a job for the hay-scales. Oh, stop growing, Margaret dear!

With lots of love
S L C

CLEMENS TO HELEN ALLEN

[Bermuda]
February 14, 1910

I know a precious little witch,
    And Helen is her name,
With eyes so blue, the asters say,
    "they bring our blue to shame";
And cheeks so pink the eglantines,
    That by the roadway blow,
Shed all their leaves when so they fail
    To match the dainty glow
That steals across from ear to ear,
    And down from eyes to chin,
When that sweet face betrays the thoughts
    That hidden lie within.

I am hers, though she's not mine;
    I'm but her loyal
                    Valentine.

FROM NOTEBOOK 39
[A PORTRAIT OF HELEN ALLEN][1]

Did last Power of Atty abrogate the 1907 one? No. There is danger there. Hasn't Francesca written?

At this very day Ashcroft is manufacturing forgeries to rob Clara with when I am dead. Keep Lark & Stanchfield always, to be ready for him.[2]

She has a most winningly sweet nature, tempered by outbursts resembling the wrath of God.

She will break out in an amazing fury over any little disappointment. This is not an uncommon divine and human characteristic; but along with it she has a characteristic which *is* uncommon, & is a golden quality, a splendid quality: to-wit: her resentment masters her for only a little while, then she masters *it*, & drives it away & is her fine & sunny self again.

By nature & instinct—not by training & study—she is courteous. It would be impossible for her to be impolite to any persons or other animals except her parents & me. Of that I am sure. She is not impolite to me with words, but only with silences;—& pretty impressive silences they are, sometimes, & humiliating. Politeness comes natural to her, & nothing but training can remove it. She has been trained (unintentionally) to be impolite to her father & mother. But where her behavior has been left to itself, untrained, only hypercriticism could find fault with it.

All her life her parents have scolded her in the hearing of persons not entitled to hear. A frightful insult, an inexcusable insult. This could have only one result—it would train her to *talk back*, it would *compel* her to talk back; it would entitle her to return insult for insult, by authority of the strong character born in her, & this training could not go on long, before she would rise to her rights & begin to exercise her privilege. No parent has a right to insult a child. No parent can do it & not damage the child. *Ich bin mit Keinem bekannt gewesen*[3] who was not morally, God's superior, in one or two or even more particulars. Such as pity, mercy, forgiveness, justice, fairness, goodness, kindliness, generosity, charity, etc. I have not been intimate with any one who was so largely lacking in these qualities as God appears to be, by the testimony of His Bible & of His professional friends.

Her native good manners have survived this dreadful training—except in the cases mentioned (the Three.) When her parents scold her, or even when they deny her an absolutely preposterous & impossible favor (such as a moonlight ride with a man qualifying as neither groom nor gentleman but blending both capacities)[4] she retorts (right before people) with language & manner which must be heard & seen to be believed, so far do they go beyond the bounds of anything resembling ladylike manners & speech.

Can she be cured? She needs no curing. It is her parents that need it. As she grows older they will naturally modify their ways with her. This is the law of nature & custom, & will be obeyed. In a year or two from now they will be as courteous to her as they are to the servants. She will be sure to respond in kind.

She has 3 sharply-defined moods, & these are as sharply & definitely reflected in her face: (1) dreamily reposeful; (2) sour-hostile, resentful, touch-me-not; (3) animatedly sweet & winning.

None but God can foresee these moods—they always come as surprises. The one you are expecting is absolutely certain to be the one that does not arrive. None but God can forecast the moment when one of the moods is going to vanish from the face & another take its place; & not even He can tell the *reason* of the change. The change is startlingly sudden; it is summer one moment & winter the next. The *why* of it is her own secret.

She is (substantially) destitute of curiosity. It is astonishing—stunningly, bewilderingly astonishing. I have never been intimately acquainted with any one before, of whom it could be said: "This person is without curiosity." If she were dull, sluggish, inane, stupid, unintelligent, one might *partly* understand it, maybe—but she isn't. She is bright, smart, *alive,* energetic, determined, high-tempered, *intense.* Her spirit fairly *burns*—when the fire of a certain few interests is applied to it. It goes promptly out when a certain dozen other excitants are offered. For instance, she has a passion for romance-literature, but reads no poetry, & falls silent the moment you mention a poem, remains silent through all your artful attempts to get her to express a feeling one way or the other about it. Dear me, she makes you feel so baffled, defeated, ashamed! In your distress you try a pause. The pause never fails with any other person—*cannot* fail with any other person. Continued for two solemn & sombre minutes that dismal stillness will become unbearable, and that silent person will *have* to break it & say something—cannot help it. But in her case? It has not the slightest effect upon her pulseless composure[?]—she could maintain her silence a week without turning a hair. She talks with strong interest & fine discrimination about the romances that have pleased her, but she does not much care to talk about her school studies. She has a liking—not very warm—for English, French & American history, but you may skirmish around over all other histories, ancient & modern, hunting for a joint in her armor of mute indifference & you will not find it, she will utter not a word. You may try to stir her up with the latest splendid news from the observatories—you are wasting your time: astronomy does not interest her, Halley's comet & the Martian canals are nothing to her, you cannot coax even a whisper out of her.

Undmirabile! sie ist ohne Dankbarkeit, ganz und gar![5]

1. Clemens was a guest of Helen Allen's parents from early January until 12 April 1910, giving him the opportunity to study an angelfish more closely. This notebook entry and the two Helen Allen manuscripts that follow are among the last things Clemens wrote. The first two manuscripts were certainly written while Clemens was living with the Allens; the third may have been written during his return voyage.

2. Before giving his full attention to Helen Allen and her family, Clemens reveals the extent to which his unnecessarily paranoid cast of mind was still vilifying Ralph Ashcroft and Isabel Lyon.

3. The German translates: "I don't know anyone."

4. Helen's boyfriend, Arthur.

5. The German translates: "Unbelievable[?]! She is completely without gratitude!"

HELEN ALLEN TO CLEMENS

Bay House
March 5, 1910

Received of S.L.C.

two Dollars and forty Cents in return for my promise to believe everything he says hereafter.

Helen S. Allen

[*on the reverse side*]

FOR SALE

The proprietor of the hereinbefore mentioned Promise desires to part with it on account of ill health and obliged to go away somewheres so as to let it reciprocate, and will take any reasonable amount for it above 2 percent of its face because experienced parties think it will not keep but only a little while in this kind of weather & is a kind of proppity that don't give a cuss for cold storage nohow.[1]

1. In his deteriorating physical condition Clemens dictated most of his letters, either to Helen or another member of the Allen family. This page, most likely dictated to Helen, was included with a letter to Albert Bigelow Paine, reassuring him that Clemens remained in good spirits.

HELEN ALLEN MANUSCRIPT 1

1. Has no strong likings yet, except for the lower animals, but plenty of indifferences.

has momentary predilections which look like strong likings—A,[1] for instance—but they are only Darwinian floating islands, they are not anchored to the bottom.

Can frequently get over the sharpest disappointment amazingly. Often blows it away with a fractious outburst of feeling, & is presently not only composed but cheerful and friendly. Doesn't often pout, & holds resentments & hostilities only a reasonable length of time.

Has absolutely *no* curiosity.

Takes a strong interest in clothes & dancing & the theatre, & riding & canoeing & picnicking, & a prodigious interest in any & all members of the male sex, under 45, married or single.

Will not even answer when one proposes to point out a radiant chapter in a book; sits silent, expressionless, limitlessly indifferent—looks bored.

She is 15½. Has she ever read any poetry? Probably not. Not a line, I think. Never mentions it. Kipling lies on the parlor table untouched.

But she has read several excellent books, high-class literature and fervently likes them.

She is splendidly appreciative of "Sandhaven" & misses not one single point in that brilliant book when it is being read aloud; but she will listen to other fine books—for a long stretch of ten minutes—great and choice passages—& look wooden & atrophied; & when you are through, will thank you for your trouble with a perfectly ghastly silence!

You are astonished & embarrassed; you are ashamed; it is as if someone to whom you were offering a politeness, has slapped you in the face; you feel that somebody's got to *speak*—or make a noise of some kind or other, the silence is so uncomfortable; so you say—

"It's *good!*—*isn't* it good!"

"Y-e-s."

That is all. It is her entire opinion. You will get nothing more. Only just that one little word—little frosty word—little frozen word; lifeless, colorless, indolently uttered.

She doesn't utter any thanks for your effort to interest her, for she doesn't *feel* any, in such cases. You have been allowed the privilege of making your effort, & that is compensation enough.

1. Helen's boyfriend, Arthur.

Clemens to Dorothy Quick

Bay house

Hamilton [Bermuda]

[13 March 1910]

Sunday

Dorothy dear, I am so sorry to hear the sad news that hurries you and your mother home. Yesterday you did not come to us, & we wondered if something was wrong. I could not go out at night yet, & had been shut up with my cough since Wednesday morning in a fresh accession to it—so I sent my man servant to inquire, & he brought word from the hotel that you have received a cable that your uncle was very ill & you had taken ship at once. The world seems full of trouble for us all.

The young people came yesterday afternoon, after the rain, & played tennis, but I did not go out doors; I was out Thursday afternoon & played games but had a hard night to pay for it. This is now the fourth day that Helen has been in bed, & I think her mother *ought* to have been in bed yesterday, but she stayed up to take care of the company. All this illness comes of my catching a cold in the head 3 weeks ago from a visitor who brought it from America. The household caught it from me. Mine ran into bronchitis.

The Colliers arrived last Friday, but I only learned it this evening, for they sent me no word & will have to be scolded. Mr. Collier is ailing —the New York Winter has been too much for him.

I am so sorry you had to go away, for I think a few weeks' rest in this climate would be good for you, dear.

Please give your mother my kindest regards. With lots of love.

SLC

Helen Allen Manuscript 2

When you are present I do not miss you, but when you are absent I do.[1]

Deck stewards are very well, Helen Dear, but there are some deficiencies which they cannot supply.

Yours is the best disposition & the patientest I have met with, Helen. A rare compliment, a good strong compliment, but I could add to it & keep within the facts.

Send this book to Arthur, Helen. There is a page in it which is poisoned.

I wish I could trade places with Teddy.

I think ⁓/⁓ ⁊ ⁊ and)./ and ♂ ₐₙ⁊ Helen—in fact I *know* it.[2]

If I were as polite as I ought to be I would Miss you when you are present; but at any rate I always miss you when you are absent. ⸜·⊦⊱⁊ It will be best to tell you in private, Helen.[3]

Up to 18 we don't know. Happiness consists in not knowing.

Helen lay to heart this wisdom, uttered by PW: Consider this pro[?]

The kindly and cordial and incautious diamond beams upon all corners alike and presently lands in the shirt-front of the barkeep. Helen, out of my jealous heart I drink to your barkeep.

If I catch him around these premises again, I will carve him up with his own Excalibur.[4]

I would God I had some Paine-killer[5] (Peter wouldn't get it this time.)

Helen, I intend to tell Mrs. Col. Wilkins[?] how that outcast has been trying to alienate your affections from me, & she will tell her mother. Then there will be doings[?].[6]

He will come with me once again;

Just once again;

Only once again;

And after a time & two times & half a time he will go down the stairway that looks upon the sea:

And lo, the places that knew him once will know him no more forever!

Always the diamond gets caught in the blue clay—ho! sunshine and fog wedded! Be cautious, watchful, wary, dear—break the age-worn rule![7]

1. Several references here suggest Clemens wrote this piece either on shipboard while returning from Bermuda, or perhaps just before sailing for home. All but the first line have been crossed out.

2. Clemens's special code probably reads: "You are very pretty and sweet and dear and cute" (*MTGF* 261).

3. The code probably translates "Who is saccharine?" (*MTGF* 261).

4. Excalibur, the sword of the legendary King Arthur, is presumably another guarded reference to Helen's boyfriend, Arthur, who seems to have been employed as both a groom and a bartender.

5. A double entendre, referring to both the codeine Clemens had been taking and to the doting presence of Albert Bigelow Paine.

6. Presumably this passage and the lines that follow again refer to Arthur.

7. There is no indication that Helen or her parents ever saw this or the preceding Helen Allen documents.

ALBERT B. PAINE TO DOROTHY QUICK

Stormfield
April 21, 1910

Dear Dorothy:

May I be permitted to send you thanks for your thoughtful expression, which I am sure Mr. Clemens would appreciate if he were well enough to receive the same. His health at this time is very poor, but we hope for speedy improvement.

Very sincerely yours,

A. B. Paine

My regards to your mother.

AFTERWORD

In his study of Clemens's last decade, Hamlin Hill reports that the Helen Allen manuscripts were sequestered for decorum's sake by Albert Bigelow Paine (*MTGF* 260). Since Clara Clemens and Paine were the principal agents in the suppression of any materials that might have disturbed Mark Twain's reputation, it is remarkable these final manuscripts survive. Clara became so touchy on the topic of the Bermuda angelfish that Paine had to warn Elizabeth Wallace, when she was writing her book about Clemens in Bermuda, "I should avoid any '*affectionate*' photographs with young girls. Clara feels pretty strongly about that" (*MTGF* 268).

With the possible exception of Clemens's final visit with the Allen family, restraint and discretion seem to have characterized his relationship with the angelfish. They were always carefully chaperoned, and, according to his rules, when they turned sixteen or were no longer schoolgirls, they would become "honorary" angelfish.

His extended visit with the Allen family was doubtless difficult for Clemens. Not only was his health rapidly deteriorating, he was obviously disturbed by what he saw of Helen Allen's life. Although the final manuscripts reveal his jealousy of and vindictiveness toward her boyfriend, Arthur, the evidence of his life and writings suggests he did not wish to be her lover so much as her older friend and protector. His last written words to Helen urged her to "be cautious, watchful, wary," and to guard the "diamond" of her innocence above all else, to avoid becoming "besmirched." The rapidly maturing Helen Allen challenged Clemens to define further his complex role as "Slave of the Aquarium."

In addition to being a friend and servant to schoolgirl innocence, he must be, if required, its protector and defender as well.

Clemens's fullest fictional tribute to adolescent female innocence and purity is his *Personal Recollections of Joan of Arc* (1895). Although Joan was older than sixteen at the time of her martyrdom, she was both sexually underdeveloped and inexperienced. Hamlin Hill and Albert E. Stone have argued that Clemens believed girls became spoiled as they entered the age of sexual maturity, which he associated with age sixteen. His considerable concern over the ages of his angelfish, with pleadings that they stop aging, certainly supports this interpretation.

An even more poignant revelation of his thinking on the subject comes from his image of the "platonic sweetheart," in which Twain is always seventeen and his love is an innocent maid of fifteen. Their love is neither the love of passionate lovers nor the mere affection of a brother and sister, but something finer, more exquisite, "more profoundly contenting." Clemens told more than one angelfish that although he was old of body, in his mind he was still a lad of seventeen. It appears that the idea of a platonic sweetheart that had occupied his dreams for many years and entered his fiction also influenced his relationship with the angelfish. Clemens played with a wide variety of roles in his relationship to these young women: father, grandfather, Chief Shark, Admiral, slave, and platonic sweetheart.

Inevitably, questions have been raised regarding Clemens's inordinate interest in girls, his mental health during this period, and the reactions of the angelfish themselves. As Clemens observed in his notebook and dictations, he suffered from loneliness and longed for school-age girls who would write and visit him like grandchildren and remind him of his daughters when they were younger. Beyond that, Clemens was probably in love with his memory of himself as a boy or young man. He overcame his sense of loss and fulfilled his formula for happiness by surrounding himself with young women. His angelfish behavior was certainly unusual, even obsessive, but it was also the final expression of a lifelong love affair with his teenage years. Beyond these autobiographical considerations, Albert Stone argues that Clemens's preoccupation with childhood reflects the generation that grew up prior to the

Civil War: "These Americans tended to look back upon their village boyhoods and girlhoods as simpler times of idyllic happiness. They recollected in present turmoil the tranquil past" (*IE* 265).

The Aquarium gave Clemens great pleasure during a period that was otherwise filled with bitterness and unhappiness; there is no evidence to suggest real impropriety or scandal in connection with any of the angelfish. Perhaps his greatest crime was stereotyping and idealizing the lives of these young women. He talked of renting, buying, and collecting them as one might discuss inanimate objects or pets. They were alternately his fish, his gems, his butterflies. He tried to fix them in the amber of an endless adolescence. By pleading that they stay young and innocent, he was perhaps attempting to deny that, as they and the world continued to age, so must he.

Of course, they continued to grow and mature despite his pleadings to the contrary. Dorothy Quick, for example, profitted from her "Author's League" with Mark Twain; her long writing career resulted in fifteen volumes of poetry and fiction, as well as her reminiscence, *Enchantment: A Little Girl's Friendship with Mark Twain*. The other angelfish seem to have had fond memories of their friendship with Mark Twain, and his letters to them reveal but another dimension to his complex personality. For all his personal loss during his last years, his pessimism, his rages against nature—both human and divine—he remained faithful to his lifelong dream of a platonic sweetheart, which found its final and fullest expression in the angelfish of his Aquarium.

A CALENDAR OF LETTERS

THIS CALENDAR follows the chronological sequence of this edition. The date indicated is that of the writing of the letter, unless unavailable, in which case the postmark on the envelope is given. In cases where no date or only a partial date is available, letters have been placed where they seem most likely to belong in the context of the correspondence. The location indicated is that of the correspondent at the time the letter was written. A date or location followed by a question mark indicates a likely date or location. The source refers to the present location of the original manuscript, with two exceptions for fragments that exist only in a previously published text. When the original is not known to survive or is unavailable, the location of a typescript (ts), transcription (tr), photocopy (ph), or other source (*) is indicated. Letters not included in this edition are indicated with a dagger (†). Fragments are identified (inc), inscriptions (ins). Mark Twain's previously unpublished works are identified by a double dagger (‡). These works are protected by copyright (see page iv).

The following abbreviations are used for the correspondents:

ABP	Albert Bigelow Paine	GN	Gertrude Natkin
C	Samuel Clemens	HA	Helen Allen
CC	Clara Clemens	HM	Hellen Martin
CW	Carlotta Welles	IG	Irene Gerken
DB	Dorothy Butes	IL	Isabel Lyon
DH	Dorothy Harvey	LP	Louise Paine
DQ	Dorothy Quick	MB	Margaret Blackmer
DS	Dorothy Sturgis	MBr	Marjorie Breckenridge
FN	Frances Nunnally	RA	Ralph Ashcroft

To	Location	Date	Source
GN to C	New York	27 December 1905	MTP-ts
C to GN‡	New York	28 December 1905	MTP
GN to C	New York	31 December 1905	MTP
C to GN‡	New York	1 January 1906	MTP
C to GN‡	New York	3 February 1906	MTP
GN to C	New York	3 February 1906	MTP
C to GN‡	New York	8 February 1906	MTP
GN to C	New York	13 February 1906	MTP
C to GN‡	New York	14 February 1906	MTP
GN to C	New York	17 February 1906	MTP
C to GN‡	New York	20 February 1906	MTP
GN to C	New York	22 February 1906	MTP*
C to GN‡	New York	2 March 1906	MTP
C to GN‡	New York	4–9 March 1906	MTP
GN to C	New York	10 March 1906	MTP
IL to GN	New York	13 March 1906	MTP
C to GN‡	New York	16 March 1906	MTP
GN to C	New York	17 March 1906	Yale
C to GN‡	New York	18 March 1906	MTP
GN to C	New York	21 March 1906	Yale
C to GN‡	New York	24 March 1906	MTP
GN to C	New York	early April 1906	MTP
IL to GN	New York	3 April 1906	MTP
C to GN‡	New York	8 April 1906	MTP
GN to C	New York	16 April 1906	MTP
GN to C	New York	18 April 1906	MTP
C to GN‡	New York	19 April 1906	MTP
C to GN‡	New York	27 April 1906	MTP
GN to C	New York	early May 1906	MTP
C to GN‡	New York	10 May 1906	MTP
C to GN(ins)‡	New York	13 May 1906	MTP-ph†
GN to C	New York	late May 1906	MTP
GN to C	New York	after 30 June 1906	MTP
GN to C	New York	30 November 1906	MTP
C to GN‡	New York	30 November 1906	MTP
GN to C	New York	25 December 1906	MTP
C to GN‡	New York	December 1906	MTP
C to GN‡	New York	31 December 1906	MTP
C to GN‡	New York	January 1907	MTP
GN to C	New York	20 February 1907	MTP
C to DB(ins)‡	New York	22 April 1907	MTP-ph

To	Location	Date	Source
C to CW‡	aboard the SS *Minneapolis*	June 1907	MTP-tr
C to CW‡	aboard the SS *Minneapolis*	17 June 1907	MTP-tr
C to CW(ins)‡	aboard the SS *Minneapolis*	17 June 1907	MTP-tr
C to FN(ins)‡	New York	1 July 1907	Huntington†
RA to CW	London	5 July 1907	MTP-tr
C to FN‡	London	7 July 1907	Huntington
C to CW‡	London	8 July 1907	MTP-tr
C to FN(ins)‡	London	9 July 1907	Huntington†
FN to C	London	12 July 1907	MTP
C to FN(ins)‡	London	12 July 1907	Huntington†
C to CW‡	London	12 July 1907	MTP-tr
C to DQ‡	Tuxedo Park, N.Y.	late July 1907	MTP
C to DB‡	Tuxedo Park, N.Y.	late July 1907	Columbia
C to DQ‡	Tuxedo Park, N.Y.	31 July 1907	MTP†
DQ to C	Plainfield, N.J.	31 July 1907	MTP
C to DQ‡	Tuxedo Park, N.Y.	early August 1907	MTP
C to FN‡	Tuxedo Park, N.Y.	3 August 1907	Huntington
FN to C	London	3 August 1907	MTP
C to DQ(ins)‡	Tuxedo Park, N.Y.	5 August 1907	MTP-ph†
C to DQ‡	Tuxedo Park, N.Y.	9 August 1907	MTP
C to DQ‡	Tuxedo Park, N.Y.	11–15 August 1907	MTP
DQ to C	Plainfield, N.J.	16 August 1907	MTP
C to DQ‡	Tuxedo Park, N.Y.	17–22 August 1907	MTP
C to FN‡	Tuxedo Park, N.Y.	18 August 1907	Huntington
DQ to C	East Rockaway, N.Y.	26 August 1907	MTP
C to DQ‡	Tuxedo Park, N.Y.	26–27 August 1907	MTP
IL to DQ	Tuxedo Park, N.Y.	31 August 1907	MTP
C to DQ‡	Tuxedo Park, N.Y.	1 September 1907	MTP
C to DQ(ins)‡	Tuxedo Park, N.Y.	1 September 1907	Berg†
IL to DQ	Tuxedo Park, N.Y.	2 September 1907	MTP
C to DQ‡	Tuxedo Park, N.Y.	8 September 1907	MTP
C to DQ‡	Tuxedo Park, N.Y.	12 September 1907	MTP
C to DQ(ins)‡	Tuxedo Park, N.Y.	13 September 1907	MTP†
DQ to C	Plainfield, N.J.	13 September 1907	MTP
IL to DQ	Tuxedo Park, N.Y.	19 September 1907	MTP
DQ to C	Plainfield, N.J.	20 September 1907	MTP
C to FN‡	New York	25 September 1907	Huntington
IL to FN(inc)	New York	25 September 1907	MTP-ph†

To	Location	Date	Source
C to DQ‡	Tuxedo Park, N.Y.	26 September 1907	MTP
FN to C	New York	26 September 1907	MTP
FN to C	New York	27 September 1907	MTP†
C to DQ‡	Tuxedo Park, N.Y.	2–3 October 1907	MTP
FN to C	Catonsville, Md.	2 October 1907	MTP
C to FN‡	Tuxedo Park, N.Y.	4 October 1907	Huntington
IL to DQ	Tuxedo Park, N.Y.	7 October 1907	MTP
C to DQ‡	Tuxedo Park, N.Y.	19 October 1907	MTP
DQ to C	Plainfield, N.J.	after 19 October 1907	MTP
FN to C	Catonsville, Md.	27 October 1907	MTP
C to FN‡	New York	28 October 1907	Huntington
DQ to C	Plainfield, N.J.	1 November 1907	MTP
C to MB‡	New York	14 November 1907	Berg
C to FN‡	New York	18 November 1907	Huntington
C to DQ‡	New York	18 November 1907	MTP
FN to C	Catonsville, Md.	23 November 1907	MTP
C to FN‡	New York	27 November 1907	Huntington
DQ to C	Plainfield, N.J.	27 November 1907	MTP
FN to C	Catonsville, Md.	29 November 1907	MTP
GN to C	New York	30 November 1907	MTP
DQ to C	Plainfield, N.J.	19 December 1907	MTP
C to DQ‡	New York	December 1907	MTP†
C to FN‡	New York	20 December 1907	Huntington
C to FN‡	New York	29 December 1907	Huntington
C to DQ‡	New York	29 December 1907	MTP
DQ to C	Plainfield, N.J.	30 December 1907	MTP
C to CW‡	New York	30 December 1907	MTP-ts
C to DQ or DB‡	New York	early January 1908	MTP†
DQ to C	Plainfield, N.J.	12 January 1908	MTP
C to DQ‡	New York	13 January 1908	MTP
CW to C	Paris	14 January 1908	MTP
C to FN‡	New York	15 January 1908	Huntington
C to DQ‡	New York	17 January 1908	MTP
C to DQ‡	New York	18 January 1908	MTP
FN to C	Catonsville, Md.	18 January 1908	MTP
C to FN‡	New York	21 January 1908	Huntington
C to DQ‡	New York	21 January 1908	MTP
DQ to C	Plainfield, N.J.	21 January 1908	MTP
FN to C	Catonsville, Md.	22 January 1908	MTP
C to FN‡	New York	8 February 1908	Huntington
C to DS‡	New York	13 February 1908	Columbia
DQ to C	Plainfield, N.J.	18 February 1908	MTP

To	Location	Date	Source
C to DQ‡	New York	20 February 1908	MTP
FN to C	Catonsville, Md.	20 February 1908	MTP
FN to C	Catonsville, Md.	21 February 1908	MTP
DQ to C	Plainfield, N.J.	21 February 1908	MTP
C to DQ‡	New York	23 February 1908	MTP
MB to C	Briarcliff Manor, N.Y.	24 February 1908	MTP
C to FN‡	Bermuda	24 February 1908	MTP
MB to C	Briarcliff Manor, N.Y.	28 February 1908	MTP
C to IG(ins)‡	Bermuda	29 February 1908	Berg†
C to MB‡	Bermuda	2 March 1908	Yale
DB to C	London	4 March 1908	MTP
FN to C	Catonsville, Md.	4 March 1908	MTP
DQ to C	Plainfield, N.J.	6 March 1908	MTP
C to DQ‡	Bermuda	10 March 1908	MTP
C to FN‡	Bermuda	10 March 1908	Huntington
C to DQ‡	Bermuda	12–16 March 1908	MTP
IG to C	New York	13 March 1908	MTP
C to FN‡	Bermuda	14–16 March 1908	Huntington
C to FN‡	Bermuda	24 March 1908	Huntington
FN to C	Catonsville, Md.	25 March 1908	MTP
C to DQ‡	Bermuda	28 March 1908	MTP
DQ to C	Plainfield, N.J.	29 March 1908	MTP
C to DQ‡	Bermuda	31 March 1908	MTP
C to FN‡	Bermuda	31 March 1908	Huntington
MB to C	Briarcliff Manor, N.Y.	1 April 1908	MTP
FN to C	Catonsville, Md.	4 April 1908	MTP
C to DS‡	New York	13 April 1908	Columbia
MB to C	Briarcliff Manor, N.Y.	14 April 1908	MTP
C to MB‡	New York	14 April 1908	Yale
DS to C	Boston	14 April 1908	MTP
C to MB‡	New York	15 April 1908	Yale
C to DQ‡	New York	16 April 1908	MTP
DQ to C	Plainfield, N.J.	16 April 1908	MTP
HM to C	Montreal	17 April 1908	MTP
C to HM(inc)‡	New York	17 April 1908	MTP*
C to DS‡	New York	19 April 1908	Columbia
DS to C	Boston	23 April 1908	MTP
C to DQ‡	New York	24 April 1908	MTP
C to HA‡	New York	25 April 1908	Berg
C to DS‡	New York	late April 1908	Columbia
HA to C	Bermuda	27 April 1908	MTP
DQ to C	Plainfield, N.J.	27 April 1908	MTP

To	Location	Date	Source
C to DQ‡	New York	28 April 1908	MTP
FN to C	Catonsville, Md.	30 April 1908	MTP
C to FN‡	New York	1 May 1908	Huntington
DS to C	Boston	2 May 1908	MTP
C to DQ‡	New York	4 May 1908	MTP
C to DQ‡	New York	8 May 1908	MTP
C to DS‡	New York	9 May 1908	Columbia
C to DQ‡	New York	9 May 1908	MTP
FN to C	Catonsville, Md.	10 May 1908	MTP
C to DQ‡	New York	12 May 1908	MTP
DQ to C	Plainfield, N.J.	12 May 1908	MTP
HA to C	Bermuda	13 May 1908	MTP
DS to C	Boston	13 May 1908	MTP
DQ to C	Plainfield, N.J.	14 May 1908	MTP
C to DS‡	New York	15 May 1908	Columbia
DS to C	Boston	17 May 1908	MTP
DS to C	Boston	21 May 1908	MTP
C to DS‡	New York	24 May 1908	Columbia
C to MB‡	New York	25 May 1908	Yale
DQ to C	Plainfield, N.J.	25 May 1908	MTP
HA to C	Bermuda	26 May 1908	MTP
DS to C	Boston	27 May 1908	MTP
C to CW‡	New York	29 May 1908	MTP-ts
DQ to C	Plainfield, N.J.	30 May 1908	MTP
C to DQ‡	New York	2 June 1908	MTP
C to DS‡	New York	2 June 1908	Columbia
C to FN‡	New York	3 June 1908	Huntington
FN to C	Catonsville, Md.	4 June 1908	MTP
DQ to C	Plainfield, N.J.	5 June 1908	MTP
C to FN‡	New York	6 June 1908	Huntington
C to DS‡	New York	7 June 1908	Columbia
C to DQ‡	New York	7 June 1908	MTP
DQ to C	Atlantic City, N.J.	11 June 1908	MTP
C to DQ‡	New York	14 June 1908	MTP
C to DS‡	New York	14 June 1908	Columbia
C to DQ‡	Redding, Conn.	19 June 1908	MTP
C to MB‡	Redding, Conn.	20 June 1908	Yale
C to FN‡	Redding, Conn.	20 June 1908	Huntington
C to DQ‡	Boston	28 June 1908	MTP
ABP to DQ	Boston	29 June 1908	MTP
ABP to DQ	Boston	29 June 1908	MTP
C to DQ‡	Boston	29 June 1908	MTP†

To	Location	Date	Source
C to DS‡	Redding, Conn.	July 1908	Columbia
C to DQ‡	Redding, Conn.	2 July 1908	MTP
C to MB‡	Redding, Conn.	7 July 1908	Yale
C to DB‡	Redding, Conn.(?)	25 July 1908	MTP
C to DQ‡	Redding, Conn.	26 July 1908	MTP
C to FN‡	Redding, Conn.	29 July 1908	Huntington
C to HA(inc)‡	Redding, Conn.	Summer 1908	MTB(1471)
C to MB(inc)‡	Redding, Conn.	Summer 1908	MTB(1438–39)
C to DS‡	Redding, Conn.	3 August 1908	Columbia
C to DQ‡	Redding, Conn.	10 August 1908	MTP
C to DQ‡	Redding, Conn.	12 August 1908	MTP
C to MB‡	Redding, Conn.	13 August 1908	Yale
C to DS‡	Redding, Conn.	15 August 1908	Columbia
DQ to C	Hampton Beach, N.H.	2 September 1908	MTP
C to DQ‡	Redding, Conn.	3 September 1908	MTP
FN to C	London	4 September 1908	MTP
C to MB‡	Redding, Conn.	18 September 1908	Yale
C to FN‡	Redding, Conn.	18 September 1908	Huntington
C to DQ‡	Redding, Conn.	18 September 1908	MTP
C to MBr‡	Redding, Conn.	19 September 1908	Cooley
MB to C	New York	20 September 1908	MTP
C to FN(ins)‡	Redding, Conn.	28 September 1908	Huntington†
C to LP‡	Redding, Conn.	30 September 1908	MT Library
C to DS‡	Redding, Conn.	30 September 1908	Columbia
C to MB‡	Redding, Conn.	6–9 October 1908	Yale
C to MB‡	Redding, Conn.	7 October 1908	Yale
C to MBr‡	Redding, Conn.	7 October 1908	Cooley
C to DQ‡	Redding, Conn.	7 October 1908	MTP
C to FN‡	Redding, Conn.	10–12 October 1908	Huntington
C to MB‡	Redding, Conn.	11 October 1908	Yale
C to MB‡	Redding, Conn.	24–29 October 1908	Yale
C to FN‡	Redding, Conn.	24–31 October 1908	Huntington
C to DS‡	Redding, Conn.	27 October 1908	Columbia
C to Margery‡	Redding, Conn.	30 October 1908	MTP
C to DH‡	Redding, Conn.	30 October 1908	MTP-ts
C to MB‡	Redding, Conn.	1 November 1908	MTP-ts
C to FN‡	Redding, Conn.	1 November 1908	Berg
C to LP‡	Redding, Conn.	4 November 1908	MTP-ph
C to DQ‡	Redding, Conn.	5 November 1908	MTP
C to MB‡	Redding, Conn.	29 November 1908	Yale
C to MBr‡	Redding, Conn.	1 December 1908	Cooley
C to DS‡	Redding, Conn.	6 December 1908	Columbia

To	Location	Date	Source
C to FN‡	Redding, Conn.	9 December 1908	Huntington
C to DQ‡	Redding, Conn.	10 December 1908	MTP
C to DQ‡	New York?	10 December 1908	MTP
C to DS‡	Redding, Conn.	26 December 1908	Columbia
C to FN‡	Redding, Conn.	29 December 1908	Huntington
C to GN‡	Redding, Conn.	31 December 1908	MTP
C to DQ‡	Redding, Conn.	1 January 1909	MTP-ts†
C to DQ‡	Redding, Conn.	2 January 1909	MTP
C to MB‡	Redding, Conn.	3 January 1909	Yale
C to DS‡	Redding, Conn.	31 January 1909	Columbia
C to MB‡	Redding, Conn.	5 February 1909	Yale
C to FN‡	Redding, Conn.	9 February 1909	Huntington
C to FN‡	Redding, Conn.	17 February 1909	Huntington
C to MB‡	Redding, Conn.	20 February 1909	Yale
C to DQ‡	Redding, Conn.	3 March 1909	MTP
C to DS‡	Redding, Conn.	3 March 1909	Columbia
C to DQ‡	Redding, Conn.	5, 31 March 1909	MTP
C to FN‡	Redding, Conn.	28 March 1909	Huntington
C to FN‡	Redding, Conn.	29 April 1909	Huntington
C to FN‡	Redding, Conn.	18 May 1909	Huntington
C to MBr‡	Redding, Conn.	26 May 1909	Cooley
C to DQ‡	Redding, Conn.	26 May 1909	MTP
C to DQ‡	Redding, Conn.	4 June 1909	MTP
C to FN‡	Redding, Conn.	7 June 1909	Huntington
C to FN‡	Redding, Conn.	18 June 1909	Huntington
C to MBr‡	Redding, Conn.	6 July 1909	Cooley
C to DQ‡	Redding, Conn.	11 July 1909	MTP
C to FN‡	Redding, Conn.	15 July 1909	Huntington
C to FN‡	Redding, Conn.	27 August 1909	Huntington
FN to C	Waterbury, Conn.	5 September 1909	MTP
C to DQ‡	Redding, Conn.	10 September 1909	MTP
C to MB‡	Redding, Conn.	15 September 1909	Yale
C to FN‡	Redding, Conn.	27 September 1909	Huntington
C to MBr‡	Redding, Conn.	Fall 1909	Cooley
C to HA(ins)‡	Redding, Conn.	16 October 1909	MTP†
C to MB‡	Redding, Conn.	18 November 1909	Yale
C to DQ‡	Redding, Conn.	18 November 1909	MTP
C to HA(ins)‡	Bermuda	25 November 1909	MTP-ts
C to FN‡	Bermuda	14 December 1909	Huntington
GN to C	New York?	December 1909	MTP
C to FN‡	Bermuda	17 December 1909	Huntington
FN to C	?	December 1909	MTP†
C to DQ‡	Redding, Conn.?	21 December 1909	MTP

To	Location	Date	Source
C to HA(ins)‡	Bermuda	1910	MTP-ph
C to MB‡	Bermuda	17 January 1910	Yale
C to Margaret‡	Bermuda	26 January 1910	MTP
C to MB‡	Bermuda	26 January 1910	Yale
C to HA‡	Bermuda	14 February 1910	MTP-ph
C to HA	Bermuda	5 March 1910	Pr. Col.
C to DQ‡	Bermuda	13 March 1910	MTP
ABP to DQ	Redding, Conn.	21 April 1910	MTP

INDEX

Illustration pages are indicated in italic.